COSTA RICA

Paul Glassman

PASSPORT PRESS

Champlain, New York

1989

ISBN 0-930016-12-2

Photos courtesy of Instituto Costarricense de Turismo

Cover by J. S. Houghton

Published and distributed by:
    Passport Press
    Box 1346
    Champlain, New York 12919
    U.S.A.

Printed in the United States of America

Contents

Introduction

In a region where the watchwords are rebellion, repression, corruption and suffering, Costa Rica can be described almost endlessly by what it is not. There is no long tradition of military takeovers. Indeed, there is not even an army, and elections have been free and fair for longer than in many European countries. No class of people has been placed at the margin of society, toiling to enrich a small class of landowners, and the social tensions of neighboring lands are lacking. Typical street scenes reveal few beggars or hustlers, refugees are not the most current export, and almost all people can read and write. Hardly anything happens to attract attention from far away, and no visions of dark, unofficial doings need trouble a traveler to the country.

But for the visitor, Costa Rica is more than a curious island of stability in a strife-torn area. The ordinary historical sites to which visitors elsewhere are taken as a matter of course and obligation are few; but natural wonders and opportunities for sport, adventure and relaxation abound. Volcanoes are at hand for rugged ascent by foot, or in the comfort of a car or bus. Within sixty miles of the capital are cloud forest, dense jungle, sandy beaches, tropical savannah and piney highlands with rushing rivers and white waterfalls. Birds from humdrum sparrow to exotic macaw, beasts from deer to jaguar to monkey, are equally at home. Experienced sportsmen find fishing on two coasts that is unsurpassed in the hemisphere. Comfortable lodging, civilized dining and excellent transportation are all widely available at reasonable prices in a tropical setting that has yet to be heavily travelled. A self-confident people welcomes visitors

1

as equals, not adversaries. There are few surprises but pleasant ones—which is the best surprise.

Costa Rica has in the past been covered briefly in guidebooks for all of Central America, and for Costa Rican tourism today, this is too bad. Interest in seeing all of Central America has waned. But facilities in Costa Rica have continued to expand, and curiosity about the country is on the rise.

I hope to help remedy the lack of detailed, current information about travel and living in Costa Rica with this book. History, culture and geography are covered. But this book is also about places and how to visit them; about the capital city of San José and how to live well there at modest expense; about beaches and fishing villages and small towns, and the buses and chugging trains and canal boats that take you to them; about what to take along in your travels and where (and whether) you will find a comfortable place to sleep.

Read this book all the way through if you wish, or consult the table of contents and index to find what you need to know. And if there's something missing, or if you discover in your travels something that you want to share with others, please write to me in care of my publisher.

I hope that you enjoy your visit to Costa Rica.

1984

Readers of previous editions will find that in many ways this is a new book. I've taken into account hotels that have opened in the last few years; non-traditional activities and unconventional ways to explore; new roads, and better transportation on old ones. Maps have been improved. The emphasis of coverage is somewhat different, and, I hope, more practical for most readers.

1989

Costa Rica
Large and Small

Costa Rica stretches from sea to sea. Sandy beaches fringed by palms, grassy savannahs, warm inland valleys, temperate plateaus, smoking volcanoes, frosty peaks, forested slopes and steamy jungles succeed each other across the landscape. Twice as many species of tree are native to the many regions of the country as to the continental United States. More than a thousand types of orchids flourish. The national wildlife treasures are still being discovered and inventoried.

Yet, by most standards, Costa Rica is small. From north to south or east to west, the country runs only 200 miles. The shortest distance between oceans is only 75 miles. With an area of 19,575 square miles (50,700 square kilometers), Costa Rica compares to Vermont and New Hampshire combined, or to the province of Nova Scotia. But the influences of two seas and seasonal tropical winds, earthquakes, volcanic eruptions that have enriched the soil, and altitudes that vary from sea level to nearly 4000 meters, make of Costa Rica a continent in miniature.

Costa Rica drapes itself upon a jagged, mountainous spine that runs from northwest to southeast, part of the great intercontinental Sierra Madre-Andes chain. The volcanic Guanacaste, Tilarán and Central ranges, separated from each other by relatively low passes and valleys, rise successively higher down the northern two-thirds of the country. Traversing the south of Costa Rica and continuing into

3

Panama is the Talamanca range, which encompasses the highest points in the country. Cool and even frigid, the mountain slopes remain for the most part in their natural, breathtaking, forested condition, exploited here and there only as pasture.

South of the volcanoes of the Central Range is the Meseta Central, or Valle Central—the Central Plateau, or Central Valley—in every sense the heart of Costa Rica. Measuring only about 20 by 50 miles, the Central Valley covers an area roughly equivalent to that of metropolitan Los Angeles. Yet packed into it are not only the capital city and most of the major population centers, but the richest farmland. Ranging from about 3000 to 5000 feet above sea level, with rolling, forested and farmed terrain, the valley also abounds in natural beauty.

For centuries from the arrival of the Spaniards, virtually the only organized settlement in Costa Rica was in the Central Valley. Even today, this small area is a virtual city-state, dominating every aspect of national life. It claims well over 60 percent of the nation's population, concentrated in the capital, San José, and in the nearby cities of Cartago, Heredia and Alajuela, and in dozens of small towns. Almost all industry clusters around the capital. Small farms crowd all cultivable land, producing vegetables for home use, as well as most of the nation's main export crop, coffee

East of the Central Valley, between the Talamanca Range and the Pacific, is the valley of the General River, which was isolated from the rest of the country until the construction of the Pan American Highway in the 1950s. Here, at elevations lower and warmer than those of the Central Valley, is Costa Rica's fastest-growing concentration of family farms, many operated by migrants from the more crowded core of the country.

Toward the Pacific, Costa Rica tilts precipitously down a slope broken by fast-flowing rivers, some of them harnessed to provide electrical power. In the northwest, on the edge of the hilly Nicoya Peninsula, are miles of sandy beach where Costa Rica's new resort industry is concentrating. Just inland are the savannahs of Guanacaste, populated mostly by fat, grazing cattle, Opposite Nicoya on the mainland is Puntarenas, the nation's major port. Near Panama are stretches of fertile lowland—once important banana-producing areas—as well as the hilly Osa Peninsula. The remainder of the Pacific coastal area consists of low hills, with a narrow, flat, fertile strip along the water. Temperatures all along the coast are regularly in the eighties and nineties (Fahrenheit), in contrast to the comfortable seventies of the Central Valley.

With its multiple bays, inlets, peninsulas, and hills that plunge into the sea, the Pacific coastline measures more than a thousand kilometers (630 miles), though a straight line from border to border is only half that length. The less broken Caribbean coastline runs only about 212 kilometers (133 miles).

To the northeast of Costa Rica's mountainous spine, the land slopes down to a broad, low-lying triangle of hardwood forest and jungle, with two sides formed by the Caribbean Sea and the 300-kilometer (186-mile) border with Nicaragua. This is the land of eternal rainfall, where coastal storms can blow in at any time of the year. Elsewhere in Costa Rica, the central mountains block Caribbean storms, and it rains only from May to November, when the winds are from the Pacific.

For many years, the eastern lowlands were the impenetrable Costa Rica. Heat, disease, swamps and apparent lack of resources kept the first European explorers even from crossing the area, and the highlands were settled from the Pacific coast. It was only with the construction of a railroad to the sea at the end of the last century, and the immigration of workers from Jamaica, that permanent settlements were established. Even today, communication is difficult and population sparse. No roads disturb the landscape in the forests along the border with Nicaragua, and most transport is by riverboat and canoe.

With its varied climates, the Costa Rican earth can and does produce all the fruits and vegetables of the temperate zones, along with tropical plants, from mangoes, papayas, pineapples and oranges to *chayote, anona, pacaya, zapote* and many others whose names in English are either non-existent, or so unfamiliar as to be meaningless.

But for all the diversity of the land, Costa Rica has always relied mostly on a handful of crops. Corn and beans dominated the subsistence scratched from the earth for centuries as a colony, and are still the staples of most Costa Ricans' diet, along with rice. Coffee, grown in and around the Central Valley, and bananas, grown along both coasts, turned Costa Rica from a poor backwater into one of the better-off nations of Latin America. Sugar, in the lower elevations, and cotton, from the Pacific lowlands, are newer exports, along with beef from the grazing lands of Guanacaste. On these few products, with their rising and falling prices and years of lean and bountiful harvests, the prosperity of the nation depends.

A Short History

Here are some paradoxes:

Hardly a building survives in Costa Rica from the colonial era, though such relics abound elsewhere in Central America. There are few public historical monuments. Yet Costa Ricans, unlike their neighbors, refer almost constantly to the past to explain why they are the way they are; hardly a visitor escapes acquaintance with the country's post-Conquest history.

In museums and shops, exquisite ceramics and wrought gold recall pre-Columbian Indian cultures. Yet virtually no Costa Rican feels a link to the first inhabitants of the land.

The proudest moment in Costa Rica's history was a military intervention in a neighboring country. Yet Costa Rica claims a peaceful tradition of non-interference that sets it apart from other Latin American nations.

PRE-COLUMBIAN COSTA RICA

Even before the first Spaniards arrived, what was to become Costa Rica differed from neighboring lands. To the north, in what are now Mexico, Belize, Guatemala, Honduras and El Salvador, and to the south, in mainland South America, civilizations arose based on the cultivation and harvest of bountiful crops of corn by large groups of settled people. Some societies were so powerful and complex that they altered the landscape with great cities, subjugated peoples for hundreds of miles around, traded regularly with distant lands, wrote histories, and made complex astronomical calculations.

But the Costa Rica of that time was off civilization's beaten track. Armies and traders moved south from Mexico and Guatemala, and north from Peru. Some left their influences in Costa Rica. But none succeeded in dominating the land. Costa Rica was for both cultural regions a distant backwater, removed from the main communication routes. Mountains and swamps impeded passage. Population was sparse. Abundant food and water allowed the native groups to move easily from place to place, which made them difficult targets for conquest. As well, there were few riches in the area to arouse long-term interest by outsiders. Contacts existed between north and south—Peruvian gold and seashells have been found in Mayan tombs—but the path of least resistance was by sea.

The peoples living in Costa Rica when the Spanish arrived belonged to five major cultural groups. Caribs, of South American and Antillean origin, inhabited the Atlantic region. Borucas, related to peoples of Colombia, lived in the lower Pacific coastal area. The Corobicís, the oldest of the native groups, lived in small bands in the valleys of the north. There were also a few Nahuatl-speaking Indians recently arrived from Mexico. The Chorotegas, the most numerous, lived in the Nicoya Peninsula, which was not to become part of Costa Rica until the end of the colonial period. More advanced and settled than the other groups, they cultivated corn and beans for subsistence, and cacao for trade. In all, about 25,000 persons inhabited Costa Rica at the beginning of the sixteenth century, mostly in groups isolated from each other by rivers and mountains and jungles. Even related bands spoke mutually unintelligible languages. They made war on each other, and sacrificed or ate captured enemies.

Archaeologists have been able to trace a shadowy cultural history of the first peoples of Costa Rica, using the objects they left behind. Pottery from Nicoya from before the time of Christ shows similarities to Mesoamerican styles of the period, with red coloring on a buff background. Elsewhere in Costa Rica, pottery was made in a single color, as in South America. A few hundred years later, jade appeared in Nicoya and central Costa Rica, probably imported from Guatemala. The northern influence is evident also in the appearance at the same time of the Mexican god Tlaloc on pottery in

Guanacaste, in the northwest. In the sixth century, gold from South America began to appear in southern Costa Rica, possibly following the fall of the empire of Teotihuacán in Mexico, and the disruption of maritime trade routes. By 1000 A.D., multicolored pottery was the norm in Guanacaste and Nicoya, and houses were built in rectangular shapes, all attributes of cultures to the north. Elsewhere in Costa Rica, houses were circular, while pottery featured appliquéd decoration, both characteristics of areas to the south. But while some of the influences of north and south are evident, the dividing line between the two in Costa Rica was generally faint and meandering.

SPANISH OCCUPATION

In densely settled parts of the Americas, the Spanish conquest followed a set pattern. The Spaniards made hesitant contacts with the natives of the coast, learned of a ruling civilization inland, marched to the interior, made war and alliances along the way, and finally subjugated the capital of the native empire, along with everything it ruled. Gold was sought by adventurers, souls by the Church, and glory by both. A new order was imposed, as Indians were parceled out to Spaniards to be converted, resettled, and put to work. Slaves were imported as necessary to replace those who did not survive war, disease, abuse and outrage. Spaniard married native, and a new set of classes, with the native-born Spaniard clearly on top, replaced in a few decades what had existed before.

In Costa Rica, events took a somewhat different turn, though not for want of effort on the part of the Spaniards. Indian battled Spaniard, but there was no empire to be subdued, and usually no surrender. Riches were elusive, and few slaves were imported. Soldiers and fortune-hunters gave way to subsistence farmers. With the passage of time, the settlement came to have more in common with English and French colonies in North America than with other Spanish dominions.

It was Christopher Columbus himself who discovered Costa Rica, and whose sailors were the first Europeans to be discovered by the natives of Costa Rica. The encounter took place on or soon after September 18, 1502, when Columbus, on his fourth voyage to the New World, took shelter from a storm at what is now Uvita Island, just off the port of Limón. No account survives of the impression that the intruders, with their white skins and huge ships, made upon the natives. But the Spaniards noted straight off the golden disks and animal-form decorations worn by the inhabitants, and acquired some of them in exchange for junk jewelry. And through native playfulness or cunning, or faulty interpretation, or wishful thinking on the part of the newcomers, the Spaniards departed with the impression that there were treasures aplenty in all landward directions. Thus, and with similar exchanges on succeeding expeditions, did the nickname of Costa Rica—the Rich Coast—become applied to the land that the Spaniards officially called Veragua.

Attempts to subdue the land and its peoples, and appropriate its reputed treasures, however, faltered. A party led by Diego de Nicuesa in 1506 explored the Atlantic coast of present-day Costa Rica and Panama. But the close-knit native bands viewed all outsiders with mistrust, and none made the fatal mistake, so common elsewhere, of allying itself with the newcomers against traditional enemies. Attacked by Indians who vanished into the jungle, ravaged by heat, diarrhea, yellow fever and assorted diseases to which they had no resistance, tormented by clouds of mosquitoes, drenched by seemingly inexhaustible rains, bogged down in mud, unable to replenish supplies, the men of the Nicuesa party departed without founding a permanent settlement, and later expeditions likewise came to grief.

Frustrated on the Atlantic side, the Spaniards turned their efforts to the Pacific shore. Here the terrain was less of a morass, the vegetation less impenetrable, the inhabitants more permanently settled and less intractable. Spanish attempts to conquer were less of a failure. The expedition of Gil González Dávila in 1522 succeeded in peacefully converting many Chorotega Indians under Chief Nicoya to Catholicism. Quantities of gold were carried off as well. The price was over a thousand men dead from the familiar trio of hunger, disease and raids. Francisco Fernández de Córdova later founded a town called Bruselas near present-day Puntarenas, but infighting among Spaniards led to its abandonment. Short-lived settlements were established on both coasts, but for more than half a century from the arrival of Columbus, there was no permanent Spanish foothold. Finally, in 1561, Juan de Cavallón, with a party of Spaniards and domestic animals, founded the successful settlement of Garcimuñoz in the Pacific lowlands. For lack of finding gold, however, Cavallón himself withdrew.

It was under Juan Vásquez de Coronado, Cavallón's successor as governor, that Costa Rica's course began to differ from that of the other Spanish provinces. Vásquez moved the main settlement from the lowlands to the temperate Central Valley, and renamed it Cartago, or Carthage. The search for gold was abandoned, and Vásquez attempted to deal with the natives in friendship. Spaniards cultivated crops for their own consumption, lived mostly in peace, but achieved no great prosperity. Cartago was not the sort of outpost that attracted adventurers, but at least it survived. The luck of Costa Rica in being governed by Vásquez, however, did not extend to him personally: he was lost at sea after a voyage to Spain to seek financial aid for the colony.

COLONY AND NATION

Despite the initial peaceful settlement of the valley, conflict with the natives was inevitable, and the Spaniards dealt with them in characteristically harsh fashion. A few were subjected, and came to live peacefully alongside the Spaniards, to serve them and eventually to intermarry with them. Others were conquered and removed to areas where they could be easily watched over. By far the largest numbers refused to submit. Some simply moved on to remote areas of the lightly populated country. Most either died violently or succumbed to the diseases brought by the Spaniards, to which they had no resistance. There was no Indian problem in the parts of Costa Rica settled by Spaniards simply because there were soon few Indians.

Without native labor to exploit, without crops to grow for export on a large scale, restricted in trade by Spanish mercantile policy, hemmed into a small valley by hostile environments, Costa Rica stagnated, and the very name of the colony must at times have seemed a cruel hoax. No great public buildings were erected. Little moved out of the province but small amounts of meat, cacao, honey and potatoes. Traders faced a journey to port made hazardous by Indians. Sea traffic was ravaged by pirates. Manufactured goods were in short supply. Costa Rica was virtually isolated from Nicaragua, and communication with Panama existed only by a mule trail that was often impassable.

Spain responded to piracy by closing the ports in 1665. Trade plummeted, though smuggling to Panama and illegal contacts with Dutch and English merchants continued. The shortage of money forced the colonists to revert to the traditional Indian medium of exchange, cacao beans. Cloth was so scarce that tree bark and goat hair were used to make clothing. Even the governor had to grow his own food.

The forlorn colonists remained isolated on their farms, not even coming to town to attend church, not least because they had nothing to wear. Family life was disorganized, and church officials complained of the licentiousness of the populace. A few immigrants drifted in, but the colony hardly grew; more than a hundred years after its founding, Cartago, the capital, was barely more than a village, with fewer than a hundred houses, and a single church. It was destroyed almost entirely by the eruption of the volcano Irazú in 1723.

Costa Rica's last century as a colony saw some improvement in the standard of living, and even a modicum of prosperity. Religious authorities, alarmed at the depths of poverty and ignorance, the low level of morality, and their declining influence, in the late eighteenth century ordered the populace to resettle and concentrate around the churches. Trade with the other colonies was officially re-opened toward the beginning of the eighteenth century. Cacao plantations near the Caribbean expanded as the coastal area was fortified, and by the end of the eighteenth century, Costa Rica was exporting tobacco, sugar, wheat and flour, as well as cacao. To the first towns of Cartago and Aranjuez were added Heredia, San José, Alajuela and Escazú, all organized in the eighteenth century as agriculture and settlement pushed westward from Cartago.

But progress was relative. In comparison with neighboring colonies, Costa Rica still remained poor, isolated, sparsely populated, a social misfit in its lack of a class structure.

There were probably no more than 20,000 persons in Costa Rica at the opening of the nineteenth century, most descended from the few score families that had first settled the colony. Less than one-eightieth of the land had any significant settlement.

Independence, when it came, had little initial effect on Costa Rica. Spain had administered the five Central American provinces from Guatemala; toward the end of the colonial period, Costa Rica was reduced to the status of a dependency of Nicaragua. In practice, however, Costa Rica had long gone its own way. Without the ambitions and class conflicts of the other colonies, living at subsistence, Costa Rica required only minimal government.

News of the independence of Central America, declared in Guatemala on September 15, 1821, reached Costa Rica at the end of the year. A provincial government was hastily formed, and soon acceded to annexation to Mexico. Opinion on the association was divided, however, and a short civil war was fought. The forces of the town of San José, rejecting Mexico, gained the upper hand. In the end, the Mexican empire collapsed in 1823, and Costa Rica joined the United Provinces of Central America, with full autonomy in its internal affairs. The most important result of independence was the elimination of Spanish trading restrictions, but since the world was not beating a path to Costa Rica's door, even this freedom was of limited value.

With little administrative heritage from Spain, Costa Rica's form of government varied over the years. At times it was frankly experimental, as the legislature changed from bicameral to unicameral and back again, and the capital was rotated between towns on a trial basis. Internal strife also came with independence, though to a lesser degree than elsewhere in the region.

Costa Rica's first elected president, Juan Mora Fernández, held office until 1833, and began the policy of encouraging coffee cultivation. Civil war broke out toward the end of his term over the location of the capital. Braulio Carrillo, chosen for the presidency by congress in 1835, succeeded in stabilizing the country politically and financially, and planted the capital firmly in San José. Carrillo extended his term by coup d'etat, and ruled as a benevolent dictator until over-thrown in 1842 by Francisco Morazán, a Honduran and Central American federalist. Morazán's extra-national ambitions led to his own overthrow and execution in 1843. Costa Rica made do with a weak central government after Morazán, and even abolished its army for a short time. In 1848, all connections with the moribund Central American federation were severed. A strong leader emerged once again in 1849 with the election to the presidency of Juan Rafael Mora, a representative of the new coffee aristocracy.

Mora's term saw the one glorious military episode in Costa Rica's history. The American adventurer William Walker had taken control of Nicaragua, and Mora responded to the challenge by raising an army to oppose him. Aided by Britain and by American business interests, Costa Rica played the major role in ousting Walker from the isthmus.

Following the Nicaraguan adventure, Mora was over-thrown, and was subsequently executed when he attempted a comeback. A military government gave way to a series of constitutional presidents who represented the aristocracy. In 1879, Tomás Guardia overthrew the government, and ruled as a military strongman until his death in 1882. The presidency then passed in turn to two of Guardia's relatives.

DEVELOPMENT AND EXPANSION

The topsy-turvy politics of Costa Rica in the nineteenth century were only a sideshow to the economic changes that were taking place. Costa Rica was transformed, as coffee came to be cultivated on a large scale.

Coffee was first grown in Costa Rica toward the end of the colonial period. The plant was so eminently suited to the highland volcanic soil and held such obvious promise that the newly independent republic granted it exemption from a number of taxes. By 1829, coffee was Costa Rica's most important product. In 1831, the government began to give away land on which to plant the crop. Production grew from 50,000 pounds in 1832 to 9 million pounds in 1841, and by the 1880s, annual harvests approached 100 million pounds.

Inevitably, the rewards of coffee cultivation were not distributed evenly. Some families acquired large expanses of land, transformed their wealth into political power, and developed tastes for culture and the finer things in life that the nation had done without for so long. But despite the emergence of a class structure, there appeared to be land and profit enough for all, and no sector of society failed to advance.

Although he was autocratic, Tomás Guardia saw himself as a benefactor of his people. Under his government and those of his two successors, roads were built and improved, public buildings erected, capital punishment abolished, and primary education made free and compulsory, and independent of the church. Coffee earnings, and borrowings against future earnings, financed the expenditures.

The problems of shipping coffee led indirectly to the development of a second major export crop. Coffee was sent by oxcart to the Pacific port of Puntarenas, then on a long voyage around South America to markets in the eastern United States and Europe. To shorten the journey, President Guardia ordered the construction of a railroad line to the Atlantic. Bananas were planted as a stop-gap measure to provide revenue for the financially troubled project. The new crop proved immensely profitable, and large areas were soon planted in the fruit.

DEMOCRATIC COSTA RICA

Costa Rica's modern, democratic tradition started with the election of 1889, the first that was honest, open and direct. No masses clamored for reform at the time. In a typically Costa Rican way, President Bernardo Soto called for the free election whose time, he felt, had come. José Joaquín Rodríguez, a candidate opposed by Soto, won the election and, against expectations, took office. The course of democracy was to have its ups and downs thereafter. Presidents attempted to amend the constitution in order to succeed themselves, and dismissed uncooperative legislatures. But peaceful transitions of power, and more active participation in politics by all sectors of the population, characterized the years that followed.

The major challenge to the democratic trend came in 1917. Claiming that the government was corrupt, Minister of War Federico Tinoco Granados seized power and ruled as a dictator. Opposition by the United States helped force his resignation after two years, and elections were held for a successor.

In the 1930s, Costa Rica began to show signs of social unrest. Many of the benefits of coffee wealth had gone to relatively few families. An extraordinarily high rate of population growth had led to repeated division of the smaller landholdings, and many workers owned no land at all. A strike in the banana plantations succeeded in obtaining higher pay, and agitation was threatened elsewhere.

The response of those in power was to take the lead in distributing wealth more evenly and improving the security of workers. President Ricardo Jiménez Oreamuno organized a government insurance company, and in 1935 began the distribution of United Fruit Company land to farmers, in small plots. Under Rafael Angel Calderón Guardia, a physician who became president in 1940, the measured pace of reform continued as the first social security legislation was enacted.

Calderón was to be one of the more controversial figures in modern Costa Rica. His social programs—including paid vacations, unemployment compensation and an income tax—and his early declaration of war on Germany, offended many of his original conservative supporters. Calderón sought to broaden his political base by allying himself with the Communist-influenced Popular Vanguard party. The polarization of the country continued under Calderón's successor, Teodoro Picado. Conservatives considered the government radical, while liberals, led by José Figueres Ferrer, felt reform programs were ineffective.

In 1948, Calderón ran again for the presidency, and lost to Otilio Ulate. But the government claimed fraud, and the legislature annulled the results. Tensions rose, and finally broke out into an open rebellion led by José Figueres. Armed by the governments of Guatemala and Cuba, the rebels prevailed in a few weeks over the army. The short civil war was the bloodiest in Costa Rica's history, with more than 2000 killed.

MODERN COSTA RICA

José Figueres led an interim administration that attempted to restore order to a disrupted nation. Banks were nationalized and taxes restructured. Most curiously following a civil war, and amid threats from domestic plotters and opponents in exile, Figueres and his allies chose not to purge and restructure the army, but to abolish it altogether, retaining only those elements of the old security forces that they considered appropriate in the Costa Rican context: a national police force, and the military bands.

A constituent assembly proceeded to write a constitution that rejected some of Figueres' proposals, but extended social welfare programs, gave the vote to women, ended discrimination against blacks, and established an electoral tribunal with broad powers to ensure the honesty of elections. Following the legislative elections of 1949, Figueres stepped aside, and Otilio Ulate, the victor of the disputed 1948 vote, assumed office as president.

Despite the bitterness of the civil war, politics in Costa Rica since 1948 have been remarkably peaceful and democratic. Exiles have threatened invasions on two occasions, but have found no internal support, and their movements have fizzled. José Figueres himself has twice served as president, from 1953 to 1957 and from 1970 to 1974, and his National Liberation Party has dominated electoral politics. But it has only twice held the presidency for more than a single term.

Social and economic progress since 1948 has contributed to stability. With revenues growing as a result of high coffee prices and expanded cultivation, the government acted to improve living conditions and modernize agriculture and industry. Social legislation was implemented without the heavy-handed opposition by business interests that plagued Costa Rica's neighbors. By 1981, social security programs— medical care, health services and income maintenance— served 90 percent of the population, took 40 percent of the national budget, and were the largest employer in Costa Rica. Education accounted for 30 percent of the budget, and basic schooling was widespread. Government clinics and private agencies have provided birth-control information to a people concerned not with surviving but with maintaining its standard of living. A population growth rate that was one of the highest in the world at mid-century was reduced from over four percent to well under three percent. Life expectancy has meanwhile risen to 68 years for men and 72 years for women, respectable figures for any country.

Economically, Costa Rica has diversified considerably. Industry expanded at phenomenal annual rates of over ten percent in the sixties, as manufactured goods were exported to the new Central American Common Market. Exports to other areas remained largely agricultural, but expanded to include meat, lumber, sugar, cacao, and flower seeds, along with coffee and bananas.

Massive public works have helped to improve living standards. Hydroelectric projects have brought power to most homes in the Central Valley. An intracoastal canal along the Atlantic has improved access to parts of the lowlands. The highway system has been extended even to the once-forbidding Caribbean region. Government land continues to be available to those who are willing to work it. Foreigners and foreign investment have been equally welcome, and tourism has grown, as have the numbers of retired residents from abroad.

But not everything has been rosy for Costa Rica. Through the 1980s, unstable coffee prices, oil bills, disruptions of trade in the Central American Common Market, the arrival of refugees from Nicaragua, the shutdown of banana plantations in the face of higher taxes and labor strife, and the costs of social programs have all given the society and economy a jolt. The government has at times been hard-pressed to meet payments on loans from abroad, which take up most export earnings, and the currency has been regularly devalued. National income has fallen in some years, and unemployment has risen.

Attempts have been made to stimulate a stagnating economy through diversification of agriculture and development of new sources of revenue, such as manufacturing and distribution in duty-free zones, but results have been illusory. Grantsmanship has helped to see the country through difficulties: on a per-capita basis, Costa Rica ranks second only to Israel as a recipient of U.S. aid.

Elsewhere in the region, economic crises of these proportions have led to turmoil and bloodshed. In Costa Rica, administrations that have failed to stabilize the economy have been turned out of office democratically. But while Costa

Ricans are proud of their stability, it has provided little consolation when they have had to make do with less.

Internationally, Costa Rica has continued to exert a strong moral influence as a nation that has renounced the use of arms. Administrations have generally been pro-Western, and some have given more than passive support to armed movements in neighboring countries. Most recently, reconciliation between all parties in conflict in Central America has been actively promoted. For his key role in putting together a regional peace plan, president Oscar Arias was awarded the 1987 Nobel Peace Prize.

A Mystery of
National Character

"The Switzerland of Central America" . . . "more teachers than policemen" . . . "peaceful and idealistic" . . . "no sharp class distinctions" . . . Costa Rica sometimes sounds like an earthly version of heaven, where all live in peace, and the cares of a less civilized age have been transcended.

No nation could live up to such a billing, however, and the facts bear sorting out. The relative lack of beggars and street urchins indicates that in at least *this* Central American country, there is a minimal social justice. Citizens do, indeed, respect authority and national institutions, rather than fear them.

But there are also elements of more fallible societies. Most Costa Ricans are moderately poor, though poverty is buffered by social services. The bloodiest war in the nation's history occurred only 40 years ago, political exiles have attempted, unsuccessfully, to invade and stir general uprising, and terrorist incidents, attributed to foreigners, have occasionally taken place. There is no army, but the police forces are organized along military lines. As in other parts of Latin America (and in many "advanced" countries), though to a much lesser degree, corruption is part of the way things work.

Still, in its usual state of social peace, in its profession of and adherence to democratic values, Costa Rica is more like nations in North America or Europe than its seething neighbors. It is the social democracy, rather than the Switzerland,

21

of Latin America. That it is so is the primary mystery of the place to many first-time visitors.

There are no easy explanations, no easy descriptions of this regional anomaly. Costa Ricans are Latins, like most of their neighbors to the north and south. But they are a paler shade of Latin. Literally this is so, for though Costa Ricans come in all colors and mixtures of European, native American and African, the European strain predominates. But also in their ways, Costa Ricans are just like their neighbors, only—to turn an ethnic punch-line around—less so. Costa Ricans profess the sanctity of the family as much as other Latins, and social life centers on the home, but the family is not quite the unassailable bastion of elsewhere. Catholicism is ingrained in national life, but public displays of religious fervor are relatively restrained. A Costa Rican male will maintain as strongly as any Latin that sex is a major occupation or preoccupation, but unbridled machismo is rare.

Why are the Costa Ricans a little bit different? Relative prosperity, inevitably, has something to do with it. But a few American nations have had fortune and circumstances comparable to those of Costa Rica. Argentina comes to mind immediately as a country that is fairly well off, even more European-descended than Costa Rica, and mostly middle class. Yet Argentines as a whole are volatile and ultranationalistic, and so fractious in their political expression that many consider dictatorship a necessity to sort themselves out. Costa Ricans are nothing of the sort.

Costa Ricans themselves usually find the explanation in their history. The national myth that informs the way Costa Rica looks at itself arises out of the hardships of the colonial period. In that time, all were small farmers, equally poor and equally proud; all had to labor to sustain themselves. There were no slaves, no social classes, no wealth for anyone to accumulate, nor differences of race or privilege. No man could hold himself to be the better of another. Colonial Costa Rica was a natural democracy.

The national myth is, indeed, only a myth today. Costa Ricans are no longer equally poor. Opportunities to advance did finally present themselves in the era of coffee expansion, and there were no barriers to getting ahead other than those of talent and will. Most Costa Ricans now aspire to be part of the middle class, and a few are wealthy. But they still uphold equality of opportunity, independence, self-reliance and hard work, concepts converted from everyday facts of colonial life into generally accepted values. The heritage of social tensions of other Latin American countries—race against race, class against class—is not ingrained, if not entirely missing. Individually, and as a nation, Costa Ricans erect few barriers against each other, and against outsiders.

Not everything about the Costa Rican character, however, is unique, different, or even positive. Some of the shadings of variation from neighboring lands are rather delicate, and easily over-emphasized. Nobody who visits Costa Rica has any doubts about what region of the world he is in. Attitudes about time are relaxed, bureaucracy is stifling, and logic sometimes follows a non-western course. But few fail to notice, as well, a fresh air of difference.

To themselves, and to those who know them, Costa Ricans are *Ticos*. The nickname derives from the way they speak. Diminutives are common in the language of Latin America. A moment becomes a "little moment," a *momentito*, to indicate "in a little while." But in Costa Rica, the word is *momentico*, and the peculiar ending is applied to the people who use it.

Like their Spanish language, which was locked away for centuries from the outside world by mountains, jungles and seas, Costa Ricans are gracious, courteous, traditional, even a bit archaic. The *retreta*—that circling of boys and girls in the central square on weekend evenings, with shy glances that could, just could, lead to romance—hung on in Costa Rica even as it was disappearing from elsewhere in Latin America and Spain. Now, dating is the norm. But old-fashioned prudishness survives in public. Movies, for one, are heavily censored.

The sense of tradition and what is proper extends to marriage, of course. Most couples are married in church, and the common-law unions that elsewhere in Latin America may outnumber legal marriages are in Costa Rica the small minority. Marriage is usually life-long. Divorce is technically legal, but scandalous. If a marriage fails, the family stays together, though a husband sometimes spends his nights away from home. And even in successful marriages, the sexual wanderings of men are said to be tolerated, while women's are limited by social pressures and home duties; though how this can be is, of course, a great statistical mystery.

More than 95 percent of Costa Ricans are Catholic. The government contributes money to the Church, and religious education is part of the public-school curriculum, though technically optional. The missionary Protestant evangelism that has spread to Latin America from the United States has so far had little impact in Costa Rica. Sudden modernization, disruption of isolated village life, prolonged warfare, natural disasters, and the hopeless poverty that elsewhere have loosened ties with the traditional church exist to a lesser degree or not at all in Costa Rica. Some Protestant sects have their headquarters in San José not because Costa Rica is a fertile field, but because it is centrally located for their Caribbean and Central American efforts, and because life in San José is pleasant.

Catholicism is so unchallenged in Costa Rica that it is somewhat taken for granted. Men especially are lax in their practice, and for many persons, baptisms, weddings and funerals are the only occasions for seeing the inside of a church. Religious holidays dot the calendar, and the saints' days of the towns and villages are regularly celebrated. But mystical devotion that transcends the hardships of everyday life is simply not part of the Costa Rican national experience. Fiesta processions pale before those of other Latin American countries. The country is short of priests, and most of the clergy is Spanish, Italian, Irish or American, rather than Costa Rican. Nevertheless, if challenged, as they sometimes are by missionaries, Costa Ricans feel their allegiance to the Church becoming stronger.

Civic pride is said to be the second great religion of many Costa Ricans. The *fiestas cívicas*—the year-end celebrations—bring out more parades, floats, dancing, puppeteers and music than any church commemoration. And national elections—when the peaceful governmental tradition is most evident—are the occasion for the largest celebrations. Costa Ricans are conscious that their national traditions and

24

values differ from those of their neighbors, and are protective of their separateness. To outsiders, they may be Latin Americans. And a Guatemalan or a Honduran, when outside his homeland, may allow himself to be called a Central American. But a Costa Rican is always a Costa Rican. Education and culture are national icons. A sense of what is proper and of the importance of being a well-mannered person are part of the way people live, not merely lessons taught in school. The high rates of literacy and school attendance are facts of life sometimes repeated ad nauseam. Culture in the highbrow sense is a near-mania.

The reason why is one of Costa Rica's mysteries. Only 150 years ago, as the coffee era began, Costa Ricans were just emerging from the era of barefoot, dirt-poor, ignorant backwardness. Not only was there no widespread literacy at the time, there was no national culture, no music, nothing but hard work to survive. Costa Rica's present love of the finer things traces back to the frontier days not at all, except, perhaps, as overcompensation, an obsession with what was once out of reach, and with being a people worthy of relative prosperity.

And how the Costa Ricans have tried to catch up! Long before oil sheiks gave out contracts to raise universities in the desert, Costa Rica invested coffee wealth in crash programs to expand primary education. When opera companies invited from afar had no place to perform, the coffee growers taxed themselves to finance the construction of a national theater to rival any hall in Latin America. When local folk traditions were found to be somewhat pale or even nonexistent, the dances and music that were imported with the annexation of Guanacaste province were adopted by all Costa Ricans; the *punto guanacasteco*, performed to the accompaniment of guitar and the xylophone-like gourd marimba, became the national dance, and the national folk music became what was played on the *quijongo*, ocarina and *chirimía*, wind instruments of pre-Columbian origin. Most recently, when President Figueres cast his glance about, and saw that classical music was good, but that Costa Ricans were not adept, he arranged for the importation, whole, of a national orchestra and music school, to be staffed, eventually, by national counterparts in training.

25

Unlike some notorious opera houses that stand empty in jungles and deserts, the imported elements in the case of Costa Rica were brought to fertile ground, and have taken root. A respectable literature includes novels of social realism about exploitation on the banana plantations, and of *costumbrismo,* depicting the everyday happenings and ways of the cities and small towns. Modern and classical composers are appreciated on a broad scale. The best of the visual artists, such as engraver Francisco Amighetti Ruiz, have reached audiences outside of Costa Rica.

Strangely, for a people that has grabbed hold of its destiny and managed it fairly well, Costa Ricans have a strain of fatalism. This is said to come from their Hispanic heritage, and the churchly lessons of submission and obedience repeated over the years. It also comes out of hundred of years of poverty that could not be transcended until relatively recently. The values of working hard and bettering oneself predominate, but these don't necessarily go along with planning ahead and being prudent. Costa Ricans are poor savers, and some big-ticket public investments were financed by foreign loans that are now burdensome. But with a sense of limited control over the future, and a past of deprivation, they are consumers par excellence. Those who can afford it, and those who can't, eat, drink and dress well, buy all the consumer gadgets they can get their hands on, and enjoy life while they can.

Two minority groups—blacks and Indians—maintain ways different from those of the vast majority of Costa Ricans.

Blacks were present in early colonial Costa Rica in small numbers as slaves, but those who survived the harsh conditions and ill treatment of that era merged into the general population. A later generation of blacks arrived in Costa Rica at the close of the nineteenth century, from Jamaica and elsewhere in the West Indies, to construct the railroad from San José to the Atlantic, and remained to labor on the banana plantations established by Minor Keith.

The newcomers were not welcomed with open arms. Blacks were confined to the coast by a prohibition against spending a night in the Central Valley. But in the lowlands they prospered, taking the best jobs on the plantations, and in commerce in the port of Limón. When Panama disease forced the relocation of the banana industry to the Pacific lowlands in the thirties, many blacks became small farmers, or labored on cacao plantations. The 30,000 blacks in the country today more and more consider themselves Costa Ricans. All legal discrimination ended with the constitution of 1949. Most blacks who attended school since that time learned Spanish as well as English. Bilingualism has earned some good jobs in commerce and the travel industry in the Central Valley, though, as Protestants, they stand apart from other Costa Ricans.

Indians, or native Americans, are Costa Rica's forgotten minority. Their numbers are few—20,000, perhaps even less—and they live in small groups away from the centers of population.

The original Indian tribes of Costa Rica fragmented and regrouped as a result of war, disease, and exile. The Indians of today range from those whose ways are indistinguishable from those of other Costa Ricans, to jungle groups who have only recently made contact with the outside world.

The Indians of the Talamanca group live in the forested valleys north of the Talamanca mountain range, and in the adjacent Caribbean lowlands. Their ancestors were forced into the area from central Costa Rica and from the Caribbean coast, and there they have remained, except for some who have migrated to the Pacific region. Two tribes survive, the Cabécar and the Bribri, composed of the remnants of a number of pre-Conquest tribes.

For many years, the Talamancan Indians were ruled only nominally from San José, through a native king. As banana operations pushed into their territory, many Talamancans came into regular contact with outsiders; but some of the inland groups remain steadfastly isolated and hostile even to Indians not of their own clan.

The most traditional Talamancan clans are dominated by women, and maintain peculiar customs that include relocating a corpse after a year's burial, isolation of a woman at birth, and native healing rituals.

27

The Borucas of the southern Pacific coastal area, near Panama, still live largely where they did before the Conquest. Aside from working their land communally, they live like other rural Costa Ricans. But by their racial heritage, their particular devotion to the celebration of the Immaculate Conception, and through pre-Columbian ritual that survives as superstition, the Borucas maintain a separate identity.

Other Indian groups are the Chorotegas of the Nicoya peninsula, who lost the use of their separate language years ago, and are almost indistinguishable from the mestizo, or mixed-blood, Costa Ricans of the area; and a few Guatusos, who live in the northern border lowlands east of the Guanacaste mountains.

Around Costa Rica

The pages that follow cover the major towns, national parks, beaches and other points of interest in Costa Rica; how to get to them and what you'll find; where to stay, and what you should keep in mind before you go. Of course, not all appropriate travel advice can be repeated for every destination, so you'll also want to read the chapters of practical information at the back of this book before you set out for any place.

Prices are quoted in U.S. dollars, and, in the case of hotels, include the 13 percent room tax. These are subject to change, and should be taken as approximate. You can easily check the latest hotel rates through a travel agent, or by calling toll-free telephone numbers, where these are given. Restaurant prices include tax and service charge, and indicate the approximate tab for a meal appropriate to the establishment.

Bus, railroad and airplane schedules are, of course, also subject to change. I've given recent schedules to show the ease or difficulty of getting around by public transportation, and to help you plan your time. The tourist office in San José has the latest schedules for public transportation from the capital, or will get them for you. For travel from intermediate points (say, from Nicoya to one of the Pacific beaches), call the hotel where you plan to stay, in order to confirm the latest timetables.

For additional information and directions, the tourist office on the Plaza of Culture in San José is your best bet. Elsewhere, simply ask any handy Costa Rican. I do not know of another country where so many people will drop whatever they are doing, and take you, practically by the hand, to wherever it is you are trying to get to.

Not all hotels in Costa Rica are listed in this book, but I've tried to give a range, from basic *pensiones* and beach *cabinas* to first-class and luxury establishments. In general, when traveling around Costa Rica, I'd plan to spend the night in towns for which accommodations are listed. Phone ahead for reservations when you can, either directly or through someone else who speaks Spanish. At holidays and on weekends, this will guarantee you a room. At other times, a call will allow the hotel to have your room ready and to lay in supplies—an important factor at some of the beaches where food is not easily available.

Most distances and other measures are given in the metric system. Population figures are extrapolated from the latest official estimates.

Complaints about prices, service or abuses should be addressed to the Costa Rica Tourist Board, Apartado 777, San José, along with proof, if available. I would appreciate having your complaints as well, along with more pleasant discoveries and tidbits of advice that you care to send to me, in care of my publisher.

San José

Population: 300,000; Metropolitan Area Population: 725,000; Altitude: 1182 meters (3877 feet)

San José, the capital of Costa Rica, is many towns. At its center are steel-and-concrete towers, shops with plate-glass windows displaying the latest fashions and consumer electronic gadgetry, thoroughfares busy with traffic, and sidewalks crowded with neatly dressed businessmen and office workers. All might have been transplanted from a medium-sized Spanish city.

Just west of the main square is the bustling market area, much more Central American in character, where tinkerers, wholesalers and vendors of food and every necessity of daily life eke out their livings from tiny shops and market stalls and street stands, where buses and delivery trucks and taxis battle to advance through the throngs and commerce overflowing the sidewalks. Here, the buildings are one- and two-story, relatively dingy, and mostly unseen by the casual observer for all the activity around them.

Farther west of downtown San José, and in some of the surrounding suburbs, are the areas of gracious living, where huddled constructions give way to spacious, ranch-style houses with green lawns, always surrounded by substantial fences. This is where California- and Florida-style living— all the amenities in a benign climate—has grafted itself onto the local scene.

And there are the working-class neighborhoods as well, once-independent villages that lodge in simple, neat and non-unpleasant houses the thousands of people who make San José run.

CENTRAL
SAN JOSE

300 METERS
1000 FEET

ZOO

EL PUEBLO

CALLE 19

NACIONAL PARK

LIMON
TRAIN
STATION

NATIONAL
LIBRARY

CASA AMARILLA

LIQUOR FACTORY

JADE MUSEUM

METALICO BUILDING

ESPAÑA

MORAZAN PARK PARK

CALLE 15

CALLE 11

LEGISLATIVE ASSEMBLY

PLAZA OF
DEMOCRACY

NATIONAL MUSEUM

CALLE 9
CALLE 7
CALLE 5
CALLE 3
CALLE 1
CALLE CENTRAL
CALLE 2
CALLE 4
CALLE 6
CALLE 8
CALLE 10
CALLE 12
CALLE 14
CALLE 16

AVENIDA 11
AVENIDA 9
AVENIDA 7
AVENIDA 5
AVENIDA 3
AVENIDA 1
AVENIDA CENTRAL
AVENIDA 2
AVENIDA 4
AVENIDA 6
AVENIDA 8

TELEPHONE COMPANY

POST OFFICE

BORBON MARKET

CENTRAL MARKET

PASEO COLON

COCA COLA
BUS STATION

SAN JUAN DE DIOS
HOSPITAL

MERCED CHURCH

CARRILLO PARK

MELICO SALAZAR
THEATER

PLAZA OF CULTURE

VISITORS' INFORMATION

NATIONAL THEATER

SOC. SECURITY
"LA CAJA"

PARQUE CENTRAL

CATHEDRAL

Costa Rica © Paul Glassman

The city was founded in 1737 as Villa Nueva de la Boca del Monte del Valle de Abra, as the expanding population of the colony of Costa Rica moved westward from Cartago, then the capital. One of dozens of farming centers in a valley of forests, pastures and little plots of subsistence crops, San José—the name of the town was shortened to that of its patron saint—became the capital of Costa Rica during the brief upheavals that followed independence. Only slowly, though, did it grow into a national center, as commerce in coffee and bananas brought substantial revenues to government and business, along with new administrative requirements. But even as San José grew to encompass nearby villages, it never lost its small-town ways. *Josefinos*—the people of the capital—still know most of their neighbors by name, not simply as familiar faces. They shop at the corner store—the *pulpería*—as often as at the supermarket, to pick up the local gossip along with their eggs, coffee and beans. And they gather at *sodas* and bars—their own counterparts of cafés and pubs—to while away spare time and discuss the latest upswings and downturns of their fortunes.

San José sits at the bottom of a teacup valley, the mound-shaped volcano Barva to the north, a ridge of hills to the south, the slopes of both honeycombed with farms. Hardly a part of the city is out of sight of these pastoral surroundings. San José's best moments come in the late afternoon of any day in the rainy season, after a storm has blown through on a near-furious wind, soaked the land, and cooled the air that for an hour or two borders on hot or humid at the coffee altitudes. The sky turns blue again, and wisps of cloud stick to the northern slopes of patchwork fields. As evening falls, clusters of lights turn on in the surrounding higher villages, and twinkle on into the night.

Travelers use San José as a takeoff point for excursions to the many beaches and natural wonders of Costa Rica. Obligatory points of interest are few. But the hotels, country clubs, fine dining, recreational opportunities and measured pace invite the visitor to linger, especially when the weather at home is unpleasantly cold or oppressively hot. Costa Ricans tend to view their capital as a city without a heritage, but I do not think that this is so. For the outsider with time and interest, there are a few fine baroque and Renaissance-

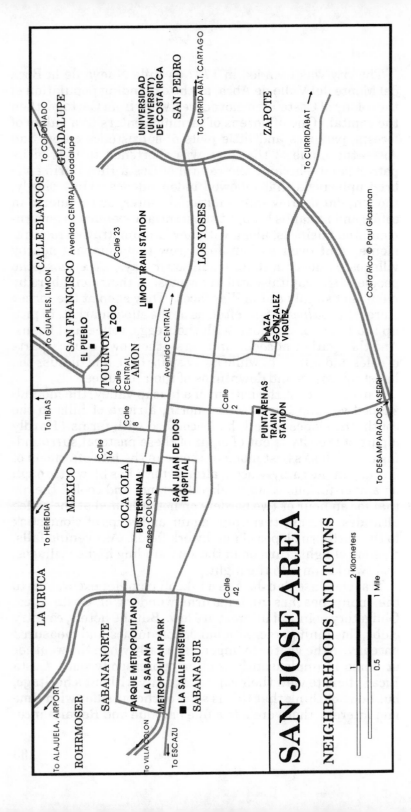

SAN JOSE AREA
NEIGHBORHOODS AND TOWNS

style buildings to view, with fantastic turrets and towers, and steep tin roofs, relics of the years of the coffee boom; visits to the magnificent National Theater, and to museums that display the jade and gold and other artistic treasures of the nation; plays and concerts to attend, and local ways to observe from the table of a sidewalk café or from the bench of one of the many little parks. The city is low-key, a pleasant place in which to live, and therefore a nice place to visit.

ORIENTATION

Avenidas in San José run from east to west, with odd-numbered avenidas north of Avenida Central, or Central Avenue, and even-numbered avenidas to the south. *Calles*, or streets, run north-south, with odd-numbered calles east of the Calle Central, even-numbered streets to the west. You'll quickly get used to this scheme as you go around the city, though you'll probably confuse your avenidas and calles at first.

The two main areas of interest are the central business district, around the intersection of Avenida Central and Calle Central, and the high-toned Paseo Colón district, to the west. Paseo Colón is a continuation of Avenida Central. From the western end of Paseo Colón to the center of the city is just over a mile, a distance easily negotiated on foot or by the many city buses that run along Colón.

North, east, west and south of the central area are the *barrios*, or neighborhoods, of the capital—Los Yoses, Sabana Sur, Bellavista, and several dozen others. Adjoining municipalities, such as Guadalupe and San Pedro, comprise the *Area Metropolitana* (Metropolitan Area) with San José, and are, for practical purposes, part of a single city.

Josefinos navigate around their city by inertial displacement from known landmarks. An ad for a certain restaurant might say that it is 200 meters west of and 150 meters north of Edificio Chile Picante. "100 meters" is another way of saying "one block" in Costa Rica (though a block is, in fact, somewhat shorter). The translation, then, is: From the Chile Picante building, go two blocks west, then one-and-a-half blocks north. This system has its charm, and is fine if you know the city, but if you're a first-time visitor, you're sunk. You'll have to seek clarification (e.g., "Where is Edificio Chile Picante?") if you get an address in this form.

Fortunately, a somewhat clearer form is generally used for addresses in the downtown area. The address of the Chalet Suizo restaurant is Avenida 1, Calles 5 y 7. This means that it's on Avenida 1 between 5 and 7 Calles. The address of the Hotel Balmoral is Avenida Central y Calle 7, meaning that it's at the corner of Avenida Central and Calle 7. In this book, I'll give such addresses as "Avenida 1, Calles 5/7," and "Avenida Central, Calle 7." Of course, you'll have to search out the Chalet Suizo restaurant along the block indicated, but that's the way the Ticos do it.

Believe it or not, buildings also have numbers, but they're rarely posted, so an address giving a house number is of little use.

For obvious reasons, I will not always give addresses and directions in the local manner.

HOTELS

The best hotel values in San José are to found at the *upper* end of the price scale, but there are also a few good buys in the medium and budget ranges. In general, rooms are larger in the Paseo Colón area than downtown, so you might well give some thought to staying in the west end, at little sacrifice in convenience. Most of the budget hotels are downtown.

Reservations are advisable at any holiday period. Take advantage of toll-free telephone numbers for this purpose, if you can. Otherwise, the airport branch of the tourist office will help you find a room in your price range when you arrive.

There are other hotels than those listed below, in outlying areas, some of them very attractive. But I think that most first-time visitors will want to stay near the central area of San José. For longer visits, consult the ads for guest houses and furnished apartments in the *Tico Times*.

BETTER HOTELS—WEST END

Hotel Cariari. Ciudad Cariari, tel. 390022. 160 rooms. $107-$158 single/$119-$158 double. (May to October: $82-$111 single or double.) Mailing address: Apartado 737,

Centro Colón, San José. U. S. reservations: tel. 800-325-1337 + 221 or 800-327-9408.

The Cariari is not in San José at all, but eight kilometers west of the city, along the Cañas expressway, halfway to the airport. This is a tasteful, modern resort and country-club complex, with a dramatic rotunda entry. The hotel has a pool, sauna, whirlpool, and casino, as well as many shops. For a fee, guests can use an 18-hole golf course, tennis courts, olympic-size swimming pool, basketball courts, and gym. Rooms have color televisions and air conditioning, and there are car rentals and assorted other amenities, including a mini-shopping center with supermarket. The La Flamme French restaurant serves many imported specialties. The coffee shop (Terraza Tropical) serves a buffet-style breakfast and is open 24 hours, as are the seafood restaurant and bar. Shuttle bus service is available to San José every two hours, at a charge. The mountain views from the extensive grounds are lovely, and I wouldn't blame anybody for spending a whole winter vacation here. The upper crust of San José society and politics frequents the facilities.

Hotel Sheraton Herradura, Ciudad Cariari (P.O. Box 7-1880, San José), tel. 390033. 120 rooms. $60-90/$65-105. U.S. reservations: tel. 800-325-3535.

The Herradura is another large and modern hotel, constructed in Spanish-colonial style. Comparable in facilities to the Cariari, but not as well-run. Rooms are among the nicest in or near San José, and have television and air conditioning. There's a large pool. The Bon Vivant restaurant, open evenings, serves French cuisine; Tiffany's serves steaks, chops, and shrimp during the day. And there's even a chapel. Members of AAA and of various other groups get a 25% discount when reservations are made through Sheraton's 800 number.

Hotel Irazú, Autopista Gen. Cañas, tel. 324811. 350 rooms. $55/$62 (slightly less without air conditioning). Mailing address: Apartado 962, San José. U.S. reservations: tel. 800-223-0888 (Canada: 800-268-7041).

The largest hotel in San José, always lively with tour groups, the Irazú is four kilometers west of downtown, in the municipality of La Uruca. Rooms are air-conditioned, and there are two restaurants, lighted tennis courts, pool, sauna, massage service, and numerous shops and real-estate salesmen in the bustling lobby. The location is not far enough from town to be suburban or quiet, and not near enough to be convenient to attractions, but the landscaping and a U-shaped building effectively disguise the urban setting. An hourly shuttle bus to downtown is available. Lower room rates are sometimes offered on site.

Hotel Corobicí, Calle 42, Avenida 5 (P.O. Box 8-5480) tel. 328122. 275 rooms. $60/$70. U.S. reservations: 800-325-1337 + 221, or 305-594-1560.

A modernesque, cream-colored structure that towers over western San José, the Corobicí is under the same management as the Cariari. The facilities here are very attractive, and include a large pool area, health spa, air conditioning and television, a 24-hour coffee shop as well as restaurant, and a courtesy bus to downtown. Though the climate doesn't demand it, there's a huge and impressive Hyatt-style towering indoor lobby.

BETTER HOTELS—DOWNTOWN

Gran Hotel Costa Rica, Avenida Central, Calle 3 (P. O. Box 527), tel. 214000. 104 rooms. $44/$59. U.S. reservations: tel. 800-327-9408 or 305-588-8541

Most Central American capitals have a fine, elegant old hotel, and this is San José's. Across from the national theater and fronting on a small park, the Hotel Costa Rica has renovated, modern rooms, all with television, a chandeliered rooftop dining room, and tasteful, sedate public areas. The Parisien Café on the ground floor is a good locale for observing the goings-on in the center of the city.

Hotel Balmoral, Calle 7, Avenida Central (P. O. Box 3344), tel. 225022. 140 rooms. $50/$59. U.S. reservations: 800-223-9868 or 212-757-2981. Canada: 800-261-9300.

One of the better hotels downtown, with good-sized rooms done in modern decor (with air conditioning and t.v.), ample seating in the lobby, a shopping arcade, and a casino. The Altamira restaurant on the ground floor, recently redone in a garden-style, light decor, is easy on the senses. Pastas and meat main courses $3 to $5.

Hotel Europa, Calle Central, Avenida 5, (P.O. Box 72) tel. 221222. 75 rooms. $36-52/$49-64. U.S. reservations: tel. 800-223-6764, 212-714-2323.

A modern hotel, with air-conditioned rooms, television, and the advantage of an outdoor pool. Not a terrific building, but the level of service distinguishes the establishment. The restaurant is pleasant, and reasonably priced, open from 6:30 a.m. for breakfast. Reduced rates are sometimes available from September to December—look for the ad/coupon in the *Tico Times.*

Aurola Holiday Inn, Calle 5, Avenida 5 (P.O. Box 7802), tel. 337233. 200 rooms. $95-$115/$100-$125. U.S. reservations: 800-465-4329.

Best-equipped of the downtown hotels, with standard Holiday Inn rooms (which are large for San José), non-offensive beige two-story lobby, pool under a dome, sauna, gym, cable television, spa, underground parking, and many shops. There are also a casino, a no-smoking floor, and several bars and restaurants. The rooftop El Mirador features continental cuisine, unsurpassed views, and high prices. Good service, no surprises. This 17-floor hotel is San José's major downtown landmark.

Hotel Bougainvillea, Barrio Tournon, P.O. Box 69-2120 Guadalupe, tel. 336622. 77 rooms. $39-$50/$45-$56, extra person $7.

This is a new and quite attractive hotel, in the style of an Arizona country resort, with soaring beamed ceilings, fireplaces and huge plants in public areas, and wood floors, carpets and generally soothing furnishings in the rooms. The location—eight blocks north of Avenida Central along Calle 3, a short taxi ride from downtown—gets you out of the fumes that sometimes afflict the city center, and is convenient to the El Pueblo shopping and entertainment complex. Solar-heated pool, whirlpool, protected parking, shops, air conditioning. All in all, a very good value. The owners have another, more tranquilly situated hotel in the nearby town of Santo Domingo de Heredia.

MODERATE HOTELS—WEST END

Tennis Club, Sabana Sur (opposite Metropolitan Park), P.O. Box 4964, tel. 321266. 26 rooms. $27-43/$34-50. U.S. reservations: tel. 305-925-2700.

This is a fun place to stay, a lively country club with many of the features of the Cariari and Herradura, but in more modest quarters. Guests have use of tennis courts, pools, sauna, bowling alley, and billiard tables, with some restrictions. The restaurant has a limited but reasonably priced menu. No shops or travel services here.

Hotel Torremolinos, Avenida 5 bis, Calle 40, P. O. Box 2029, tel. 225266. 73 rooms. $56/$63.

In a nice residential neighborhood not far from the Paseo Colón. Travel agency, pool, bar, and moderately priced restaurant.

Hotel Ambassador, Paseo Colón, Calle 28 (P. O. Box 10186), tel. 218155. 70 rooms. $29-42/$37-50.

Plain, good-sized rooms, Italian restaurant.

Apartotel Napoleón, Calle 40, Avenida 5 (P. O. Box 86340-2000 San José), tel. 233252. 32 units. $26-32/$33-40.

This is a hotel of housekeeping units consisting of large bedrooms with attached kitchenettes. Good location, not far from Paseo Colón. Rooms have t.v. and air conditioning, and there's a pool and coffee shop. This and the other "apartoteles" listed below are among the best values in San José, if you don't need the shops, travel agency and room service provided by conventional hotels.

Apartotel Castilla, Calle 24, Avenidas 2/4, tel. 222113. 15 units. $30/$45.

Somewhat worn on the outside, but the units, with one and two bedrooms, are comfortable. Near Paseo Colón.

Apartotel Ramgo, Sabana Sur (one block south of Metropolitan Park), P. O. Box 1441, tel. 323823. From $28 single to $49 for four persons. U.S. reservations tel. 305-925-2700.

Plain but large apartments, each with two bedrooms, kitchen, dining room, laundry area, and terrace, and cable t.v., in a stark building in a residential area on the western edge of San José. Near shopping and bus to downtown. A good value for families or compatible groups.

MODERATE HOTELS—DOWNTOWN

I'm sorry to say that most downtown hotels in this category are more modest in their facilities than in their prices. Most appear to have been sliced from the same modern office cube, according to the size of the available lot, and set down in place. All have limited public space—usually a couple of chairs and sofas in a miniature lobby—and would fit more appropriately in the crowded confines of Amsterdam. Some, indeed, have Dutch names. Don't shy away from these establishments if you want to stay in the middle of the downtown action, but in most cases, don't expect more than a modest room, either.

Hotel Royal Garden. Calle Central, Avenida Central, P. O. Box 3493, tel. 570023. 54 rooms. $35 single/$40 double. U. S. reservations: tel. 800-223-6764 or 212-758-4375.

Exit San José, and enter the mysterious Orient through the front door of the Royal Garden. An elevator takes you to the second floor, where, at 9 a.m., Chinese music tinkles, curtains keep out all but thin shafts of daylight, and smoke floats over the blackjack tables. An unexpected milieu in Central America. Air-conditioned rooms with television, well-managed. The restaurant features a *dim sum* (Chinese breakfast from carts of goodies), as well as American food. Casino hours are 5 p.m. to 11 the next morning. You can't get more central than this hotel. And never dull.

Hotel Plaza, Av. Central, Calle 2/4 (P.O. Box 2019), tel. 225533. 40 rooms. $27/$41.

Central location, restaurant and bar, carpeted rooms with television, some with balconies.

Hotel Amstel, Calle 7, Avenida 1 (P. O. Box 4192), tel. 224622. 55 rooms. $32/$35. U.S./Canada reservations: tel. 305-532-0726.

Air-conditioned rooms in various sizes, less claustrophobic than other downtown hotels, well-run. The restaurant, of no particular genre, is popular with residents, and reasonably priced—$5 for the set lunch. Good location just off Morazán Park.

Hotel La Gran Vía, Av. Central, Calles 1/3 (P. O. Box 1433), tel. 227737. 32 rooms. $29/$33.

The usual tiny lobby, small carpeted rooms, some of which are air-conditioned and have balconies for watching the action on Avenida Central. The restaurant serves a set lunch for about $4.

Hotel Alameda, Avenida Central, Calle 12 (P.O. Box 680), tel. 213045. 52 rooms. $20/$24-$26.

If you have to be near the bus station and market area, this hotel is probably your best choice. Facilities include a full-service restaurant with a few quite reasonably priced items. This is a faded gem with decor straight out of the fifties— flecked carpets, mirror walls and Formica panelling—but then, a lot of San José is mired in that time.

Hotel Presidente, Avenida Central, Calles 7/9 (P.O. Box 2922), tel. 223022. 51 rooms. $40/$51. U.S. reservations: tel. 800-826-6842 or 305-532-1052.

Refurbished hotel, some rooms air conditioned, basic restaurant, bar, a few suites, and the ever-present casino. One of the curiosities here, in a reception room, is a mural of the five-colón note, which itself is a copy of a mural in the National Theater.

Hotel Talamanca, Avenida 2, Calles 8/10 (P.O. Box 449-1002), tel. 335033. 56 rooms. $22/$25. U.S. reservations: tel. 305-925-2700.

Located in the noisy bus terminal and market area. Some rooms have t.v. 24-hour restaurant, bar, casino.

Apartamentos Lamm, Calle 15, Av. 1 (P. O. Box 2729-1000) tel.214920. 19 units. $29 single/$33 double/$36 triple/$51 for six.

Small housekeeping units, each with one bedroom, living room with sofa bed and t.v., and kitchen. Some units have three bedrooms, two bathrooms, terrace, and a larger kitchen. In a central location off National Park, near the Legislative Assembly. Discounts by week and month.

Apartotel San José, Avenida 2, Calle 17/19, tel. 220455. 14 units. $23-28/$28-34.

Similar to Apartamentos Lamm, in a more commercial area with traffic noise.

Hotel Don Carlos, Calle 9, Avenidas 7/9 (P. O. Box 1593), tel. 216707. 10 rooms. $31/$38.

A good, intimate hotel in a remodelled mansion, with comfortable rooms. Centrally located on a quiet street. Management quite helpful. Rates include light breakfast. Television room. Apartments available for about $250 per week.

Hotel Galilea, Av. Central, Calles 11/13, tel. 336925. 24 rooms. $18/$21.

Modern and plain, fair value, near the bus for Cartago, otherwise not a good location.

Hotel Fortuna, Avenida 6, Calles 2/4 (P. O. Box 7-1570), tel. 235344. 24 rooms. $15/$22.

Newer than most hotels in this area (c. 1958), with hot water, private bath, phones in rooms.

Hotel Park, Avenida 4, Calles 2/4. 16 rooms. $20 for one bed, $25 for two beds.

A modest hotel, run by Americans who appear to know what their clients want. Three "suites"—more attractive wood-panelled rooms out back, facing the light well—go for $31 daily. This is a man's world.

BUDGET HOTELS

Hotel Cacts, Avenida 3 Bis, Calles 28/30 (P. O. Box 379-1005), tel. 212928. 20 rooms. $9/$14, or $12/$17 with private bath.

It's hard to call this a budget hotel when you get so much for your money: quiet location just a few blocks from Paseo Colón, modern, airy rooms, free airport pickup with three-day stay, cable and satellite t.v. in the lobby, beverage service and continental breakfast, congeniality, even secretarial services if you need them. Family owners are around to help. Some units have cooking facilities.

Hotel Ritz, Calle Central, Av. 8/10, tel. 224103. 16 rooms. $13/$16.

A modest hotel with small, plain, but clean rooms, and the special asset of warm, helpful American owners. Doubles have private bath. Breakfast only served, coffee on the house, reading area. Upstairs.

Petit Hotel, Calle 24 No. 39. 12 rooms. $12-21/$16-34.

A converted private home, with rooms far more ample and light and airy than at budget hotels downtown. Excellent location one-half block south of Paseo Colón, within walking distance of most intercity buses. Friendly, good value. The lower rates are without private bath.

Costa Rica Inn, Calle 9, Avenidas 1/3, P. O. Box 10282, tel. 225203. 15 rooms. $12/$18. U.S. contact: P. O. Box 59, Arcadia, LA, tel. 318-263-2059.

Tidy and homey, on a quiet street near the city center. All rooms with private bath, and all suffering from the budget-hotel blues of San José: little light and ventilation. But a relatively good value. Rates slightly lower by the week.

The above hotels are the best of the budget establishments in San José. Here are some others, which I mention without particular enthusiasm, because of what they are or where they are:

Hotel Cocorí, Calle 16, Avenida 3, tel. 330081. $9/$11.

I wouldn't want to stay in the noisy area near the bus station, but if you have to, this hotel is all right, of recent vintage, clean and secure. Rooms have private bath and hot water.

Another cheap, relatively safe hotel in the area is the **Boruca,** Calle 14, Avenidas 1/3. There is no end of other places to bed down, if you're not fussy.

Hotel Johnson, Calle 8, Avenidas Central/2 (P. O. Box 6638, tel.237633). 40 rooms. $10/$12.

Your Central American businessmen's hotel—dark, woody, soap operas on t.v. in the lobby, with families crowded around. Relatively large rooms with private bath. Bar, breakfast. Good value.

Gran Hotel Centroamericano, Avenida 2, Calles 6/8, tel.213362. 50 rooms. $8/$12-16. Rank after rank of small rooms, no exterior windows, prison-like. Rooms with musty carpeting cost more.

Hotel Boston, Avenida 8, Calles Central/2, tel. 216944. $6/$10. Large, dark rooms. The **Prince,** a hotel of a similar genre, is around the corner at Avenida 6, Calles Central/2.

A few blocks to the north, comparable hotels include **Hotel Central,** Avenida 3, Calles 4/6 ($9/$11, telephone in room, private baths) and **Hotel Capital,** Calle 4, Avenidas 5/7.

Hotel Asia, Calle 11, Avenidas Central/1, tel. 233893. $5/$8. Simple, with tiny rooms and little light, but clean. Chinese-run, as you might guess. Upstairs.

EASTERN SAN JOSE

Eastern San José is carbon monoxide alley, where, for a good part of the day, buses, trucks and cars back up as they try to get into or out of town along Avenida Central. Nevertheless, there are some attractive accommodations in the middle- and upper-class residential districts out this way. Hotels away from Avenida Central are preferable.

Toruma Youth Hostel, Avenida Central, Calles 31/33. A neoclassic tin-roofed mansion, right on Avenida Central. You stay in dormitories, and have access to laundry service, game rooms, and the special atmosphere of a younger, international crowd. Some food service. $3 or so with international youth-hostel card, more without. Front door open from 6 a.m. to 11 p.m.

Apartotel Conquistador, P. O. Box 303, San Pedro, tel. 253022. 29 units. $26/$31 Television, phone, pool, kitchen.

Apartamentos Scotland, Avenida 1, Calle 27, tel. 230833. One-bedroom, furnished, garden-type apartments, each with separate entrance, from $155 weekly, $385 monthly, linen and electricity extra at the monthly rate. A few lower-priced apartments also available.

Apartotel Los Yoses, Avenida Central, Calle 43 (P.O. Box 1597), tel. 250033. 23 units. $20-$30/$23-$34. Small, modern units for up to six persons. Pool, cooking facilities

WEST OF SAN JOSE

Attractive accommodations are available in suburban Escazú (mentioned later in this chapter). Rooms at the **Hotel Mirador Pico Blanco** (P.O. Box 900 Escazú, tel. 283197, $30 to $40 double) offer sweeping views of the Central Valley from their balconies. **Posada Pegasus** (P.O. Box 370-1250 Escazú, tel. 284196) is somewhat similar, with a country atmosphere, less than a half-hour from downtown San José. There are only a few rooms at either place, so call before you go.

Luxurious suburban garden apartments are available at **Apartotel María Alexandra**, Calle 3, Avenida 23, San Rafael de Escazú (P. O. Box 3756-1000 San José, tel. 281507, 14 units, $30 triple to $45 for a five), a block off Escazú's main street in a pleasant residential neighborhood. Units have washing machines, air conditioning, and cable television, and the complex includes a pool and sauna, bar, restaurant, and travel agency.

The bus to Escazú leaves from Calle 1, Avenida 16/18, San José.

CAMPING

The only trailer park currently operating near San José is in San Antonio de Belén, eight kilometers west of the city, not far from the airport. Take the San Antonio turnoff from the Cañas expressway, then continue two kilometers to the entrance, opposite the Seaboard Marine depot—there is currently no sign. This is a pleasant parking area with lots of trees, though facilities are limited. Rates are about $5 per day. Telephone 412270 or 412595.

RESTAURANTS

Some very good food, indeed, is to be found in and near San José. Numerous restaurants specialize in Swiss, Central European, Spanish, French, Italian and Chinese cuisine, as well as steaks and seafood. There are many clean, reasonably priced luncheonettes, and a very few restaurants even serve native Costa Rican specialties.

The best chefs take advantage of the beef, fish (usually *corvina*, or sea bass), chicken and fresh fruits and vegetables that are abundant at all times of the year. Shrimp and lobster are usually available and are attractively served in a number of restaurants, but are no bargain—that innocent shrimp appetizer suggested by your waiter will usually run well over $10. Drinkable wines and imported liquors are quite expensive—double or triple the American price—so you may want to consider the excellent Costa Rican beers or local rums and other spirits.

Most restaurants open for lunch from 11:30 a.m. to 2:30 p.m., and for dinner from 6:30 p.m. or 7 p.m. to 10 or 10:30 p.m. Luncheonettes ("sodas") and many of the inexpensive restaurants are open throughout the day. A good hour for dinner in San José is 7:30 p.m. or so.

Some of the better dining places are open in the evenings only. But at those that serve lunch, you'll often find an all-inclusive special for about the same price as a main course alone. Look for the *almuerzo ejecutivo*.

My selection of restaurants is mostly limited to the downtown and Paseo Colón areas, near the major hotels. Also take a look at the restaurants mentioned under hotels, above. But don't limit yourself to these. There are many more good choices, both in central San José and in the suburbs. Consult the ads and the "On the Town" column in the *Tico Times*, and *Guide* magazine. Or walk into any place that looks attractive. You generally don't have to worry about the safety of the food.

DOWNTOWN

Chalet Suizo, Avenida 1, Calles 5/7. The Swiss Chalet is nicely atmospheric, with wainscotted walls, wooden beams, brick hearth and costumed waiters. And the cuisine is authentic. The house steak, covered with ham and cheese, is excellent, and there are fondues, goulash, smoked pork chops, seafood items, fine French and Italian desserts, and much more. Most entrees run $4 to $6, the inclusive lunch $5.

Isle de France, Calle 7, Avenidas Central/2. An excellent little French restaurant. Not at all cheap for San José. A daily complete lunch goes for about $10. Specialties are paté maison, tournedos, Vichyssoise, and rich soups. Most entrees $7 and up.

Casino Español, Calle 7, Avenidas Central/1. The gastronomic tour continues with fine Spanish cuisine. Specialties are quail in wine, tripe, Asturian fabada (stew), and paella. Elegant atmosphere and service. Entrees $5 to $8, fixed-price lunch for $5.

El Escorial, Avenida 1, Calles 5/7, is a popular, popular-priced, noisy, open-to-the-street restaurant that might have been transplanted from the bullring district of Seville, music and all. At lunchtime, you can fill your plate from the self-service tables for just $2. Or choose from the many, many Spanish specialties—eight kinds of paella, Spanish sausage, Asturian stew, mixed grills and seafood platters, for $3 and up.

For more formal but still friendly Spanish food, go across the street to Goya, Calle 1, Avenidas 5/7. Rabbit in wine, beef with mushrooms, paella, $4 to $6 for a main course, tablecloths, arches and atmosphere included.

Less expensive, and less elegant, the **Casa España** restaurant, part of a private club but open to outsiders, sits on the top (sixth) floor of the Banco de San José building, Calle Central, Avenidas 3/5. $3 will get you a well-prepared *prix fixe* lunch that might include asparragus soup, sea bass in a sauce, squash, and rice. And there are a la carte paellas, filet mignon and fish for $6 and up. Don't miss the views! Open from 11 a.m.

Probably no city in the hemisphere has as many Chinese eateries for its size as San José. Chinese food generally runs in the medium price range. And you pay extra for rice. One of the better Chinese restaurants is the Nueva China in San Pedro (see below). In the downtown area, **Lung Mun,**

Calle 1, Avenidas 5/7, serves Tico-style food at its lunch buffet, for about $2. A la carte American and Cantonese food runs $2 to $4 for a main course. If you have a hankering for shrimp, you can get it in your chow mein here for much less than elsewhere. Another good downtown choice, with both western and oriental choices, and a *dim sum* on Sundays, is the restaurant of the Hotel Royal Garden, Calle Central and Avenida Central. Lunch costs just $3.

La Hacienda, Calle 7, Avenidas Central/2, is one of many restaurants in San José specializing in charcoal-broiled steaks and chops. Mixed grills, steaks or luncheon specials for $6 and up. **Kamakiri** steak house, Calle 3, Avenidas Central/1, upstairs in the arcade, is more lively, with music. **La Esmeralda**, Avenida 2, Calles 5/7, is an open-to-the-street establishment with strolling Mexican musicians. Steaks from $5, set lunches for $3, including a drink.

Balcón de Europa, Avenida 7, Calle 1. This is more than a restaurant, it's an industry. The main establishment, extremely popular, serves Italian-style meat main courses, such as scallopine, for $5, as well as pastas. House wine, at $1.50 a glass, is more inexpensive than just about anywhere else in San José. Next door, on the corner, under the same ownership, is Finisterre-Food World, a woody old bar and dining room, where the daily lunch special (example: veal in wine, soup, dessert) costs about $3. A few native combination plates are offered as well. For the price, the food is more attractively served than you might expect, and you get real vegetables, not just rice. Around the corner is still another eatery under the same management, a modest soda and bar.

La Cocina de Leña. You could spend weeks in San José and think that native-style food didn't exist. La Cocina de Leña (The Wood Stove), in the El Pueblo shopping center north of downtown, is one of the few places where you can enjoy home cooking. Tiny tables, piles of firewood, whitewashed walls, subdued lighting, and decorations of colorful enamelware and gourd beakers all re-create the atmosphere of a dark, smoky country kitchen. The menu—printed on a paper bag—is a lesson in traditional Costa Rican cooking. Some items: olla de carne (meat stew), mondongo en salsa (ox in tomato sauce), stuffed pepper or cabbage, chilasquiles (tortillas filled with meat), pozol (corn soup), and the old standby, gallo pinto (rice and beans). Most entrees are served with tortillas and beans, and run $4 to $6, or you can get the complete lunch special for $5. To get here, take the Calle Blancos bus from Avenida 5, Calles 1/3.

Also in El Pueblo are **Lancer's Steak House**, which offers complete, low-priced lunches; **Rías Bajas**, an excellent seafood house; and numerous other eating and drinking spots.

Cafés: There aren't many of these, but two are reminiscent of Europe. The Parisien Café of the Hotel Costa Rica, Calle 3 at Avenida 2, provides sidewalk seating with a view to the national theater, the Plaza de la Cultura, and the continuing activity of vendors and buskers in the adjacent small park. A fine place for extended sitting, reading, or people-watching. More elegant is the café across the street in the National Theater itself where, at marble-topped tables, surrounded by works of art and bathed in recorded chamber music, you can enjoy a sandwich and coffee for less than $3, or a luncheon special for slightly more.

Buffets: The Gran Hotel Costa Rica, Avenida Central at Calle 3, serves buffet breakfasts, lunches and dinners in its ground-floor Jardín restaurant for $6 to $7. At the Holiday Inn, Calle 5, Avenida 5, a breakfast buffet is served in the main floor coffee shop for $7, and there are Italian and seafood buffets during the week and Sunday brunch for $10 to $12. The rattan furnishings are attractive. The regular menu in the coffee shop is nothing special.

Smokey's Garden of Eatin', in the courtyard-light shaft of the Hotel Park (Av. 4, Calles 2/4) serves breakfasts from the U.S. South (pancakes, grits, waffles, sausage patties and the like) and Reuben and pastrami sandwiches from the U.S. North (or maybe Miami Beach). Also chili con carne. $3 for anything. American and friendly.

Sodas are San José's all-purpose coffee shops and diners, where in simple, soda-shop surroundings you can enjoy anything from a cup of coffee or a drink to a sandwich or a steak. The blue-plate luncheon special usually runs $3 or less with tax and service. At **Soda Sina**, opposite the Hotel Amstel at Calle 7 and Avenida 1, complete breakfasts are about $2, shots of rum less than a dollar, main meat and fish courses

$3 and up. Similar fare and clean surroundings are available at almost any soda in San José. Among them are:

Soda Central, Avenida 1, Calles 3/5. A hole in the wall with cheap sandwiches and drinks.

Soda Palace, Avenida 2, Calle 2, on Parque Central. Good seats for watching the main square. Mainly drinks and sandwiches. Opposite the Palace, the **Restaurant Boruca** serves American breakfasts, and a $2 lunch special. And a block to the east, the soda of the Melico Salazar theater, at Avenida 2, Calle Central, offers mostly beverages, and less of a view.

Soda Yuré, Avenida 2,, Calle 3, downstairs in the arcade next to the Gran Hotel Costa Rica. Open 7 a.m. to 4 p.m., Monday through Friday.

Soda Vishnu, Calle 3, Avenidas Central/1, is vegetarian, with fruit and vegetable cocktails, and an Indian-flavored lunch special for $2.

Soda La Casita, Avenida 1, Calles Central/1, sits you down in booths and serves you fresh fruit drinks, pastries, and *empanadas* (meat-filled pastries).

Risas, Calle 1, Avenidas Central/1, is somewhere between a soda and a restaurant/bar. Ceviche (marinated-fish cocktail), stews and steaks for $4 and up, fishburgers and American-style (large) hamburgers in several decorations for $1.50 to $2.50. Open 11 a.m. to midnight.

Also somewhere in-between is **Spoons,** on Avenida Central, Calles 5/7, with light lunches and heavy desserts. About $4 for lunch with lasagna, a salad or the plat du jour, or $2 for something gooey with coffee.

Fast Food: McDonald's, familiar and reliable, is at Calle 4, Avenidas Central/1. Prices are about the same as in the States—$1.80 for a Big Mac—and they have refreshing iced tea with lemon. Another location is at Avenida Central, Calles 5/7, opposite the Plaza of Culture. McDonald's clones include Woopy's, Avenida 2, Calle 2, and Hardee's, Avenida Central, Calle 1. Pollo Kentucky (Kentucky Fried Chicken) has outlets at Avenida 2 and Calle 6, and Avenida Central and Calle 2. The colonel's lunch runs $3 to $4. Archi's, Avenida Central, Calles 5/7, is a cross between McD's and the Colonel, serving two pieces of chicken and a roll for about $2. Don Taco, Avenida 1, Calles Central/2, serves tacos, burritos, and similar Tex-Mex fare, along with hamburgers. $2 to $3 for a light meal. Last and not so fast is Pizza Hut, serving pizzas, subs and spaghetti, at Avenida 1, Calles 3/5; and Calle 4, Avenidas Central/2. $5 and up for a large pizza, $1.50 salad bar.

Inexpensive Food: There are cheap eateries all along the block of Calle 5 facing the Plaza of Culture (Avenidas Central/2). **Rincón de España**, a bar, has a daily lunch (example: chicken and rice) with a drink for under $2. Elsewhere, **Restaurant Poás,** Avenida 7, Calles 3/5, is an inelegant, hole-in-the-wall joint, more fun than the sterile places nearer to Avenida Central. Set lunch specials go for about $2 or less. Some of the plates, like *casado* (meat with cabbage and rice and beans) and *olla de carne* (stew) are home-style Costa Rican classics. Breakfast and dinner are served as well. For a whole array of cheap, inelegant eateries, hasten to the **Central Market**, Calle 6, Avenida 1, where you can fill your stomach with cabbage, rice, beans, eggs, and stew for $2.

Self-Service: The point-and-shoot method of ordering is useful if you're in a hurry, or if your Spanish produces unpredictable results. **Chips**, on Calle 5 opposite the Plaza of Culture, has lasagna, chicken and pizza. $3 and up for lunch. **El Escorial**, Avenida 1, Calles 5/7, and **Lung Mun**, Calle 1, Avenidas 5/7, both mentioned above, have cafeteria set-ups at lunchtime where you can fill your plate for about $2.

Snacks: Pops, Avenida Central, Calles 1/3 (and just about everywhere else in San José) has the best ice cream in Costa Rica. From 40 cents for a cone. **Pastelería Schmidt**, Avenida 2 at Calle 4, sells excellent breads and pastries, which may be eaten in, with a cup of coffee, or carried out. Another location at Avenida Central and Calle 11. **Churrería Manolo**, Avenida Central, Calles Central/2, serves those greasy, finger-shaped Mexican donuts (*churros*), and sandwiches. San José's ubiquitous fruit carts sell bananas and pineapple and papaya at almost every corner. At Christmas, they offer apples and grapes, which are great and expensive delicacies. And there are many hamburger and hot dog vendors as well.

WEST END

La Masia de Triquell, Avenida 2, Calle 40. Spanish and Continental cuisine in a large old house with plenty of arches and stuccoed walls. Paella for $10, sea bass in bearnaise sauce and steak in garlic sauce for about $8.

La Bastille, Paseo Colón at Calle 22, is a fine French restaurant, where food preparation is painstaking. Assorted soups such as consommé with sherry, appetizers like caviar, and classic beef preparations as a main course: stroganoff, filet mignon, tenderloin Provençal in Café de Paris sauce; also sea bass in an interesting wine sauce with apples, grapes and peaches. $15 and up.

Le Chandelier, Paseo Colón, Calle 30. The storefront is unpretentious, but inside, this is an intimate, elegant restaurant—walls covered in brocade, and, yes, a chandelier. And there's nothing unpretentious about the fine, creative continental dining, some of the best in San José. Meats and poultry are served in delicate sauces, vegetables are crisp, and service and presentation are faultless. On a recent visit, I had one of the specials of the evening, breasts of chicken in morel sauce, which, aside from being delicious, was easily double the portion I would expect in Manhattan or Montreal. Paté, a cheese plate and cookies come courtesy of the house. Regular items on the menu include Caesar salad for two, three tenderloins in café de Paris sauce, and sea bass quenelle. You'll spend at least $20 here for dinner—it's worth it—but the tab can run much, much higher. If prices put you off, there's a modest soda next door, also called Le Chandelier, with lunch plates for under $4.

Beirut, Avenida 1, Calle 32. Your classic neighborhood Lebanese eatery, anything but elegant, but clean and pleasant. You eat in one of several rooms in an old wooden house. Kibbeh, kabba, schawarma, kebabs and combinations thereof, all for about $4. Lebanese food is always good. Closed Monday, lunch only on Sunday.

La Fontana di Trevi, in the Hotel Ambassador, Paseo Colón, Calle 28. The value here is the $4 fixed-price lunch, which includes soup, a main course such a chicken in wine, a dessert such as cassata, and coffee. Also a la carte pasta and meats from $5. Open from 11:30 a.m. for lunch, from 6 p.m. for dinner.

Antojitos Cancun, Paseo Colón, Calles 24/26, next to Pizza Hut, downstairs, has Tex-Mex tacos, enchiladas and burritos in assorted combinations for $1.50 to $5, and all the beer you need to wash it down. Kiddy seats available.

La Mallorquina, Paseo Colón, Calles 28/30. The owners are from Mallorca, but the cuisine is a combination of Spanish and French. Not unlike a restaurant in Spain, with Flamenco music in the background, fans wafting the air, and arches, though not excessively formal. Main courses run from $7 to $12, anything with shellfish $16 and up. A recent luncheon special included a crisp salad, blanquettes of veal in white wine sauce (something like an elegant stroganoff), followed by an excellent custard, for $7. There's a large selection of expensive wine, and the snacks are free at the bar.

Lobster's Inn, Paseo Colon at Calle 24. Good seafood. Lobster and shrimp are expensive—$20—but sea bass (corvina) is reasonable at about $7, served in a variety of ways, and there are continental beef main courses—veal cordon bleu, chicken chasseur. Not quite the environment of the Chandelier, but not the prices, either.

Ana, Paseo Colón, Calles 24/26. An unpretentious and inexpensive Italian restaurant serving lasagna, spaghetti, veal and non-Italian dishes for $3 to $5. Pleasant surroundings, especially in the upstairs dining room. **Piccolo Roma,** Avenida 2, Calle 24, has more home-style Italian food. Many pastas, pepper steak and seafood for $4 to $7, complete lunches for $3.50.

Arirang, at Paseo Colón and Calle 38, in the Centro Colón building, is your standard Korean family restaurant. You're served various combinations of pork or beef or chicken with vegetables, or tempura, at Formica tables. It's very good, and at $3 or so for a main course, the price is right.

El Chicote, Sabana Norte (facing the north side of, and near the west end of, Metropolitan Park). An excellent steak house with a nice arched interior, and reasonable prices. All sorts of steaks and chops go for $6 and up, and there are a few creative specialties, such as tenderloin stuffed with shrimp. To get here, take the bus marked "Sabana Estadio" from Avenida 3 between Calles Central and 1, or from along Paseo Colón.

Farther west, and south, in suburban Escazú, is the **El Churrasco** steak house. Here you get more atmosphere—brick surroundings, and pottery decorations. Steak comes in assorted cuts and sizes, draft beer is served, and there are salads and appetizers. $10 and up. Drive, or take the Escazú bus from Avenida 1, Calles 16/18, San José. The restaurant is half a block off Escazú's main street—look for a sign pointing the way.

Soda Tapia, Calle 42, Avenida 2, opposite Metropolitan Park. More a café than a soda, good for sandwiches and fruit salad at the outdoor tables.

Fast Food: There's a **McDonald's** on Calle 42, a couple of blocks south of Paseo Colón. **Pollo Kentucky** (Kentucky Fried Chicken) has an outlet at Paseo Colón, Calles 32/34 which, whatever its culinary virtues, is a common reference point for giving directions. **Pizza Hut** is at Paseo Colón and Calle 28.

San José 2000 is not a restaurant, but a shopping center. If you're staying at the Hotel Irazú next door, you'll find some good alternative eating here. **La Fuente de los Mariscos** offers seafood at prices much lower than elsewhere in the city: shrimp from $3 to $10, depending on the size, a combination dish for $4. **El Tapatío,** a Mexican restaurant, serves several kinds of mole, for about $5, and there's a Chinese restaurant as well. From the Paseo Colón area, you can walk out to San José 2000 along the Cañas expressway; or else take an Alajuela bus.

SAN PEDRO/EAST END

This is not an area that most visitors get to on their first trip. But you'll go out this way to be near a university crowd, or if you visit the insect museum. The **Nueva China,** Calle 11, Avenida Central, San Pedro, is everybody's recommended Chinese restaurant. The decor and ambience are authentically oriental, right down to the imported tile. The menu has two sections, Chinese and "international" (if you want it). Peking duck can be prepared with a day's notice, but on a walk-in basis, you can try shrimp soup, garlic-honey chicken, or chicken Szechuan. Main courses come in two sizes, and run $5 to $8. Remember to order your rice separately if you want it. And *insist* on spicy if you like it that way. Chinese white wine is available. A dim sung is served at breakfast on Saturday and Sunday. My fortune cookie: *"La prisa puede llevarle a cometer errores importantes."* To reach the Nueva China, take the San Pedro bus from Avenida 2, Calles 5/7.

BARS

Drinking is a pastime that most Costa Ricans feel comfortable with, and the visitor, in turn, will feel comfortable in any halfway-decent-looking bar. All are reasonably priced, with domestic drinks for $1 or less. Bocas (snacks) are served on the side, sometimes at a price in the fancier establishments. Many of the downtown bars are good places to rendezvous with other foreigners. Among them:

Piano Blanco Bar, Avenida Central, Calles 7/9. A popular spot for those in transit to the coast.

Disco Túnel del Tiempo, Avenida Central, Calles 7/9. A discotheque, not a bar, probably more to local tastes than yours, but centrally located.

Key Largo, Calle 7, Avenida 3, on Morazán Park. Nice, old house with a few nautical motifs in the yard and Tiffany lamps in one of the dark drinking rooms, not quite the Bogart atmosphere that the management advertises. Casino, live music, ladies of the evening, happy hour most afternoons,

Nashville South, Calle 5, Avenidas 1/3, is your light-wood, down-home bar where serious music is played.

The bar at the **Park Hotel**, Av. 4, Calles 2/4, is a gathering spot for Americans and other foreigners on extended stays. The neighborhood is just a little bit seedy, but not in a dangerous way.

Bar México, Avenida 13, Calle 16. A bright spot in a run-down neighborhood, painted on the outside in red, white and green, well-kept with polished wood tables in the arched interior. Marinated fish and snacks are served with the drinks, but the attraction is mariachi music. Open from 3 p.m., from 11 a.m. Saturday, closed Sunday. Walk from the Coca-Cola bus terminal area, or take the Barrio México bus from Avenida 2, Calles 6/8. Next to the bar is the neighborhood church, visible from many parts of San José, huge and multidomed on a bare, concrete utility-building base.

El Pueblo shopping center, mentioned above under restaurants, has numerous bars and *boites*, as well as trinket shops for an evening of browsing in a pleasant mock-colonial environment. Take the Calle Blancos bus from Avenida 5, Calles 1/3.

Club Cocodrilo, on Calle Central in San Pedro (see East End, above) is a university hangout, with continuous movies, flashing lights, videos, and a namesake over the huge bar. Immensely popular. Steaks for $5, burgers and fries for $3, all well presented.

THE SIGHTS OF SAN JOSE

San José does not have all that much in the way of obligatory sights to see. If your time is short, limit your rounds to the high points: the National Theater and Plaza of Culture, the National Museum, and the Jade Museum. These can be seen in a half-day, or between excursions to the volcanoes and countryside around San José. At a more leisurely pace, you can cover the itinerary below, and get to know the city better, in a couple of days or more. Most of the places mentioned are within a half-mile or so of the Central Park.

Any walking tour of San José starts at the Parque Central (the Central Park, or main square), bounded by Calles Central and 2, and Avenidas 2 and 4. Bus after city bus stops and accepts the long queues of commuters along all four edges. Horns beep incessantly and traffic slams into gear and races ahead at the change of lights on wide Avenida 2. Office buildings and advertising billboards tower overhead. But the park is an oasis in all this, a neat, gardened square where workers on their breaks and anyone with a few moments to spare will sit on the benches, pass the time of day, read a book, and, perhaps, engage the visitor in conversation

Central San José

about such favorite themes as Costa Rican democracy, Costa Rican economic problems, Costa Rican foreign policy, and Costa Rican women. A massive bandstand squats at the center of the park, sheltering a children's library in its base. Public concerts are offered on most Sunday mornings in this musically concerned city.

Across Calle Central from the park is the Catedral Metropolitana (Metropolitan Cathedral), one of the many undistinguished churches of relatively recent vintage in San José. Cream-colored, blocky on the outside, with neo-classical pediment and columns at the entry, the Cathedral has a massive, barrel-arched interior. Much more interesting is the ecclesiastical administration building attached to the rear of the Cathedral, done in the charming and disappearing nineteenth-century San José style, with a European face—in this instance stone-cased windows and pediments straight out of Renaissance Italy—and a red tin roof.

On the north side of the square, at the corner of Calle Central, is the restored Melico Salazar theater, a period piece of pre-depression tropical urban architecture, with fluted

Corinthian columns, balconies, and stuccoed relief sculptures in the pediments.

A couple of blocks down Avenida 2, at the corner of Calle 3, stands the Teatro Nacional, the National Theater, which over the Years has come to embody San José and its self-image as a cultural center. And with good reason, for a more impressive public structure is to be found in no city for a thousand miles to the north or south.

The construction of the theater came about in a fit of national pique, after an opera company cancelled a performance in San José in 1890, for lack of a suitable hall. In response, the coffee growers of Costa Rica levied a cultural tax on their exports, engaged the appropriate experts, and had their theater completed seven years after the insult.

Though sometimes advertised as a replica of the Paris or Milan opera, the block-long National Theater is neither, and stands on its own. Columns and pediment and window arches are carved into the massive stone blocks of its majestic Italianate neo-classical facade, which is crowned with allegorical statues of Dance, Music and Fame. The sides of the building are less elegant, faced with cement plaster, and the tin roofing is purely San José.

Astride the entrance to the theater stand statues of Beethoven and the Spanish dramatist Calderón de la Barca; in the vestibule are allegorical figures of Comedy and Tragedy. In the Costa Rican tradition of importing and assimilating Culture, these were executed by European masters. Belgians designed the building and fabricated its steel structural members. And Germans, Spaniards and Italians collaborated on the architectural work and interior decoration. But Costa Rica is present as well. The sculpture called Heroes of Misery, in the vestibule, is the work of native Juan Ramón Bonilla; and the stairway paintings depict themes of Costa Rican life and commerce—coffee and banana harvest and shipment, and local fruits and flowers. The parquet flooring in much of the theater is made from native hardwoods.

Especially impressive inside the theater building are the foyer, upstairs, with its three-part ceiling painting representing Dawn, Day and Night; the interior marble staircases;

National Theater and Plaza of Culture

the gilt decorations throughout; and, of course, the multi-tiered great hall.

The National Theater is the locale of regular concerts by the national orchestra, which was transformed into a full-time professional and teaching organization in 1971, with the acquisition of a number of foreign musicians; and of performances by the youth orchestra, and native and foreign drama companies and artists. Tickets are sold in advance at the little building alongside the theater, for as little as $2. Admission for sightseeing costs about $1.

Opposite the entrance to the National Theater is a little park where vendors of handicrafts—model oxcarts, dolls, jewelry and leather—display their wares. Adjacent is the stately Gran Hotel Costa Rica, with its pleasant ground-floor café. There's another café in the theater itself.

Along Avenida Central between Calles 3 and 5 is the Plaza de la Cultura (Plaza of Culture). The commercial buildings that once occupied the site were razed to create an open expanse decorated with flowers and benches, and platforms, where outdoor performances are sometimes given. To preserve the broad vista to the adjacent National Theater, a complex of exhibit halls has been constructed below ground level. Foremost of the displays is the exquisite gold collection of the Banco Central de Costa Rica, with over a thousand pre-Columbian decorations, mostly from burial sites in the southern Pacific coastal region of Costa Rica. Also included are jade ornaments from Costa Rica and other countries. Currently, the exhibit is only open on weekends from 10 a.m. to 5 p.m.

Near the entrance to the exhibit area, at the corner of Avenida Central and Calle 5, is the information center of the Costa Rican Tourist Board (Instituto Costarricense de Turismo), where the personnel are quite helpful in answering questions, providing maps, schedules and brochures, and generally orienting the visitor.

Six blocks east of the Plaza of Culture, and up the hill known as the Cuesta de Moras, is the National Museum (Museo Nacional), housed in the old Bellavista Fortress, once the headquarters of the now-defunct army.

Of major interest in the museum is the pre-Columbian collection, one of the largest of its kind. All of the materials are shown quite logically, divided into the three major cultural zones of the country, and arranged chronologically for each. Many but not all of the exhibits are labelled in both English and Spanish, and a map helps to explain Costa Rica's importance as a meeting point of three cultural traditions. It's fascinating to see in a few minutes the progress of pottery in the Nicoya region, over a period of more than a thousand years, from plain and primitive figurines to the exquisite polychrome vases in anthropomorphic form that were manufactured at the time of the Spanish conquest. In the Atlantic region, the figures are less sophisticated, in buff and brown, but no less beautiful. The Diquis region is represented by its own pottery styles, and by its fabled, near-perfect stone spheres, some of which are up to two-and-a-half meters in diameter. There are, as well, examples of goldwork, including pendants and pectoral discs, and jade from the northern half of Costa Rica.

The National Museum also has an extensive collection of colonial furniture; printing presses and historical imprints from the era of independence; period costumes; portraits of presidents and politicians; and a cellar of religious art, in-

Nicoya Pottery in National Museum

cluding saints in wood and plaster, vestments, and paintings executed over the period from colonial times to the present.

Bellavista fortress itself is one of the few colonial-style structures in San José, dominating the central part of the city, massive, towered, gray and brusque on the outside, pocked by bullet holes from the 1948 civil war, but quite lovely from the inner gardened courtyard, with tile roofs, whitewashed walls, and covered passageways. All of the exhibit rooms have high, beamed ceilings. On sale at the museum shop are examples of Talamanca Indian weaving, bows and arrows, and gourd crafts, which are some of the best souvenirs available in San José.

The National Museum is open every day except Monday from 8:30 a.m. to 5 p.m. (Sunday from 9 a.m.) There is a small admission charge.

Across Calle 15 from the National Museum is the Plaza of Democracy, dedicated in 1989 to mark 100 years of popularly elected governments. Like the Plaza of Culture, this open area was created by demolishing houses and offices, replacing them with terraces suitable for cultural activities, and, with the Legislative Assembly just to the north across

Avenida Central, no doubt for political demonstrations as well. The legislature is a cream-colored, Moorish-style building. You may go in the side door and look around, but it's all quite unprepossessing and uninteresting, except, perhaps, as an artifact of Costa Rica's rather un-Latin non-aggrandizement of its political institutions.

North of the legislature is Parque Nacional (National Park), one of San José's nicely landscaped shady squares. The city planners have gone in for tall trees that make for a wonderful cool shade in the middle of the day. The park's centerpiece is an allegorical statue depicting the five Central American nations in arms, driving out the American adventurer William Walker, who had installed himself as ruler of Nicaragua in 1856. Across from the north side of the park is the National Library (Biblioteca Nacional), a modern and not particularly attractive airline-terminal sort of building, decorated with a splotchy mosaic of the sun. There are exhibit areas inside.

Northwest of National Park is the block-square compound of the National Liquor Factory. Liquor is a big business in Costa Rica, in terms of the size of the country, and most of it is the business of a government-owned company. There are branch operations elsewhere in the country.

West of the liquor factory, between Avenidas 5 and 7, at 11 Calle, is Parque España (Park of Spain), also known as Parque de la Expresión, an enchanting little enclave of towering tropical trees transplanted from around the country. On Sundays, many of San José's artists display and sell their work here.

On the north side of Parque España, at Avenida 7 and Calle 11, is the modern office tower of the Instituto Nacional de Seguros, the government insurance monopoly. On the eleventh floor is the Museum of Pre-Columbian Jade (Museo de Jade), open Monday through Friday from 9 a.m. to 3 p.m. The name of the museum is somewhat misleading, for the collection is comprehensive, with contemporary pottery, tools, weapons and dress of the surviving native peoples of Costa Rica; exhibits showing how jade and gold and stone were worked; and a fascinating assortment of utilitarian art, with such pieces as *metates* (grinding stones) in anthropomorphic form. Of course, there is much purely decorative art, including jade pendants and necklaces produced by cultures that have now been obliterated.

The museum also offers from its high perch some excellent views of San José and environs—to the north and the volcanoes from the lounge, and to the south and the city center from the vestibule. The first building visible to the south is the Edificio Metálico (Metal Building), an unusual structure designed in France by Victor Baltard, architect of Les Halles. Incongruous and green-painted, with rusting roof panels, the Edificio Metálico was one of the first of the prefabs, shipped in pieces from Europe. It's now used as a school.

Across Calle 11 from the insurance building is the attractive, Spanish-style Casa Amarilla, which houses Costa Rica's foreign ministry.

North of Parque España is one of the more traditional neighborhoods of San José. Here are large, older homes in wood, decorated with fretwork and crowned with steep tin roofs; and stuccoed brick homes with Renaissance and baroque elements, sometimes painted in pastel colors. See this tropical wedding-cake architecture while you can. Construction in San José has slowed down with the economic problems of recent years, but these buildings are sure to disappear.

At the northern edge of downtown is Parque Zoológico Simón Bolívar (Simón Bolívar Zoological Park). Follow Calle 7 north, then Avenida 11 east to the entrance. Here are turtles, monkeys, macaws, peccaries, vultures, jaguars, alligators, ducks, and much else brought from all parts of Costa Rica to a rain forest planted in the middle of the city, complete with palms, bromeliads and aromatic plants. The zoo is well worth a visit if you have even a mild interest in the wildlife of Costa Rica. Also here is an information center for the national parks where publications are on sale. Bolívar Park is open Tuesday through Friday from 8:30 a.m. to 3:30 p.m., weekends and holidays from 9 a.m. to 4:30 p.m., with a small admission charge.

South of the zoo, back in the central part of the city, is Parque Morazán, divided by heavily trafficked Calle 7 and Avenida 3 into four separate gardens. The nicest is the Japanese-style northeast section, with ponds, a temple-like gazebo, little bridges, and a kids' playground. The structure at the center of the park is the Temple of Music, another of San José's tributes to the finer things.

West along Avenida 3, between Calles Central and 1, is the former site of the United States embassy. People still commonly refer to the embassy's old location when giving directions in the downtown area. The real embassy is now located in suburban Pavas.

Farther west, on Calle 2, facing a pleasant mini-park, is the baroque palace that houses the central post office (Correos y Telégrafos, or Cortel).

The Central Market (Mercado Central), at Calle 6 and Avenida 1, is a block-long area housing vendors of flowers, baskets, vegetables, shoes, spices, and a few souvenirs. It's small and sedate by Central American standards, but worth a walk-through. Other markets nearby are the Borbón, a block north, at Calle 8 between Avenidas 3 and 5, and the Coca-Cola bus terminal and market, Calle 16 between Avenidas 1 and 3. Just as interesting as the markets is the thriving general commerce of the area, where stores, stalls and street hustlers hawk fruit, firecrackers, flypaper, firearms, and countless other articles, many of which you'd have trouble finding at home.

One last downtown reference point, bounded by Avenidas 2 and 4, and Calles 12 and 14, is Parque Carrillo (Carrillo Park), also known as Parque Merced, after the church nearby. The park is typically treed and nicely landscaped, though the neighborhood is heavily trafficked and noisy. One interesting feature, though, is the park's centerpiece, a four-foot-diameter pre-Columbian stone sphere from Palmar Sur, in the southern Diquis region. Other examples of these near-perfect forms are to be seen at the National Museum and, as originals or reproductions, on many a lawn in San José, where they are popular decorations.

North of downtown, and of interest to visitors with time to browse and shop, is the El Pueblo Shopping Center (Centro Comercial). This is a tasteful, charming collection of shops, offices and restaurants, constructed in a style reminiscent of a colonial village, with narrow lanes, wrought-iron lamps, tile roofs, whitewashed brick and stuccoed walls, and beamed ceilings. It's almost better than the real thing. Most of the action at El Pueblo takes place after dark. Take the Calle Blancos bus from Avenida 5, Calles 1/3, or a taxi.

Less than a mile to the west of downtown, at the opposite end of the upscale Paseo Colón district, is Parque Metropolitano (Metropolitan Park), or La Sabana, once the airport for San José. A drained lake has been restored, trees have grown back, and extensive sport facilities have been erected, including a pool, gymnasium, and stadium.

On the east side of the park, facing Paseo Colón, is the former airport control tower, a Spanish-style structure now converted to the Museo de Arte Costarricense (Museum of Costa Rican Art). Most of the paintings reflect an appreciation of the bucolic and the archaic that contrasts with modern Costa Rican life. Frequent subjects and motifs are idealized landscapes, Indian cultures long gone from the land, and oxcarts and whitewashed adobe houses; in other words, the simple life. Of the works displayed, Francisco Amighetti's woodcuts have earned the most fame outside of Costa Rica. The museum is open every day except Monday from 8 a.m. to 5 p.m., and there is a small admission charge. Any Sabana bus from Avenida 3, Calles Central/2, or from the Central Park, will stop near the entrance.

The Museo de Ciencias Naturales (Natural Sciences Museum), is located near the southwest corner of La Sabana park, in La Salle High School. The collection includes over a thousand stuffed birds, monkeys, and other denizens of the wild, many in mock-ups of their natural habitats. The museum is open Tuesday through Friday from 8 a.m. to 3 p.m., Saturday until noon, with a small admission charge. Buses from the Central Park marked "Sabana Cementerio" stop nearby.

The high point of San José for visitors interested in insects will be the Museo de Entomología (Entomology Museum), housed in the fine arts (bellas artes) department at the University of Costa Rica. The butterfly collection is especially good. Hours are from 1 p.m. to 6 p.m. on Wednesday and Thursday only. Take a San Pedro bus from in front of the Social Security building ("La Caja") on Avenida 2 between

Calles 5 and 7.

Once you've been in San José for a few days, you'll get some sense of the character of the city—progressive and relatively prosperous, but not ostentatious; fast-paced, but not frenetic; well-mannered and neat, but friendly and not excessively formal; respectful of tradition, but with few visible reminders of the past; a national capital, a center of commerce, but manageable in size; a collection of well-off and middling and working-class neighborhoods, with few areas of grinding poverty or ostentatious luxury. One says "but" and "not quite" rather often in describing San José, and all of Costa Rica, the country that has been called the "land of the happy medium."

But despite the progress of the last century, so evident in the efficient functioning of the capital, the crowds of customers at shops and restaurants, and the dense traffic, the economic crisis of this decade, brought on by foreign debt, unstable commodity prices, and the collapse of the Central American common market, has dealt a severe blow to Costa Rica and its self-image. The nation now teeters on the brink of re-entry into the less privileged ranks of the third world. The unemployment rate has regularly been 10 percent or higher. Purchasing power shrank following severe devaluations of the currency early in the 80s, and has never recovered. Fully 70 percent of Costa Rican families, according to official figures reported in the newspapers a few years ago, had incomes below the poverty line, then defined as $100 per month. During 1988 alone, according to central bank statistics, average salaries fell by ten percent in real terms.

And yet, the hard facts are not reflected in San José's surface. The middle class struggles to maintain its style and good taste, even with limited funds. Josefinos are generally well groomed; their clothes are fashionable, though their wardrobes are limited. Their automobiles are small, but well maintained. Straitened elegance is the style, and it's catching. I once spotted a diplomat tooling around San José in a tiny Renault with a uniformed chauffeur.

One of the great debates into which visitors are drawn has to do with the merits of Costa Rica's women, and especially those of San José, who have acquired an extra-regional reputation for their beauty and charm. At the risk of sounding blasé, I will join the controversy and say that there are as many good-looking women in other places as well. But Ticas (and Ticos as well) are generally well groomed and well dressed, and in better shape than most Americans. And their preference for clothing that appears to have been pasted onto their bodies only enhances their fame (and form).

To a casual observer, San José appears to have a high Jewish population. Many a neck is adorned by a gold or silver star of David. In fact, the star has acquired a certain cachet as a pop symbol among Catholic Costa Ricans—quite a difference from other Latin American nations, where swastikas are sometimes seen.

The liveliest time of year in San José is the month-long celebration that starts on December 1. Avenida Central is closed to traffic earlier and earlier in the day. *Chinamos*, stalls selling such seasonal goodies as apples and grapes, toys, and the makings of nativity scenes, crowd the sidewalks. Merchants open their businesses through the midday hours and even on weekends. The throngs grow larger and larger and louder and louder, and drunker and rowdier. Christmas is just a short pause in the round of parades, dancing, bonhomie, confetti-tossing, horse show, and general street partying that bursts finally at New Year's and dissolves into the traditional mass hangover. The onset of this orgy of self-indulgence coincides not with any religious or civic anniversary, but with the day when the *aguinaldo*, the yearly bonus for salaried employees, is usually paid.

What-country-are-we-in department: If you keep a sharp eye, you'll note pistol-packing guards not only at banks, but at hotels and major stores as well, just as in other Central American countries. The wielders of weapons are discreet, but they are there.

Who is that near the National Library, on Avenida 3, below 15 Calle, in steel helmet, with bayonet fixed? Just a soldier on sentry duty, you might think. Until you remember that this is Costa Rica and there *are* no soldiers. No, he's a civil guardsman.

If you read Spanish, you'll note that newspaper editorials freely criticize the government, and names of junketing legislators are published for the enlightenment of their constituents. Elsewhere in Latin America, the authorities of the day are treated with kid gloves. Yet freedom of the press is only available to licensed journalists.

This all might suggest that a certain country does not quite live up to its disarmed and disarming billing. Yet the president, according to a reader's report in the *Tico Times*, shows up without any entourage at his dentist, and waits his turn.

SAN JOSE DIRECTORY

Airport

Juan Santamaría International Airport is located on the outskirts of Alajuela, 17 kilometers west of San José. It's a small and manageable facility serving both domestic and foreign scheduled flights. Local charter flights use the smaller airfield at Pavas, nearer to San José.

Passengers arriving at the airport will come to the tourist information counter before passing through the customs check. Make reservations here for a hotel in town if you don't already have one arranged, and pick up any other information you need—they're quite helpful. To change money, you'll have to go left and back inside the terminal building after you leave the customs area. Banking hours are Monday to Friday from 6:30 a.m. to 6 p.m., weekends and holidays from 7 a.m. to 1 p.m. It's a good idea to change a fair amount at the airport in order to avoid the long lines at banks in town.

Transport from the airport to San José is available by taxi for about $8; and on the regular Alajuela-San José buses and microbuses that stop in front of the terminal, for about 25 cents. Luggage space on buses is limited, but the driver might allow you to put your bags in an otherwise empty seat for an extra fare.

To get to the airport from San José, call 216865 to arrange a taxi; or take the Alajuela microbus from Avenida 2, Calles 12/14.

When you depart Costa Rica by air, you may purchase only 50 American dollars at the bank—if they have the cash available. First check in with your airline and pay the exit tax, which is currently about $5. The usual assortment of overpriced airport shops solicits your last Costa Rican coins. The post office branch is open until 5 p.m. The duty-free shop, located beyond the immigration post in the departure area, has a good assortment of liquor, cigarettes and perfumes, and some odds and ends of other luxury goods. All items are priced in U.S. dollars, though Costa Rican currency is accepted. You may carry your purchases out the door.

Airlines
Scheduled service to San José is currently provided by:

LACSA, Costa Rica's international airline, Calle 1, Avenida 5, tel. 310033; airport, tel. 416244.

TAN-SAHSA, Avenida 5, Calles 1/3, tel. 215561.

Sansa, the domestic airline, Calle 24, Avenidas Central/1, tel. 333258.

Aeronica, Avenida 1, Calles 1/3, tel. 332483.

Eastern Airlines, Paseo Colón, Calles 26/28, tel. 225655.

Taca, Calle 1, Avenida 3, tel. 221790

Pan American, Calle 5, Avenida 3, tel. 218955.

SAM (Colombia), Avenida 5, Calles 1/3, tel. 333066.

COPA (Panama), Calle 1, Avenida 5, tel. 237033.

Iberia, Calle 1, Avenidas 2/4, tel. 213311

Mexicana, Calle 1, Avenidas 2/4, tel. 221711.

Air service to Tortuguero and other places not served by SANSA is provided by a number of companies listed in the phone book under "Taxis Aéreos."

Automobile Rental
For assorted warnings, advisories and cautions, see the practical information chapter of this book (page 240)

Among car-rental companies operating in San José are:

ADA Rent-A-Car, Holiday Inn, tel. 336957. This company will deliver cars to certain beach locations.

Budget, Paseo Colón, Calle 30, tel. 233284; also at airport.

Dollar, Calle Central, Avenida, tel. 333339; also at airport.

There are others listed in the phone book under "Alquiler de Automóviles," but none offer bargains. Costs of importing and maintaining cars in Costa Rica are quite high, which is reflected in the rates.

Banks

You'll have no trouble finding a bank in downtown San José. Most are open from 9 a.m. to 4 p.m., Monday through Friday. The Banco de Costa Rica branch at Calle 7 and Avenida 1 is open until 6:30 p.m., and is convenient to some of the larger hotels. The Banco Anglo Costarricense at Calle 3, Avenida 2 is open 9 a.m. to 7 p.m. weekdays, and Saturdays as well from 10 a.m. to 2 p.m.

Black-market moneychangers, during periods when they are tolerated, congregate along Avenida Central between Calles 2 and 4, near the post office. There's usually only a small spread between the official and free market rates.

For tales of woe about changing travellers checks, see "Money and Banking" in the chapter of practical information.

Books, Magazines, Newspapers

Books in English are available at:

Universal, Avenida Central, Calles Central/1. Large stock of English and Spanish books in a department store.

Librería Lehmann, Avenida Central, Calles 1/3. Also many English and Spanish books.

Librería Quijote, in the Arcadas mall at Avenida 1, Calles Central/2. A smaller selection of books in English, including a few used ones.

The Bookshop, Avenida 1, Calles 1/3. Most varied selection.

Casey's Donuts, Calle Central, Avenidas 7/9. "I haven't sold donuts for years," says the owner (the sign now reads "Casey's Book Exchange,"). Stacks and stacks of used books from 50 cents per.

Prices for imported books at some outlets are quite high—double the American price, sometimes more—despite a modest import duty.

For French and Italian magazines, try Librería Francesa/Librería Italiana, Calle 3, Avenidas 1/Central.

The *Tico Times* and *Costa Rica Report*, two excellent local publications in English (see page 273), as well as *Time, Newsweek,* the Miami *Herald* and other imported magazines and newspapers, are available at the bookstores mentioned above and at many hotels.

Free publications, such as *Guide* magazine, are distributed at major hotels. It's easy to dismiss these, with their ads for strip joints, investment schemes and massage parlors. But *Guide* has some useful tidbits of information and travel articles, as well as discount coupons.

Local Buses

City buses and those serving nearby suburbs provide a service roughly comparable to that in large North American cities, at a fraction of the price. The fare is usually posted near the door, and on most routes is about 10 cents.

Many bus routes start at or near the Central Park. All are identified by both a number and the name of the neighborhood or suburb they serve. These are clearly posted at the stops. In addition, 20-passenger microbuses serve some of the same areas.

Buses and their stops are given for most places of interest mentioned in this chapter. For others, ask at the tourist office.

Long-Distance Buses

Buses to various points in Costa Rica are mentioned in the coverage of towns, parks and beaches in this book. Many leave from the area of the Coca-Cola market, 16 Calle, Avenidas 1/3. For buses to other points, and to re-check schedules, inquire at the tourist office.

Service to Panama and to all Central American capitals, with connections to Mexico, is provided by Tica Bus, Avenida 4, Calle 9, tel. 218954. Currently there are departures for Panama City on Monday, Thursday and Sunday at 5 a.m. (fare about $25), and for Managua on Monday, Wednesday and Friday at 7 a.m. (fare $10). Sirca, Avenida 2, Calle 11, has service to Managua on Wednesday and Saturday. Other buses from the Coca-Cola terminal go as far as the Nicaraguan border at Peñas Blancas. Tracopa, Avenida 18, Calles 2/4, has three daily buses to the border of Panama at Canoas, another to David, in northern Panama.

Churches

Among places of worship in or near San José are:

Bahai Center, Avenida 4, Calle 22, tel. 225335.

Shaare Zion Synagogue, Calle 22B, Paseo Colón/Avenida 1, tel. 225449.

Church of Jesus Christ of Latter-Day Saints, Avenida 8, Calles 33/35, tel. 250208.

Carmelite Convent, San Rafael Escazú, tel. 281920.

International Chapel of St. Mary, Sheraton Herradura Hotel. Catholic mass Sunday afternoon in English. Tel. 390033.

Anglican Church, Avenida 4, Calles 3/5. Services Sunday at 9 a.m.

Union Church, Moravia. Sunday service at 10 a.m. Call 356709 for free transport.

International Baptist Fellowship, San Pedro, tel. 245951 or 255218.

Doctors

Emergency medical attention for visitors is available at any public hospital. The most centrally located is Hospital San Juan de Dios, Avenida Central and Calle 16, tel. 220166. For a Red Cross ambulance, call 215818.

For treatment on a non-emergency basis, try the Clínica Bíblica, a church-related organization, at Calle 1, Avenidas 14/16, tel. 236422; or the Clínica Americana, Avenida 14, Calles Central/1, tel. 221010. Both have English-speaking doctors available, and provide service 24 hours.

Plastic surgery, by the way, is a growing non-traditional earner of foreign exchange for Costa Rica. Many a foreigner flies in to have breasts, wrinkles or nose renovated at a fraction of the cost in the States or Europe. If you're interested, check the ads in *Guide* magazine.

Embassies and Consulates

Most of the addresses below are for consulates. For those not listed, look in the phone book under "Embajadas y Consulados." Most are open mornings only.

Belgium, Los Yoses (east of downtown), tel. 250351.

Canada, Cronos Bldg., Calle 3, Avenida Central, tel. 230446.

El Salvador, Los Yoses, tel. 255887.

France, Calle 5, Avenidas 1/3 (no. 140), tel. 221149.

Guatemala, Avenida 1, Calles 24/28 (no. 2493), tel. 335283.

Honduras, Calle 1, Avenida 5, tel. 222145.

Italy, Calle 29, Avenidas 8/10, tel. 246574.

Mexico, Av. 7 no. 1371, tel. 338874.

Netherlands, Los Yoses, tel. 340949.

Nicaragua, Barrio La California, tel. 339225.

Panama, San Pedro, tel. 253401.

Switzerland, Centro Colón (Paseo Colón/Calle 38), tel. 214829.

United Kingdom, Paseo Colón, Calles 38/40, tel. 215566.

U.S.A., Pavas (western suburbs), tel. 203939. Send mail to P. O. Box 10053, San José. The bus for Pavas leaves from Avenida 1, Calles 16/18, San José.

Entertainment

Admission to first-run American and other foreign films runs about $1.50 in San José. Most have subtitles, so you'll be able to hear the original sound track. A few are dubbed into Spanish ("*hablado en .español*," the ad will say). Newspapers give current attractions and sometimes the show times. Rarely, however, do they reveal the address of the theater, so look it up in the phone book under "*Cines*," or ask at your hotel desk.

Check the billboard at the National Theater for concerts, plays and recitals, some featuring internationally known artists. Tickets are bargain-priced, starting at $2. San José has a number of active theater groups, and their performances, including some open-air theater, are advertised in the newspapers. Performances are given at the restored 1920s Teatro Melico Salazar, and Teatro Laurence Olivier at Avenida 2, Calle 28, near Paseo Colón, among others. Next to the Olivier theater, Sala Garbo exhibits art movies.

On the raunchy side, supposedly staid San José has more than its share of strip joints. Some are located in the vicinity of Calle 2 and Avenida 8. Weak drinks are $3 to $4, the events last all night, and you ought to watch your pockets. Massage parlors advertise in various publications. Be protected.

74

Non-striptease musical acts are featured at the bars and night clubs of some hotels, especially the Irazú, Corobicí and Cariari. The major downtown hotels usually have bands on weekends.

Gambling
The major gaming game in town is black jack—and it's everywhere. If your hotel doesn't have a casino, go next door. A couple of casinos also offer craps.

In the provinces, a more popular game is bingo, and you may want to join in if you spend some time in any small town.

The biggest game, the earner of imagined millions and a lifetime of ease for every Costa Rican, is the national lottery. By all means buy a ticket or a fraction of a ticket from a street vendor. You have a good chance of at least getting your money back if the last digit of your number is the same as that of the winner.

Libraries
For books in English, visit the library at the Centro Cultural Costarricense Norteamericano (U.S.-Costa Rican Cultural Center), a U.S.-sponsored institution, in eastern San José. Call 259433 for current hours and directions. To borrow books, you'll have to become a paying member.

The other main libraries, in case you're doing serious research, are the University of Costa Rica library in San Pedro, and the National Library, Avenida 3 and Calle 15.

Maps
Good road maps of Costa Rica and of the Central Valley may be purchased at the main office of the Instituto Costarricense de Turismo, Avenida 4, Calles 5/7, 12th floor. Less detailed maps of San José and Costa Rica are distributed for free at the tourist board's information center at the Plaza de la Cultura.

Detailed topographical maps, of interest to hikers, are available at the Universal and Lehmann department stores on Avenida Central, downtown (see Books and Magazines, above). If the maps you want are out of stock, go to the National Geographic Institute of the Ministry of Public Works, Avenida 20, Calles 9/11. Hours are 8:30 a.m. to 3:30 p.m. Assorted geographic publications are also sold, in the mornings only. Take the Barrio La Cruz bus from the Central Park to the ministry, go through the gate, turn left, and look for the "Mapas" sign.

National Parks

The National Park Service (Servicio de Parques Nacionales) is headquartered at Calle 17, Avenida 9. Take the San Pedro bus from Avenida 2, Calle 5 ("La Caja"), or, more conveniently, stop in at the national parks information center in the Bolívar Park zoo. A booklet on the parks in English, with descriptions and travel advice, is on sale, though some of the information is outdated, and you should ask for current details about any park you intend to visit. Inquire also about seasonal conditions in the more remote parks. Some of the personnel speak English.

Pools

There are several public pools in the city, including one at La Sabana Park. The most fun, however, is Ojo de Agua, mentioned in the coverage of nearby towns, below.

Post Office

The main post office (Correos y Telégrafos, or Cortel) is at Avenida 1, Calle 2. A rate sheet is available at the counter to the left, inside the main entrance on Calle 2. General-delivery mail (lista de correos) is kept in the first large hall toward Avenida 1, at window 17—there's a separate entrance. Weigh your letters and buy stamps in the same area. The philatelic department is through a separate door off the main lobby, and upstairs.

Shopping

There are wise and worthwhile purchases to be made in San José, but they won't necessarily be items intended for tourists. The limited selection of domestic handicrafts includes leatherware and items made from wood, and crocheted and macramé articles. T-shirts and similar universal souvenirs help fill the shops, along with handicrafts from neighboring countries. For some general guidelines as to what to look for, see "Shopping" in the practical information chapter of this book (page 264). In this section, I'll mention some of the more interesting stores in San José.

Artesanías Malety, Avenida 1, Calles 1/3, and at several other locations, has shoes, attaché cases and handbags that are similar in quality to what you would find in the United States. Prices are slightly lower than at home (if the stuff at home isn't on sale). High-quality leather is also sold at Galería del Cuero, Avenida 1, Calle 5; and Del Río, Calle 9, Avenidas Central/2. Cruder leather, at much lower prices, is available at Industrias Pesapop, Calle 3, Avenidas 1/3.

La Galería, at Calle 1, Avenida Central/1, exhibits and sells paintings, painted wood articles, and bowls of rosewood and other tropical hardwoods. The grains and fineness are exquisite, but do you really want to spend up to $100 for a portion-sized salad bowl?

The National Handicrafts Market (Mercado Nacional de Artesanías), Calle 11, Avenidas 2/4, is a store with handicrafts similar to what you'll find in hotel gift shops—woodware, small cotton hats, macramé, and t-shirts. A few blocks away, CANAPI, an artisans' guild, Calle 11, Avenida 1, has a similar, larger store.

You'll sometimes find examples of weaving by Costa Rica's indigenous population on sale at the shop of the National Museum.

At the public markets, such as the Central Market, you'll find a fair selection of what crafts there are in Costa Rica, along with fruits and groceries. The ornamental plants are beautiful, and cheap, but you can't take them home. (Well, you can, but you better get the right procedures from your department of agriculture before you even think about doing so.) Tidbits of pottery, hammocks and paintings are hawked in the little park in front of the Gran Hotel Costa Rica, adjacent to the Plaza of Culture.

The largest collection I've seen of wood items, dolls, leather, t-shirts, embroidered blouses, ashtrays, pots, straw hats, jewelry, and other items ranging from silly to superb is in the gallery of stalls on the east side of Calle Central, just north of Avenida Central. Some of the leather is quite nice, and there are many items from Panama (molas) Guatemala (weaving) and El Salvador (cloth birds) to supplement local production.

La Casa del Indio, Avenida 2, Calles 5/7, sells silver ornaments at lower prices than hotel shops.

Antiques will also be found in the Central Market area, and at some hotels. Pre-Columbian pottery cannot be bought legally, and reproductions are getting scarce. But if you're interested, one place where you can look at pre-Columbian effigy mortars, pottery, and colonial antiques is through the window and inside Familiar La Viña, a family eatery at Calle 7, Avenidas 4/6. You might even go in for a bite.

Supermarkets are not hard to find anywhere in San José. A huge one is Yaohan, at the end of Paseo Colón on Calle 42, opposite the Corobicí Hotel. Like many other supermarkets, Yaohan has a selection of general merchandise—pots and pans, towels, plastic goods—in addition to food items. Inside parking is available. One centrally located general department store is Galerías Plaza de la Cultura, Avenida Central, Calles 5/7. There are others to the west along Avenida Central. Browse through any of these, and you'll soon find that the selection of locally made items is quite limited, while imported goods are expensive.

And, if you happen to be looking for an item of hardware, you can always stop in at Ferretería Glazman, Avenida 5, Calles 6/8.

Taxis

Taxis are a surprisingly economical means of transport for visitors to San José. Most trips around the city will cost less than two dollars. Fares are fixed by the government, currently at 70 cents for the first kilometer, 25 cents for each additional kilometer, and $3 per hour of waiting.

Unfortunately, not all taxis are metered, and even when they are, many drivers will claim that the meter is broken. Calculate the distance of your trip beforehand—figure nine blocks to the kilometer—and settle the price with the driver before you get in. Some overpayment is inevitable. Your hotel may be able to give you guidelines on the proper fares. Taxi drivers are not tipped.

Taxis are easily spotted—they're red (except for airport cabs, which are orange) and have roof lights. You may flag one down on the street, or have one called to your hotel.

Telegrams

Radiográfica Costarricense handles domestic and international telegrams. If you have access to a private phone, you can send your telegram by dialing 123. Otherwise, take your message to the telegraph office at Avenida 5, Calle 1, or send it through your hotel operator. Domestic telegrams are inexpensive—about 3 cents (U.S.) per word, 6 cents in a foreign language. Overseas telegrams are frightfully expensive.

Telephones

Public coin telephones are plentiful in San José, but they are not kept in good repair, nor are the appropriate coins— 2, 5 and 10 colones—always in plentiful supply. A good place to find working coin phones is outside the ICE building at Calle 1, Avenida 2. Some hotels have public phones in their lobbies.

There are several types of coin phones in use. The easiest to understand are those that require you to place your coins on a rack, to be swallowed as needed. With others, you deposit a coin when signalled to do so. If you're slow about it, your call is cut off.

Many stores and hotels will allow you to use their phones for a charge of about 25 cents (U.S.) for a local call.

Any telephone in Costa Rica may be dialed direct from San José, without using an area code. Have plenty of coins ready for a long-distance call from a public phone.

Service and emergency numbers are:

110 Collect calls within Costa Rica, and operator assistance.

112 Time of day

113 Telephone number information

116 International long distance (operators speak English)

117 San José police

118 Fire department (bomberos)

127 Rural police

Make overseas phone calls from your hotel (verify charges first), or from the offices of Radiográfica Costarricense, Avenida 5, Calle 1. For collect or credit-card calls to the United States, you can reach A.T.&T. operators directly from phones at Radiográfica Costarricense, at the Holiday Inn (Avenida 5, Calle 5), and at the international airport.

Tourist Office

The visitors' information center of the Instituto Costar-ricense de Turismo (Costa Rican Tourist Board) is located at Avenida Central and Calle 5, at the entry to the underground exhibit area in the Plaza de la Cultura. Maps, hotel brochures and a sheet of bus and train schedules are available, and extensive files are maintained on special-interest areas—cultural attractions, camping, and business services, to name a few. The personnel will usually try hard to obtain information they don't have. All speak English. For information by telephone, call 221090 or 216127.

Trains

The Atlantic Station of the Ferrocarril de Costa Rica (Costa Rican Railroad) is at Avenida 3, Calle 21, a few blocks east of National Park. Departure for Limón is currently at 10 a.m., and the trip takes from five to six hours. For a shorter ride on the choo-choo train, take the Limón train only as far as Cartago or some other intermediate point, then return by bus. To check schedules, phone 260011. Whether or not you take the train, stop by to admire the impressive steam engine of the Northern Railway (as the line was called before nationalization) on a spur in front of the station. The station is a national monument, more for historical than architectural reasons.

Trains for Puntarenas leave from the station of the Ferrocarril Eléctrico al Pacífico (Pacific Electric Railroad), Avenida 20, Calle 2, at 6 a.m. and 3 p.m., and take about three-and-a-half hours. The Paso Ancho bus from the Central Park passes the station.

Fares on both lines are low. It costs less than $4 to go to Limón, and proportionately less to intermediate points.

Water

Tap water in San José (and in most larger towns of Costa Rica as well) is safe to drink. But if you're wary of it, for reasons of taste or chemical difference from what you're accustomed to, or are just plain cautious, stick to bottled soda water (*soda*, or *agua mineral*).

Water pressure in much of San José is quite low. The better hotels have pressure tanks and pumps, but in more modest accommodations, you may get no more than a dribble from the tap.

Walking

Being a pedestrian in San José is at times a risky business. At some intersections, traffic lights are arranged so that it is technically impossible to cross in the clear. And even where the signals appear to be with you, many a driver will slip into gear and bear down on you the moment the light changes. Be cautious and fleet of foot.

Weather

The average daily high for San José varies hardly at all from month to month—it's almost always in the mid-seventies Fahrenheit (22 to 25 Centigrade). Average nighttime lows are about 60 (15 degrees Centigrade), excellent for sleeping. Even the recorded extremes are moderate—92 is the highest temperature ever recorded in San José, 49 the lowest (33 and 9 degrees Centigrade). Precipitation, however, is quite variable. It rains almost every day from May to October (Costa Rica's "winter"), with monthly totals of about 10 inches, and the air gets to be uncomfortably sticky toward the middle of the day. The rains slacken off in November, and from January until the end of April, precipitation is a freakish event. Aside from rain, there are a number of seasonal signs in lieu of sharp differences in temperature: variation in length and clarity of daylight; the flowering of poinsettia, erythrina trees, coffee plants and other species throughout the year; and alterations in the richness of the green of surrounding hills.

TRIPS FROM SAN JOSE

Costa Rica is small enough, and travel facilities are well enough developed, that you can reach many far points of the country by public transportation and return to your hotel in San José by nightfall. In order to actually *see* anything, however, you'll probably want to confine your one-day trips to the environs of San José and the Central Valley, e.g., Ojo de Agua springs, Poás and Irazú volcanoes, Cartago and the Orosi valley, and Alajuela and towns on the way to Sarchí.

These places, and details on how to reach them, are described in the pages immediately following this section.

By taking a tour or renting a car, you can extend your one-day travel range to the Pacific beaches near Puntarenas and at Jacó, and, perhaps, the port of Limón on the Atlantic. By chartered plane, you can also make a one-day trip out of a visit to the Tortuguero reserve on the Caribbean. Day outings are also arranged through travel agencies for white-water rafting, jungle exploration, cruises in the Gulf of Nicoya, and horseback riding.

Where to go first? At the risk of sounding Philistine, I will state that much of the scenery near San José is essentially similar. You'll want to be selective, especially if you're on a short trip, or wish to get down to the hard work of sunning yourself on a beach, or rafting a wild river, or fishing. Choose one volcano and one scenic circuit for starters, then see the other sights as time and inclination allow. Listed below are some nearby destinations in approximate order of interest.

Poás Volcano. Impressive cloud forest, craters and views, well-conceived visitors' center and exhibits. How many of your friends have ascended a real volcano?

Orosi Valley. Plunge into a broad, magnificent valley full of lush coffee farms, with colonial churches, lakes, and a river of rapids; stop at an unusual botanical garden on the way.

Aserrí or San Antonio de Escazú. Short excursions by city bus, miniature versions of the Orosi circuit.

Alajuela. Most pleasant of the nearby provincial capitals, on the way to Poás volcano. Excursion may be extended by meandering along the old road to Grecia, the furniture-making town of Sarchí, and Naranjo.

Irazú Volcano. Views as fine as those from Poás (if you hit a clear morning), but barer at the top, with few facilities.

Ojo de Agua. Fine for swimming and boating. You'll be interested if your hotel in San José has no pool.

Cartago. For those with reasons of religion.

Heredia. Stop if you have extra time, while on the way to somewhere else.

Santiago Puriscal. A scenic, mountainside-clinging ride.

Visit other towns, ascend to Braulio Carrillo National Park, or go horseback riding, rafting, or boating, according to your fancy and funds, before you head to the edges of Costa Rica. For travel details, read the coverage ahead.

TOURS AND TRAVEL AGENCIES

Your own style, money supply and your destination will determine whether you use a travel agent or group tours while in Costa Rica. Even if you're used to making your own way by bus and train, you'll find that only a tour, taxi or rented car will get you to the top of a volcano on certain days of the week, or all the way through the Orosi Valley without having to backtrack or trudge part of the way. And of course, tours are social as well as practical. You meet people and share experiences.

Major travel agencies are:

TAM, Calle 1, Avenidas Central/1, tel. 235111. American Express representative.

Panorama Tours, Calle 9, Avenida Central, tel. 330233.

Blanco Travel Service, Avenida Central, Calles 7/9, tel. 221792.

Excai Tours, Avenida 1, Calles 1/3, tel.230155.

Fiesta Tours, Avenida 1, Calles 5/7, tel. 233433.

Swiss Travel Service, Hotel Irazú, tel. 325362.

You'll probably book where it's most convenient, generally at your hotel. Bear in mind that agencies work on commissions, and will sometimes try to sell you the most expensive trip, no matter what your interest, e.g., a flying tour to Tortuguero, instead of a more leisurely and more interesting canal-boat excursion. If you have trouble getting what you want, do not hesitate to contact a trip operator directly. You can even consider calling from abroad—most have personnel who speak English.

Among more specialized travel agencies and trip operators are:

Ríos Tropicales, Paseo Colón, Calles 22/24 (P. O.Box 472-1200, Pavas), tel. 336455. Rafting and kayaking excursions.

Costa Rica Expeditions, Calle Central, Avenida 3 (P. O. Box 6941), tel. 239975. Rafting; coastal and river fishing; birding and national park tours. Mainly a wholesaler.

Geotours, P. O. Box 469Y, 1011 San José, tel. 341867. Specializing in tours to Braulio Carrillo National Park and Carara Biological Reserve.

Horizontes, Av. 1, Calles 1/3, tel.222022. Bus and cycling trips to national parks and wildlife reserves.

Isla de Pesca/Perfini Travel, P. O. Box 8-4390, tel. 234560. Tortuguero Canal trips, and fishing.

Interviajes, P. O. Box 296, Heredia 3000, tel. 381212 or 334457. This agency advertises day trips to Arenal volcano, the Orosi Valley or Poás volcano for as little as $15, and three-day trips to Tortuguero or one of the beaches from $75. Also, car with driver from $75 per day.

OTEC Tours (Organización de Turismo Estudiantil Costarricense), tel. 220866, specializes in travel for Costa Rican students. You can use their services if you're a student, a teacher, or are under 26 years of age, and provide two photos, though their prices are only marginally lower than elsewhere.

SANSA Vacaciones, Paseo Colón and Calle 24, tel. 234179, 332714. Costa Rica's domestic airline operates bargain excursions to a limited number of destinations. Examples: two nights at Manuel Antonio National Park, *including* air ticket, hotel, four meals, and canal cruise, for $60. (!) Two nights in Tamarindo, also including four meals, flight and hotel, $76. And there are even reduced prices for kids. Schedules are sometimes less than reliable, but the price is right.

Miss Caribe (Cotur), P. O. Box 26-1017, San José 2000, tel. 330155 or 336579. Three-day, two-night tours to Tortuguero National Park by bus and canal boat for about $100, including meals and hotel—a bargain, considering the difficulty, expense and uncertainty of going by other means. They also have mountain and coastal fishing programs.

Cruceros Mawamba, P. O. Box 10050, tel. 339964, has a low-priced package to Tortuguero similar to that offered by Cotur.

Calypso Tours, P. O. Box 6941, tel. 333617. Cruise to islands in Gulf of Nicoya, and trips to Monteverde.

Finca Ob-La-Di, Ob-La-Da, P. O. Box 1, 6100 Mora, Ciudad Colón, tel. 491179, offers day horseback riding outings through scenic farms and forests west of San José, and longer trips.

Cacts Hotel, Avenida 3 bis, Calles 28/30, tel. 212948. Rain forest and volcano-watching day and overnight trips.

Costa Rica Sun Tours, P. O. Box 1195-1250 Escazú, tel. 560659. River fishing.

Among the usual tour offerings and what you might pay if you book at a hotel travel agency:

San José city tour,$12 to $16, three hours

Irazú volcano and Cartago, $20 to $25, half day.

Lankester Gardens and Orosi valley, $12 to $16, half day, $30 full day.

Orosi Valley and Irazú volcano, $30 to $45, full day.

Poás volcano, $20 to $25, half day.

Heredia, Alajuela and Sarchí, $16 to $20, half day.

Ojo de Agua, $12; train ride to Puntarenas, $26. The most timid of travelers can do these on their own.

Braulio Carrillo Park and Limón: a drive-through trip, with some hiking, and explanation of flora, $65.

"Traditional night"—basically a meal with a view for $32.

Train ride to the Caribbean lowlands, and return by bus, $60-$80.

Bus to Puntarenas and boat cruise in the Gulf of Nicoya, $65

Trips to beach resorts, $100 per day.

Rafting on the Reventazón River, $65.

Horseback rides at a farm outside San José, $75.

Jungle tours by train or bus to Limón, then by canal launch to Tortuguero reserve, returning by air, or boat and bus, $100 to $250.

Monteverde reserve, two nights, $180.

NEARBY TOWNS

San José is surrounded by dozens of settlements, ranging from suburbs where life is a virtual extension of the urban bustle, to bucolic hillside villages where events unfold at the pace of an oxcart, within full view of the city below. You can drive from point to point in the vicinity of San José, if you have a car available. But my preference is to hop on one of the frequent suburban buses, and to look ahead and to both sides of the road, catching glimpses of local sights and goings-on, and longer views whenever the bus stops to pick up or discharge passengers. Self-made bus tours to towns near San José literally cost pennies.

MORAVIA AND CORONADO

Moravia is a handicraft center seven kilometers northeast of downtown San José. The best-known shop is the Caballo Blanco, located on one corner of the main square, where thick leather belts and furniture and a few more finely manufactured items of luggage are on display. There are various other souvenir and wicker furniture shops and stands on the road into town. The crafts alone are not enough to draw a visitor to Moravia. One also comes here to sit on the large square and watch a slower, smaller-town life than that of San José. You'll note far fewer cars on the streets than in the capital, knots of people in conversation, and an indescribable something that turns out on closer examination to be an unaccustomed quiet.

The bus for Moravia leaves from Avenida 3, Calles 1/3, San José, the microbus from Avenida 7, Calle 6. Get off at the stop in Moravia where most other passengers debark. This is two blocks from the square. To continue your tour, walk back to the bus stop and wait for a bus marked "Coronado".

Beyond Moravia, the Coronado road rises through an area of lower-middle-class suburbs, where small and well-cared-for wood and concrete-block homes stand in clusters among coffee groves and pasture. About one kilometer before Coronado, in Dulce Nombre, is the Instituto Clodomiro Picado of the University of Costa Rica, where snakes are studied. Ask the bus driver to let you off nearby if you wish to visit. A few rattlers, fer de lance and coral snakes are on display. Hours are 8 a.m. to noon and 1 to 4 p.m., Monday through Friday. On Friday afternoons, you can witness the "milking" of snakes for their venom, from which antivenin is made.

After a visit to the Institute, walk or drive up the hill to Coronado, a sleepy, pleasant farming center with a surprisingly large and impressive tropical cement-clad, tin-roofed Gothic church. Some points in town offer good views to San José, and the direct road back to the capital is lined with substantial houses that take advantage of the vistas. The direct bus for Coronado leaves from Avenida 5, Calles 3/5, San José. You can walk down to Moravia in less than an hour, and be rewarded with sights more interesting than those in the two towns themselves.

ACCOMMODATIONS

The Club Mediterráneo, on the plaza in Coronado, is a restaurant that counts among the town's attractions. Look out on the square while you enjoy rather pleasant country dining in an attractive, stuccoed room with arches, hung with plants in macramé holders. Menu choices include creative vegetables such as zucchini stuffed with spinach, antipasto, bouillabaise, steak marchand du vin, veal cordon bleu, sea bass in sauce and many other standard French items which are well and authentically prepared. Service and presentation are exceptionally competent, without being overdone. Unusually, a salad is included with your main course. At $8 to $12 for a meal, more for shrimp or lobster, it is very good for the price. A fine place to spend a rainy-season afternoon. Open for lunch and dinner, afternoon only on Sunday, closed Monday. Calle 290661 to reserve.

Beyond Coronado is one of the entry points for Braulio Carrillo National Park (see page 108).

ASERRI

The ride out to the village of Aserrí takes the visitor through the working-class suburbs of Desamparados and San Rafael, then into the crowded countryside, up and up over rolling hills, by rushing streams, and past farmhouse after small neat wooden or stuccoed farmhouse, each just in from the roadside, front yard decorated with bougainvillea, hibiscus, and poinsettia. Tiny pastures and vegetable plots pass by, islands in a sea of shiny-leafed coffee trees shaded by banana plants.

Once in Aserrí, gaze down at San José, at the bottom of the valley; take a look at the whitewashed, colonial-style church; and examine the Aserrí craft specialty, dolls of a rather simple sort. Catch the bus back down, or walk part of the way.

The hill town of Aserrí is only ten kilometers from San José, and 128 meters (420 feet) higher. Buses for Aserrí leave from Calle 2, Avenidas 6/8, San José.

SANTIAGO PURISCAL

Getting there is all the fun of this longer excursion through breathtaking, rolling countryside covered with coffee and orange trees, sugarcane, banana plants, and settlement after small settlement. Some 20 kilometers out from San José, the road starts to ascend to country of pine and oak, and precipitous mountainside pastures where some force other than gravity appears to hold cattle to earth. To either side are sheer drops of a thousand feet and more. Each hairpin turn frames a new view of the Central Valley, increasingly far below.

At about kilometer 30, on the crest of the southern ridge, is the Guayabo reserve of the Quitirrisi Indians. The Quitirrisi live like other rural Costa Ricans, but they are poorer, less well educated, and have a limited command of Spanish. Their horizons are largely limited to the boundaries of their settlement. You'll notice Indians alongside the road with bundles of baskets, which are woven from vines, and sold in San José.

Buses for Santiago Puriscal leave about every 45 minutes from the Coca-Cola station, Calle 16, Avenidas 1/3. The trip takes about an hour, but one can get off around the Indian reserve and walk for a while (take a sweater), then catch a return bus.

SAN ANTONIO DE ESCAZU

The hill village of San Antonio de Escazú features a fine Ravenna-style church, and good views down to San José, and across to the hump-shaped volcano Barva. Brightly painted oxcarts are in use as a practical means of moving goods in an era of expensive gasoline, and not merely to please the eye of visitors. On the way is the town of Escazú, where many foreigners make their homes. Rural, slow, clean, sunny, industrious and quite civilized, San Antonio appears to have been transplanted from hills somewhere above the Mediterranean Sea.

Buses for San Antonio leave from Calle 16, Avenidas Central/1; and for the central area of Escazú, from Avenida 1, Calles 16/18, San José.

ACCOMMODATIONS

Several hotels and guest houses in San Antonio de Escazú, and below in Escazú proper, provide more tranquil surroundings than you'll find in San José. See page 46 for more details.

The Central Valley

In almost every way, the Central Valley is the heart and soul of Costa Rica. Most of the population lives on this twenty-by-fifty mile plateau, bordered to the north by the Poás, Barva, Irazú and Turrialba volcanoes, and to the south by an older mountain ridge. Almost all of Costa Rica's industry, most of the all-important coffee crop, and much produce for home consumption come from here. Public administration, education and power generation are centered in this ministate.

And as if all the facts about industry and agriculture and human resources were not sufficient for one small region, the Central Valley is blessed as well with more than its share of natural beauty: great slopes carpeted with coffee trees, and broken by waterfalls, rippling streams, and rivers of rapids; pine groves and pastures on rolling hills; rocky canyons and lakes; a climate as benign and temperate as any on earth, where almost anything will grow; slumbering volcanoes, their slopes carved into farms of neat squares; and small, well-built houses everywhere. It is as close to one's idealized vision of the "country" as one is likely to get.

And yet, hardly a part of the Central Valley is really rural. Paved highways reach almost every point, giant electricity pylons step across the landscape, rivers are dammed and harnessed at every edge of the plateau. A cement factory, a knitting mill, rises amid pastures and coffee. Town gives way to fields and then to village and fields and town, each settlement with its dominating church and flowered gardens.

Nevertheless, man and nature appear for all the world to

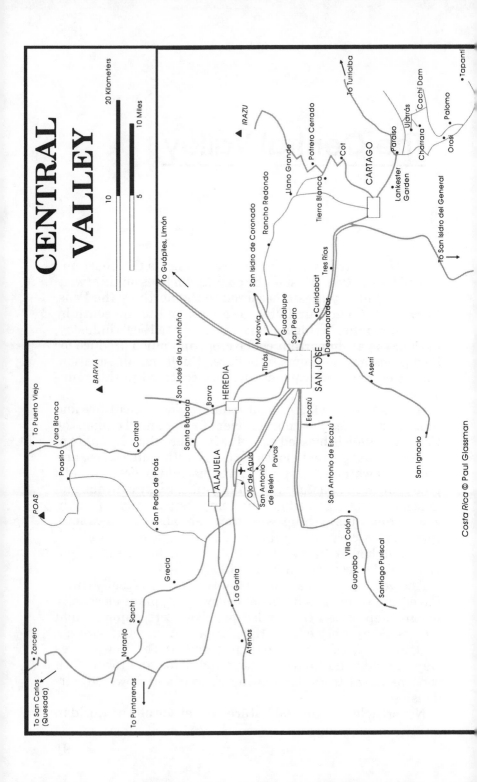

CENTRAL VALLEY

20 Kilometers
10
10 Miles
5

Costa Rica © Paul Glassman

live in beauteous harmony. All of man's intrusions might have been placed with a sense of how things look, how they interrelate, and how they are kept up. It is this machine-in-the-garden aspect of the Central Valley that is especially attractive, and unique in this part of the world.

The Central Valley is the part of Costa Rica that sometimes is called the Switzerland of Central America. In fact, there is nothing Swiss about the climate, or the tin-roofed houses. The bare statistics of per-capita income would not earn the population a place at the lowest social rung of any Swiss settlement. Only contented cows munching in mountainside pastures present a roughly comparable vista. But in the apparent industriousness of the people, in their concentration and use of all resources at hand, in their general public orderliness, it could be said that the Swiss are somewhat reminiscent of the Costa Ricans of the Central Valley.

Not that all is sublime at the heart of Costa Rica. Aside from the economic shocks of recent times, there are natural shocks. Volcanoes erupt periodically and spew ashes, boulders and destruction. Earthquakes shake down houses and cathedrals. People, too, are not always kind to the land when they live so near one to another. A close look reveals that many a gurgling stream is off-color or slimy, and lined with trash. But by the standards of the region, and of many a more developed area, most things are well.

The volcanoes of the Cordillera Central to the north are the source of the contours and the wealth of the Central Valley. Much of the land was shaped over many centuries, as volcanic ejecta and lava showered, washed down and oozed, to settle into two basins, separated by the low hills that lie between the present cities of Cartago and San José. The lava made for a natural fertility, renewed by periodic eruptions.

Pine forests dominated these basins for centuries. The Spaniards found the climate at altitudes of 900 to 1500 meters ideal for subsistence agriculture, if not for wealth-producing plantation crops, and began to cut back the natural cover. Coffee trees, of course, came eventually to be the main vegetation in the valley, complemented, according to slight differences in altitude, by sugarcane, corn, and pasture. Coffee is now to Costa Rica what citrus fruit is to Israel. Yields per acre and caffeine content are among the highest in the world.

Coffee trees are what visitors will see most as they tour the Central Valley, but how these are seen depends on the time of year. Always the trees are shiny-leafed, crowded, and usually pampered in the shade of larger trees. Shortly into the rainy season, they glisten with moisture. Dozens of delicate, white-fingered blossoms erupt on each branch, then shower down. For most of the growing season the berry (*cereza*, or "cherry") is green, turning red and finally to oxblood when ready for picking.

The rains are mostly over when the armies of coffee pickers enter the dusty fields, wrapped like beekeepers in heavy shirts and leggings and rubber boots against the abrasions of dense branches. The coffee harvest is a fabled time of hard work, crucial to the well-being of the nation, and the president himself hands out awards to the best workers. Ripe berries are selected by hand, dumped from baskets to carts, and hurried to the mills where simple machines scrape off their outer hulls. The slime that coats the beans is soaked away by a day of fermenting, then the beans are spread, sun-dried during the day on concrete platforms, and mounded and covered by night. A second skin is rubbed off, the beans are sorted and polished, and a government agency supervises the orderly marketing of the crop. Harvest time is when the plantations are busiest, but throughout the year, workers plant and prune and clear and fertilize and otherwise tend the trees.

The relatively advanced development of the Central Valley makes it easy for the visitor to explore. Roads go everywhere, and on most of them, buses both comfortable and frequent. Good hotels and restaurants are not part of the valley's blessings, though there are some establishments worthy of recommendation; and no place is far from the haven of San José.

CARTAGO

Population: 30,000; Altitude: 1450 meters (4756 feet);
23 kilometers from San José.

Defeated in their attempts to found viable settlements in
the merciless lowlands, the early Spanish settlers of Costa
Rica turned their attention to the temperate uplands. In
1564, Juan Vásquez de Coronado, the Spanish governor, was
able to write to the king: "I have never seen a more beautiful valley, and I laid out a city between two rivers. I named
the city Cartago, because this province also bears that
name."

The Guarco valley, where the new head settlement was
sited, had abundant water, fertile earth, and a population of
a few thousand who were less hostile to Vásquez than the
natives of the coast had been to his more belligerent
predecessors. While the colonists did not succeed in establishing full dominion over the colony from their new highland base, nor in subjecting native peoples to labor on vast
plantations of export crops, they at least were able to till subsistence crops and hold their own. In and around Cartago,
which remained little more than an impoverished village for
many years, was Costa Rica born and shaped.

Cartago lost its central position toward the end of the
colonial period, as Costa Rica achieved a rough prosperity
and settlement pushed westward in the Central Valley. The
relative decline of the city was affirmed shortly after independence, when the capital was moved to San José.

Costa Rica's old capital is today not at all colonial in flavor.
Virtually all structures of the pre-independence period were
damaged or destroyed by a string of natural disasters:
earthquakes in 1841 and 1910, and intermittent rains of ash
and debris from the always-threatening volcano Irazú that
looms over the city to the north.

But despite its political decline, Cartago remains a
religious capital. Ten blocks east of the main square is the
Basílica de Nuestra Señora de Los Angeles (Basilica of Our
Lady of the Angels), with its six-inch-high black statue of the
Virgin, the object of special devotion on August 2, and of
pilgrimages throughout the year.

According to tradition, the little statue was discovered on

Basilica of Cartago

the outskirts of Cartago on August 2, 1635, by a girl named Juana Pereira. It was twice removed and placed in a box, and each time miraculously reappeared in its original location. Yielding to divine will so clearly expressed, the ecclesiastical authorities decided to build a church where the Virgin had been found. The statuette twice was stolen from its shrine, in 1824 and 1950, but each time was returned. The original church was damaged in the 1920 earthquake, and the present basilica dates from 1926.

That is the religious background, which is considerably more impressive than the structure itself. The basilica stands out as an agglomeration of confused styles, roughly Byzantine at the front, with a motley collection of angels grafted on, domes bubbling overhead, barren, gray stone blocks forming the sides and rear. It is as if the officials of the Church realized that they had to do something for their Virgin, but with no national artistic tradition on which to draw, they found themselves at a loss as to how to go about it.

The interior of the basilica is no better. Vaults and columns painted in splotches of green and brown and glittering silver defocus one's attention from the altar. Poor taste completes itself will signs on the basilica's lawn advertising its soda shop.

The shrine of La Negrita, as the statue is familiarly called, is below ground level. Nearby is a room full of discarded crutches, and miniature gold and silver hands, legs, arms, and assorted other parts of the body, all testifying to the healing powers of the Virgin and of the waters that flow from the spring under her shrine.

Back at the center of Cartago are the more esthetically pleasing ruins of the Church of the Convent (Iglesia del Convento, or, more simply, Las Ruinas). Only the massive, moss-encrusted stone-block walls remain of this colonial structure, with their simple, pleasing, Moorish-Spanish contours. The roof fell in during the 1910 earthquake, after the structure had been damaged in previous tremors, and the church was abandoned. The walls now enclose a gardened space, where bougainvillea, pines and a lovely pond attract a variety of birds. The cobbled section of street in front of the church adds to the atmospherics.

VISITING CARTAGO

Aside from its religious structures, Cartago is on the routes to the Irazú volcano and the Orosi valley. Buses for Cartago leave from Avenida Central, Calle 13, San José, about every twenty minutes from 5 a.m. to 11 p.m.

Do not try to stay overnight in Cartago! All the hotels, clustered a block up from the market, across the railroad tracks, are fleabag, noisy dives of the worst sort. (I know!)

The food situation is mildly brighter in Cartago. The Salón París, on the main street opposite one corner of the market, offers main courses of simple fare for about $5, and sandwiches. Despite the name, the decor features Venetian and bullfight scenes. There are numerous other modest sodas and restaurants around, including, of course, the soda of the basilica.

IRAZU VOLCANO

At 3432 meters (11,260 feet), Irazú is the highest volcano in Costa Rica. It is also one of the most active, and certainly the most feared, a rumbling presence of continuing steaming, boiling and fuming that has practically destroyed the city of Cartago on more than one occasion, and played continuing havoc with the lives of farmers who till the soil and raise livestock on its slopes. But paradoxically, the volcano is also a benefactor. Its ash renews the richness of the soil, even while it blocks water pipes and roads.

Irazú's most recent active cycle started with a bang on March 13, 1963, when boulders and ash began to rain down on homes and farms near the volcano's peak. Over a two-year period, rivers in the vicinity of Cartago were dammed and the city flooded; corrosive ash fell like a gray snowstorm over San José, damaging water pumps, home furnishings, and many a respiratory system. Dairy production plummeted as pastures were seared or covered over, and output of coffee and vegetables likewise fell. With help from abroad, dikes were hurriedly constructed to divert deviant waters from doing further damage, and the millions of tons of ash were swept up, and carted away. Irazú's peak assumed a new form as part of the mountain collapsed into the space vacated by magma. Even today, spurts of sulphurous smoke, steam and water are part of a continuing reformation and growth of the mountain.

The distinction of Irazú among volcanoes in the modern world is that is one of the few semi-active ones that can easily be viewed up close. A paved highway climbs right to the peak, which is protected as a national park. If you happen to ascend when the peak is free of clouds—a near impossibility during the rainy season, and an uncertain condition even in dry times—you'll be rewarded with views to both oceans, or at least to a good part of the country.

The ride up Irazú proceeds slowly, through pastures and corn fields. Past the town of Cot, the air becomes increasingly windy and cold, and the trees more twisted. On the cool, ash-fertilized slopes, potatoes are the main crop, along with carrots and onions. And there are many dairy farms, all now recovered from the 1963-65 calamities, and awaiting the next ones.

Sites on the way up Irazú include the neat farming villages of Potrero Cerrado and Tierra Blanca, each dominated by a church; a pair of *miradores*, or lookout points, furnished with concrete picnic stools; and a rambling, white, tile-roofed sanatorium that takes advantage of the mountain air. About 20 kilometers out of Cartago, and 12 kilometers from the crater, is the Hotel de Montaña Gestoría Irazú, where a cool night in rustic surroundings costs less than $10 per person. Call 530827 to reserve.

Over the last few kilometers of the ascent, the face of the mountain changes dramatically, from green pasture to oak forest laden with epiphytes at the park boundary, then to a seared, boulder-strewn primeval surface of ash and bare soil where wind-beaten ferns and shrubs maintain a tenuous hold. Around the next turn, one half expects to encounter a herd of dinosaurs poking their heads through the mist. Charred tree trunks stand as monuments to the last period of intense activity, while a few younger saplings take root for what will probably be an abbreviated life in the severe surroundings.

Once atop Irazú, you can examine a small exhibit on geysers, fumaroles, mudpots, ash, and other forms and evidence of volcanic activity. Slog through the ash and view the craters—slowly. The air at this altitude is short of oxygen, and you will be short of breath, as well as buffeted by wind and mist. The Diego de la Haya crater contains a lake, tinted to a rusty hue by dissolved minerals. The main, western crater, which swallowed up several earlier craters, currently shows virtually no activity or gas emissions. There are active fumaroles on the northwestern slope. Much of this, it bears emphasizing, will not be visible because of the clouds that shroud the peak even during much of the dry season. But even when the top of Irazú is clouded over, a few minutes of exposure to the nasty environment and a glimpse of the fantasy-world landscape will be long remembered.

Visitors to Irazú should be prepared with warm clothing. A couple of sweaters will do, though a down ski jacket would not be too much. Raingear will help during the rainy season and even during the rest of the year, when wind-borne moisture will sting the skin.

TRANSPORTATION

Currently, there is no public bus service all the way to the peak of Irazú. Buses depart for Tierra Blanca, on the

The Church at Orosi

volcano's slopes, from one block east and one block north of the Cartago bus terminal. You can take one of these and hike the rest of the way—a strenuous effort in the thin air—or else look for a taxi at the end of the line. Otherwise, go in a rented car, on a tour, or in a taxi from Cartago. The crater is 32 kilometers from Cartago, or 54 kilometers from San José, and the route is well marked. There's a nominal admission charge to the volcano, usually collected only at busy times.

THE OROSI VALLEY

East of Cartago is the well-traveled scenic circuit through the Orosi Valley. The route covers only about 55 kilometers from Cartago, easily driven at a leisurely pace in a couple of hours. Bus travel requires some backtracking, but a trip to the halfway point will give you more than half the available pleasure.

About seven kilometers east of Cartago is the Lankester

100

Botanical Garden (Jardín Lankester) of the University of Costa Rica. If you're driving, you'll see the Ricalit roofing factory on the left just before the side road to the gardens on the right. By public transportation, take the Paraíso bus from the Cartago terminal to the Ricalit factory, then walk one-half kilometer down the side road to the south, to the entrance.

The Lankester Garden is most famed for its orchid collection, the largest of its kind in the world, begun as a private effort by Charles (Carlos) Lankester, a native of England. But there is much, much more in this well-planned wonderland: bromeliads and other epiphytes, acres and acres of transplanted hardwoods, fruit trees, bamboo groves, cacti, medicinal aloe plants, dreamy and deadly nightshade, and many others. Species are identified only by Latin tags, but you'll recognize some as house plants, especially in the more jungly areas, where ponds are crossed with the aid of bridges made from vines. One large section has been left untended to grow back to native forest.

Guided walks through the gardens are offered on the half hour from 8:30 a.m. to 3:30 p.m. daily. You can wander through at other times, but you'll be assigned an employee as a tail to make sure that you stick to the brick path and don't pick anything. Admission is about $1.

To continue your trip without a car, go back to the highway and pick up a bus marked "Orosi."

A couple of kilometers past Paraíso on the road to the south is a mirador, or lookout point. Take advantage of it if you can for 20-mile views down into the great Orosi valley, carpeted with pasture, sugarcane, and, of course, dark green coffee forest. The Río Grande de Orosi snakes along at the bottom and joins lesser streams to form the Río Reventazón—the Foaming River. The town of Orosi can be picked out, along with smaller clusters of houses and ranches and coffee plantation centers on hillsides and in the lesser valleys spreading out in all directions, as clearly as if you were flying overhead. In the distance is the very end of Lake Cachí. This is surely one of the most spectacular views in a country of spectacular views, superior in clarity to any road map.

The lookout point is a garden with manicured pines, hedge cedars, bougainvilleas, and picnicking and play areas and shelters. Even if you're travelling by bus, it's a good place to stop with a box lunch. Or you can pick up snacks at the adjacent stand.

After the lookout point, the road twists and descends into the valley, and finally straightens and runs flat along the river, through coffee groves to the garden town of Orosi, in colonial times a village where Indians were forcibly settled. Here is a lovely restored church dating from the mid-eighteenth century, with brightly whitewashed walls and red tile roof. The church houses a small collection of religious art. There are hot springs at the edge of town, but you can safely save your swimming for later.

A branch road two kilometers from Orosi passes the Río Macho hydroelectric works, and winds ten kilometers up yet another beautiful valley to the Tapantí forest reserve, accessible only in your own vehicle or on foot. No camping is permitted, but there are nature trails a kilometer past the entry point (you pay a small fee), with plants well marked with their names, and explanations of their roles in forest life. Signs point the way to a bouldery wading area in the rushing Río Macho, which is known as a good trout stream. Three kilometers past the hiking area is a lookout point, which offers prime views to a chute of water, and down the valley, but as vistas go in Costa Rica, this one is not of national standing.

Past the suspension bridge two kilometers from Orosi (or adjacent, by a shaky footbridge that avoids a loop of road), is Palomo. Right at the end of the bridge, without an identifying sign, is the Motel Río, which has an oversized swimming pool overlooking the Reventazón, open to non-guests at a small charge. The pleasant, cane-ceilinged pavilion dining room is best known for its river fish, and also serves steaks. Main courses cost about $5. You can phone the motel at 733057 to reserve for a night in the country. The units are not luxurious, but they're quite large—some have kitchens—and the rush of the river by your door is soothing. At about $15 double, they're a good value, indeed. If the car gate is closed when you arrive, walk in and look for the caretaker. Dinner is not served, but you can get a sandwich nearby.

Most buses to Orosi end their run near the Motel Río. Without a car, you can walk or hitch a ride toward the Cachí

Dam, or backtrack to Cartago to pick up a bus to Cachí, through Ujarrás.

Continuing by car (or tour bus), you'll proceed about eight kilometers past the spur for the village of Cachí, to the Cachí Dam, one of the larger hydroelectric projects of the Central Valley. The dam is encrusted with lilies on one side; a trickle of water spills downstream into a great chasm on the other.

Past the dam, a kilometer and a half to the west down a side road, at Ujarrás, are the remains of a Spanish mission, one of the first churches in colonial Costa Rica. According to tradition, a humble Huetar Indian fished a box from the river and carried it to Ujarrás, from where it could not be budged. When opened, it was found to contain an image of the Virgin. A church was built on the site, in about 1560. A few years later, when the British pirates Mansfield and Morgan landed at Portete, a force was hastily organized to expel the invaders. After a prayer stop at Ujarrás, the defenders marched to the Caribbean, where they defeated the superior English force. The victory was attributed to the Virgin of Ujarrás. The church was later abandoned after a series of earthquakes and floods, and the image, now less recalcitrant, was taken to Paraíso. But the ruins, in a manicured park, remain a pleasing sight. They are the locale of an annual tribute to the Virgin in mid-March.

Charrara recreation area, two kilometers from the main road down a spur from the road to Ujarrás, is something like a lakeside state or provincial park, with swimming area, basketball court, changing rooms, and a restaurant. It's well-kept and pleasant enough. Closed on Mondays, small admission fee.

The last stopping point on the Orosi circuit is the Ujarrás lookout point, high above the valley, where the highway curves back to the west, toward Paraíso (six kilometers from the Charrara turnoff) and Cartago. Take a good look before you leave the scenery behind.

TURRIALBA

Population: 28,000; altitude: 625 meters (2050 feet); 64 kilometers from San José.

Located where the Central Valley starts to slope down

toward the Atlantic jungles, Turrialba is lower, warmer, more languid, and less tidy than towns nearer to San José. Turrialba marks the approximate limit of coffee cultivation. The valley of the Reventazón in this area typically is pastured or planted in sugarcane along its lower, flatter reaches, and covered with coffee trees on its upper slopes.

Most visitors will not bother to get off the train or bus at Turrialba, which is basically an agricultural center of no great attraction. But those with a special interest in agriculture or archaeology might want to make a stop. Many rafting groups also pause here before or after riding the Reventazón.

Four kilometers east of town, on the road to Limón, is CATIE, the Tropical Agronomic Research and Education Center. Native plant diversity and the range of altitudes and environments on CATIE's more than 2000 acres of land afford a wealth of opportunities for testing plant and animal strains, and developing more efficient ways of cultivating traditional crops. The library on tropical agriculture is recognized as the best of its kind anywhere. CATIE's staff comes from many countries. Guided tours may be arranged by phoning 566431 three days ahead, or through travel agencies in San José. Or you can just drop in and look at the rather lovely and attractively landscaped estate around the main building. Take a local bus from Turrialba, or a taxi for about $3

ACCOMMODATIONS

Hotel Wagelia, tel. 561596. 18 rooms. $20 single/$30 double, or $26/$36 with air conditioning, t.v., refrigerator.

An attractive, modern hotel, very clean, with rooms around a courtyard landscaped with palm trees and boulders. Two blocks from the bus station, on the way to San José.

Lesser hotels include the Central, Chamanga and Interamericano. The latter has a few rooms with private bath. South of Turrialba, along the road to Limón, is Pochotel, where meals are served, and rooms are available for $15 double.

Near Turrialba:

Albergue de Montaña Rancho Naturalista is a mountain lodge that offers prime rain forest birding, and a wealth of butterflies, moths and fauna on the surrounding ranch. There are six guest rooms, with shared bathrooms. The daily rate of about $65 includes meals, pickup in San José with a minimum three-day stay, and horseback riding. Field trips are included with longer stays. Write to P.O. Box 364-1002 San José, or call 398036 to reserve.

Buses for Turrialba leave from Avenida Central, Calle 13, San José, about every hour from 7 a.m. to 9 p.m. The trip takes less than two hours.

About 20 kilometers north of Turrialba, on the slopes of the Turrialba volcano, is Guayabo National Monument. Although Costa Rica is especially rich in pre-Columbian antiquities, its early inhabitants lived nomadic existences, or concentrated in villages and towns built of highly perishable materials. There are no great native ceremonial centers that survive to this day, as they do in Honduras, Guatemala, El Salvador, and Mexico, or at least they have not yet been discovered. Which is why the Guayabo complex, with its constructions of natural and hewn stone, is considered important by Costa Ricans, although it is unsophisticated and relatively modest in extent.

The Guayabo site includes paved walkways, walls, and circular stone constructions that might have been foundations for houses of a South American sort. Subterranean and surface aqueducts, also signs of South American cultural influence, are still serviceable. Other finds are fluted points, scrapers and knives which show stylistic influences from both north and south; and carved stone tables, grave markers and blocks of undetermined purpose, which might have been altars. Some of the markings on the stone objects are obviously persons or gods, but most are non-representational, and remain a mystery to modern viewers.

Archeologists estimate that Guayabo was occupied by 800 A.D. and abandoned, for undetermined reasons, from 100 to 200 years before the Spanish first came to Costa Rica. In the absence of historical records, the goings-on at the site remain a mystery, though it appears that Guayabo was some sort of center for a number of nearby villages. Since it was situated on a natural route from the highlands to the Atlantic, it might also have been a trading center.

Aside from the ruins, Guayabo is a good birding area, and contains a small section of undisturbed premontane rain forest.

Access to Guayabo National Monument, 20 kilometers from Turrialba, is by an unpaved road in poor condition. Currently, the site is open *only on weekends and holidays* from 8 a.m. to 4 p.m. Buses currently leave the Turrialba bus station for Santa Teresita, five kilometers from Guayabo, daily at 11 a.m. and 6:30 p.m. A few other buses go nearer to the site during the week. Inquire at the park service in San José as to current hours if you're considering a mid-week visit.

Farther north of Turrialba is the semi-active volcano of the same name, which rises to an altitude of 3339 meters (10955 feet). Access for climbing the volcano is usually from the village of Santa Cruz, north of the town of Turrialba, or from the picturesque town of Pacayas, which may be reached by bus from San José or Cartago.

One last, adventurous excursion from Turrialba is to Moravia de Chirripó, 30 kilometers away in the mountains to the east. In the region are small settlements of Talamanca Indians, who after centuries of isolation are coming into contact with the mainstream culture of Costa Rica. Inquire in Turrialba for buses or trucks headed to Moravia.

West of San José

HEREDIA

Population: 30,000; Altitude: 1152 meters (3779 feet);
 11 kilometers from San José.

Founded in 1706 at the foot of the extinct Barva volcano by migrants from Cartago, Heredia is a short commute from San José. The Atirro coffee mill, one of Costa Rica's largest, is on the outskirts; the National University is located here; and there are some impressive mansions on the western side of town. But most of the population is working-class, and the central area has a down-at-the-heels air.

Nevertheless, there are some architectural gems in

Heredia. The main church on the central park, dating from 1797, is one of the few in Costa Rica that survive from the colonial period. With massive walls of stuccoed stone blocks stained brown and black and overgrown with moss, a triangular pediment, and an almost separate, squat bell tower, it is a near-perfect example of the public architectural style of the last years of Spanish rule. The low contours were meant to resist earthquakes, or at least control damage from vibrating, toppling towers and walls. The church is also one of the more atmospheric buildings in Costa Rica, without excessive restoration and sprucing up.

Set back from the north side of the park is El Fortín, the old Spanish fortress tower that is the symbol of Heredia. With gun slits that widen to the exterior, in defiance of standard military architecture, El Fortín stands as an unintended symbol of Costa Rica's non-belligerent nature. A number of other buildings on the square have a colonial air, with colonnades and aging tile roofs.

One last item to see in Heredia is an art deco church on the secondary square at Calle 6 and Avenida 8. It's homely, but cute in its way.

While Heredia's attractions are not to everybody's taste, the town is on the way to Alajuela and the Barva and Poás volcanoes. Do stop by if you have the time. Microbuses for Heredia leave from Calle 1, Avenidas 7/9, San José. Bus service is also available from the Alajuela terminal.

Near Heredia

In San Pedro de Barva is a museum dedicated to everything that has to do with coffee. An assortment of specialized equipment is on display, some of it dating back to the last century. The museum, four blocks north of the church, is open weekdays until 3 p.m. The bus for San Pedro de Barva leaves from Avenida 1, Calles 1/3, Heredia.

Barva, a couple of kilometers north of Heredia, is a standard Central Valley town, but for the low, thick-walled buildings with red tiled roofs that line the grassy square. It's not really colonial—the church is baroque nineteenth-century—but it's enough to make you think you're in some less-advantaged part of Central America. The bus for Barva runs from Calle 1, Avenidas 1/3, Heredia.

North of Heredia, on the slopes of Barva, is the village of San José de la Montaña, 20 kilometers from San José, where a couple of hotels take advantage of the broad views and fresh mountain air. The best is the Hotel de Montaña El Pórtico, just northwest of town, with 16 rooms, a restaurant with country lodge brick-and-beam atmosphere, sauna and pool. Rates are $35 double.. Telephone 376022, or 212039 in San José to arrange transportation. (Mailing address: Apartado 289-3000, Heredia). Farther on are the Cabañas de Montaña Cypresal, also with pool and sauna, where units have kitchenettes, and horseback riding is available. Rates are about $30 double. Phone 374466, or write to Apartado 7891, San José. Either of these places would make a fine base for touring San José and the Central Valley, if you decide to rent a car. Buses run from Heredia to San José de la Montaña. Continue to the hotels by taxi if you're not being picked up.

BRAULIO CARRILLO NATIONAL PARK

Farther north from Heredia is Braulio Carrillo National Park, which takes in the extinct Barva and Cacho Negro volcanoes. The park was established to protect the flora and fauna along the new highway to Guápiles and Limón, in the Caribbean region.

Carrillo Park, which varies in altitude from 500 to 2906 meters (9534 feet, the peak of Barva volcano), encompasses tropical wet forest, premontane wet forest, and montane wet forest, or cloud forest. All that "wet" means that branches are laden with orchids, bromeliads and mosses, while ferns, shrubs and much else compete with trees for floor space. On the Atlantic slope are numerous waterfalls and pools that evidence the great year-round rainfall. Strong winds blow through, between the Irazú and Barva volcanoes.

Common animals in Carrillo Park include foxes, coyotes, white-faced, spider and howler monkeys, ocelots, sloths, and several species of poisonous snakes. More than 500 bird species have been catalogued, including the uncommon quetzal, the long-tailed symbol of liberty whose feathers were treasured in ancient Mesoamerica. Spottings of the quetzal are usually made in the forest atop Barva.

The park is in a state of development, and it would be a

good idea to check with the park service in San José before planning a visit. There are three access routes.

One entry point is 20 kilometers from Heredia, reached via a road through San José de la Montaña, and the horse country and oak forest beyond. This route is often muddy, and is passable for certain only in the dry season. By public transportation, take a Paso Llano bus from Heredia, get off at the Sacramento crossroads, and start hiking. The first bus is at about 6 a.m. Other buses go only as far as San José de la Montaña, adding an extra hour to your walk. It's about three hours to the crater lake atop Barva. Confirm bus hours with the park service at the zoo in San José before you go.

The new toll road to the lowlands runs right through the saddle between the Barva and Irazú volcanoes, roughly following a historic cart road that connected San José with the railhead at Carrillo, before the line from Limón to San José was completed. The eerie roadside vegetation is untouched by farmers, in contrast to readily accessible terrain everywhere else in the country. The winding highway, fog, and heavy traffic make it unwise to stop just anywhere along this route, but there is one section of the park partially developed for visitors, 12 kilometers past the northern outlet of the Zarqui tunnel.

The Alto de la Palma entrance, north of Moravia, has been closed to visitors because of landslides and preservation work on the old cart road. Inquire at the park service as to current conditions. To reach this entrance, take a bus to San Jerónimo from Avenida 5, Calle 3, San José, and hike about 10 kilometers onward to the park entry.

ALAJUELA

Population: 43,000; Altitude: 941 meters (3087 feet); 23 kilometers from San José

Located just a short ride west of the capital, Alajuela is Costa Rica's second city, founded late in the colonial period, in 1790. Bustling, with a climate warmer than San José's, Alajuela is an important cattle marketing and sugar-processing center, and, increasingly, a site for small manufacturing industries. The denizens of the town are famously good humored, and well they might be, for Alajuela is the most pleasant of the provincial capitals, a place where lingering around the square is the chief diversion, and a recommendable one.

Alajuela's main claim to fame is as the birthplace of Juan Santamaría, the drummer boy who set fire to the headquarters of the American adventurer William Walker in 1857, thus helping to bring about the defeat of the filibuster forces that had taken control of Nicaragua. A statue of the Erizo (the "Hedgehog," as Santamaría is affectionately known, for his bristly hair) may be seen a block south of the main square, on Calle 2. Torch in hand, rifle at his side, he stands ready to repeat his deed.

The main square of Alajuela is a shady forest-garden, with mango and palm trees, where locals and not a small number of resident foreigners observe the passing of the day from stone benches. Also hanging out in the park, more literally, are a few two-toed sloths, those snail-slow creatures that look slug-ugly in photos but are cute and furry in the flesh. Assorted statuary and fountains complete the picture. Bordering the park are a number of substantial old buildings from the coffee-boom days, with massive walls, stone-trimmed windows, iron grilles, and, in one instance, corner turrets.

Facing the east side of the central park is the city's main church, an uninteresting neo-classical structure with simple lines. (For orientation purposes, Calle Central runs along the east side of the park, by the church, Avenida Central along the south. Few streets are marked.)

About five blocks east of the central park is a more attractive church, built in a Costa Rican simplified baroque style, with angels popping up around the edge of the façade.

A block north of the square is the Juan Santamaría Historical Museum, housed in the solid building at the corner of Calle 2 and Avenida 3. Costa Ricans and Yanqui-bashers will examine the artifacts and battle paintings of the Walker war. Others will admire the building itself, with its wide archways, massive beams, whitewashed walls and tile roof. William Walker continues to serve a rather useful purpose in Costa Rica, as an outlet for any resentments against Americans, who are generally liked. If you get into a conversation on the subject, be sure to condemn Walker's acts of more than a hundred years ago, which were, in fact, despicable. The man sought to re-institute slavery, held elections of doubtful validity, and found excuses to break numerous promises and betray his friends.

GETTING TO ALAJUELA

The city is just a short hop from San José. If you're driving, take the Cañas highway (Autopista General Cañas, or simply "*la pista*"). The turnoff for Alajuela is near the airport. Microbuses leave from Avenida 2, Calles 12/14, San José, every 15 minutes or so until about midnight, then every hour on the hour. The terminal in Alajuela is at Calle 8, Avenidas Central/1, three blocks west of the square.

ACCOMMODATIONS

The Hotel Alajuela, Calle 2, Avenidas Central/2 (P.O.Box 110, tel. 411241), a half-block from the square, is a fairly clean, homey, and relatively modern establishment, with modest rooms. At $9 to $18 single, $13 to $20 double, it's one of the better hotel buys around. Rooms on the street side can be quite noisy. There are no other decent hotels in downtown Alajuela, and only 20 rooms in this hotel, so call before you come, to make sure there's room. (Hint: Alajuela is only a half-hour from San José by frequent bus and microbus.) The Hotel Alajuela also has a few furnished apartments, and extends a discount by the month.

There are a couple of acceptable restaurants in Alajuela. The best is the Cencerro, upstairs on Avenida Central, facing the park. Charcoal-broiled steaks are the specialty, but there are fish and chicken dishes as well. About $6 to $8.

For more home-style cooking, try La Jarra, at Calle 2 and Avenida 2, a block south from the square and upstairs. About $4.

If you're planning to eat breakfast in Alajuela before catching the bus to Poás volcano, you'll have a problem. Few places are open early on Sunday, and fewer still are attractive. Limit yourself to a cup of coffee at one of the sodas near the square, then buy some pastries at ItalPan, a block and a half west of the park on Avenida Central.

Once you've made the rounds of Alajuela, you'll have your choice of continuing to Poás volcano, Ojo de Agua springs, a tropical zoo, and the towns of Grecia, Sarchí and Naranjo; which places are described below in that order.

POAS VOLCANO

Poás has several distinctions. It has the largest geyser-type crater in the world—1.5 kilometers across and 300 meters deep. It contains two lakes, one in an extinct crater, one in the fuming main crater. It is in continuing activity, in the form of seeping gases and steam, as well as occasional geysers and the larger eruptions of every few years (the last in 1978). Most practically for the visitor, it is easily reached by a paved road to the peak (2704 meters—8871 feet—above sea level), and the facilities atop the mountain are the best in the national park system.

The ascent of Poás starts at Alajuela, if you go by bus. By car, two routes are available, through Alajuela or Heredia. These converge at the little village of Poasito, high on the volcano's slopes. Either way, the visitor ascends through coffee, cattle and horse country. I won't bother to describe in detail the increasingly dramatic and grandiose vistas that are afforded of the Central Valley and of distant volcanoes and mountain ridges as the road winds onward and upward into pine and oak altitudes, such landscapes and views having been mentioned elsewhere.

The climate atop Poás is less severe than that on Irazú; the peak is several hundred meters lower, and the steam and gases burn out a smaller area. Vegetation is therefore more abundant. But on a windy day, or when the peak is enshrouded in a dripping pea soup, the visitor will find nothing benign about the environment. Nighttime temperatures well below freezing are not uncommon.

Much of the upper part of Poás is cloud forest, the enchanted, cool, moist environment where orchids and bromeliads and vines thrive at every level, along with humble ferns and mosses on the ground. The Poás cloud forest is especially rich in mushrooms and lichens. Parts of the national park are former pastures that are being allowed to return to their natural states; these contain many oak trees. Other sections near the peak are meadow-like, or are characterized by low shrubs and gnarled and twisted trees.

Wildlife in the Poás forest is not abundant, possibly due

to intense farming on the surrounding slopes. Among the inhabitants are brocket deer, coatis, sloths, cougars, and the Poás squirrel, which has been found only in this vicinity. Birds include several types of hummingbirds, trogons, and the emerald toucanet among more than 70 recorded species.

The substantial visitors' center includes an auditorium where a half-hour slide show about the national parks is given several times a day. The narration is in Spanish, but the scenes make the show worthwhile, even if you don't understand the words. Restaurant facilities may be available, but it would be wise to bring a snack just in case.

Orient yourself at the exhibit area before walking around, since you'll be covering a lot of territory. Aside from a model of the volcano and its craters, there are some wonderful peek-a-boo contraptions where you can try to identify animals by their tracks; samples of volcanic products; volcanic cross-sections; and descriptions of the extensive flora of Costa Rica.

From the visitors' center, you'll probably head first to the main crater. Along the walkway you'll notice the plant called the *sombrilla del pobre* (poor man's parasol), which is characteristic of the open areas of Poás. The leaves grow up to two meters across, which explains the name and occasional use of the plant.

Visitors are not allowed to descend into the fuming main crater, but the views from its rim are impressive. At the bottom is a lake formed by rain water, its shade of green changing according to the amount of sulfur it contains at any given time. Intermittent geyser activity results from water seeping into fissures along the bottom of the lake, then boiling and exploding upward. More likely, you'll see gas and steam escaping from fumaroles along the edge of the lake. The sides of the crater are burned and strewn with rock and ash, and only a few shrubs struggle for survival in the noxious environment at its rim.

After a visit to the active crater, climb to Laguna Botos, the water-filled extinct crater near the highest point on the volcano. The lake is named for an Indian tribe that once inhabited the area.

The last major attraction atop Poás is the nature trail, a run of about half a kilometer through a relatively undisturbed stretch of cloud forest. The signs in Spanish along the way are more poetic than informative, and some specific labels of trees and plants would be useful (says the gringo). This is the most accessible area of forest of this type in Costa Rica.

Unfortunately, it's easier to describe many of the features of Poás than actually to see them. The top of the mountain is often clouded over, at least partially. However, the clouds shift frequently. If the main crater is obscured at first, take another look before you leave. The shroud may have lifted. The view to either coast, and northward into Nicaragua, may also open up from time to time, so keep an eye peeled.

TRANSPORTATION

A public bus to Poás leaves from the southeast corner of the central park in Alajuela on Sundays—be there by 8:30 a.m. Fare is about $3. This is an all-day excursion. The ride up takes two hours, with a twenty-minute rest stop at a café high on the volcano, near Poasito. Three hours are allowed on top before departure for Alajuela. This is more than ample time to see both accessible craters and the cloud forest. On other days, buses are available from Alajuela to Poasito (lately at 5 a.m. and 1:30 p.m.). This still leaves you ten kilometers from the peak. You'll have to walk, hitch, or hire a taxi to finish the ascent. Tours operate to Poás most days from San José, or you can hire a taxi.

If you're driving, take the Cañas expressway to Alajuela, then follow the clearly marked road via San Pedro de Poás and Poasito. The peak is 37 kilometers from Alajuela, 59 from San José. An alternative and somewhat more arduous route from San José goes through Heredia, Barva, Los Cartagos and Poasito.

Rain gear will come in handy on Poás even in the dry season, when heavy winds whip clouds across the peak. Take a sweater or jacket as well. Temperatures can dip sharply in a few minutes.

OJO DE AGUA

A few kilometers south of Alajuela, just southeast of the international airport, are the Ojo de Agua springs and recreation area (not to be confused with the town of the same name, which is west of the airport). Water gushes from the earth at a rate of 200 liters per second, and most of the flow is directed into an aqueduct that supplies the city of Puntarenas, on the Pacific.

Much of the remainder is used for the amusement of the citizenry. In the tree-shaded park surrounding the springs are three pools, tennis courts, and a lake with rowboats. On weekends, this is a great place to rub elbows and much else with the locals. Go during the week if you prefer solitude, or serious swimming (or pass it up altogether if the pool at your hotel is more to your taste). Entry costs about 40 cents, and changing rooms are available. There are cheap eateries both inside and outside the gates. Through no particular logic, the recreational facilities are managed by the national railroad company.

Buses operate to Ojo de Agua from Avenida 1, Calles 18/20, San José, hourly on the half hour during the week, and every fifteen minutes or so on weekends. There are also buses from Alajuela and Heredia.

LA GARITA

West of Alajuela, along the highway to Atenas, at Dulce Nombre, is the Zoológico de Aves Tropicales (Tropical Bird Zoo), which holds an outstanding collection in a lovely landscaped setting. (In fact, the area around Dulce Nombre and La Garita is replete with beautiful gardens and plant nurseries.) Usual hours are 9 a.m. to 5 p.m. daily, admission is about 50 cents. Stop this way if you're passing through the area, or have a special interest in tropical fauna. The Atenas or La Garita bus from Alajuela passes the entrance (on the north side of the road), or you can look for a Dulce Nombre bus from the Coca-Cola terminal in San José. If you drive from San José, take the Atenas exit off the expressway, then go east, back toward Alajuela, for three kilometers.

GRECIA, SARCHI, NARANJO

The old Pan American (or Interamerican) Highway skirts the northern rim of the Central Valley, passing through the picturesque towns of Grecia, Sarchí and Naranjo. The road is in an unfortunate state of repair, and most traffic now speeds to the coast on the Bernardo Soto Expressway, to the

Oxcart Painter

south. But the old highway affords a pleasant, slow meander through rolling countryside.

Grecia is most notable for its unusual brick-red church. The surrounding hills here at the hotter, lower end of the Central Valley are largely planted in sugarcane, and much of the output is processed in Grecia.

Beyond Grecia is Sarchí, the preeminent craft center of Costa Rica, where dozens of small wood workshops line the highway. Here, tropical hardwoods are made into chairs, tables, and, of course, the brightly painted oxcarts with kaleidoscopic wheels for which Costa Rica is famous. The intricate painted designs on the carts are said to be handed down from father to son. These items are strictly for the local market, but the miniature oxcarts and statuettes are suitable for carrying off. The bi-towered church of Sarchí, with its unusual number of windows, is worth a glance. Costa Rica's country churches are, in general, charming, in contrast to the dull metropolitan temples.

The last major town on the Pan American Highway, before it drops to the coast, is Naranjo, dominated by a cream-colored baroque church.

Buses operate to Grecia, Sarchí and Naranjo every half-hour from Alajuela, and you may return to San José by a more direct route. To continue to the coast, take a San Ramón bus from Naranjo to the Soto highway ("la pista") and flag down a bus for Puntarenas or Guanacaste. You can also continue to Ciudad Quesada (San Carlos) and onward to Lake Arenal or the northern lowlands (see page 221).

The Other Costa Rica

Outside the Central Valley is another country, a Costa Rica that in many parts is as underdeveloped as any in Central America. Some of the differences from the highlands will be immediately apparent to the visitor. The population is generally sparse, and good roads are sparser. Houses are often ramshackle affairs, and the neat, flowered gardens around San José give way to dirt yards where chickens scratch for tidbits. The climate, of course, is generally hotter, and usually more humid.

More traditional Latin ways hold sway, in forms both attractive and difficult for the visitor to accept. Events unfold at times at a mañana pace, and schedules are an imperfectly understood concept. Warmth and hospitality are the norm, and the visitor can easily feel at home in any town where he lingers.

Other changes from the highlands are not visible, or slower to manifest themselves. The social-security system provides limited coverage outside the Central Valley, where there are fewer salaried employees. Electricity and drinkable water have not yet reached many smaller settlements. Large banana and palm plantations, cotton farms and cattle ranches take up more of the land than small family homesteads.

Progress, quite simply, is generally less than in the Central Valley, and much more uneven. There are pleasant, clean, bustling lowland towns such as Liberia; idyllic, nearly isolated national parks; and serene beach settlements. And there are places where, at first glance, the major elements of life appear to be liquor, litter and loud music.

119

Once you leave the main lowland routes, a flexible schedule is a must, unless you make ironclad arrangements through a travel agency. Expect simpler food and less-than-top-notch service, barer hotel rooms and lower standards of hygiene. There are a few beach and mountain resorts where these cautions don't apply, but in general, more tolerance and understanding are required. Remember to phone ahead for reservations when possible, and to reconfirm schedules off the main routes, where bus service is generally poor.

The Wild East

North and east of the mountainous backbone of Costa Rica is the triangle-shaped Caribbean coastal region, a vast area of dense tropical forest. No time of year, no remote corner of the Atlantic slope, is ever dry. Clouds blow in from the sea throughout the year. Those that don't drench the area directly shed their water against the central mountains, from where it flows back to the Caribbean in numerous rivers, and often overflows onto the low-lying, poorly drained land. Rainfall at Limón, in the center of the coastal strip, reaches 150 inches in many years, and near the Nicaraguan border, approaches 200 inches.

Despite the thick layer of plants in the lowlands, the soil is poor. Enriching ash blows only westward from the volcanoes of the highlands, and constant rain leaches nutrients. The tribes that lived in this area before the Conquest were the least settled of Costa Rica, relying on hunting and gathering for their food, as well as on corn plots that had to be frequently relocated as the earth was exhausted. The Caribbean was the locale of the first attempts by the Spaniards to conquer and settle Costa Rica. But jungle heat, endless rain, insects, poisonous tree sap, snakes, dense vegetation, yellow fever, malaria, dysentery, and a hostile population were only some of the obstacles to establishing a plantation agriculture in the region.

In the nineteenth century, as Costa Rica began to export large quantities of coffee, it became clear that a direct, all-year transport route to the Caribbean was needed. In an epic undertaking, and at a cost of thousands of lives, a railroad was completed from the port of Limón to San José in 1890.

121

Long before that date, however, a new export crop was being carried on the route: bananas. Costa Rica was the first nation to supply the world with the fruit, and within a few years, the crop was second only to coffee in earnings. But Panama disease ravished the plantations in the 1930s, and operations were relocated to the Pacific lowlands. Later, cacao, rubber and abaca (manila hemp) were planted, but none proved as profitable as bananas.

Spurred by new road and canal construction, settlements are today spreading through much of the formerly empty Caribbean region. Forests are being cut down and converted to pasture, or tilled for crops. And the once moribund banana industry is reviving, with disease-resistant varieties.

The environment in much of the Caribbean region is still largely uncomfortable, in parts threatening to human existence. Why, then, would anybody venture there, except out of necessity? The train trip to Limón, from highlands to jungle, is regarded by some as the premier travel experience in Costa Rica. The Caribbean coastline is one nearly continuous sweep of white beach, most of it deserted. Wildlife treasures abound, including green turtles in their protected nesting area at Tortuguero. Fishing, especially for tarpon, is world-famous. The blacks who form a large part of the lowland population are a fascinating culture, quite different from other Costa Ricans. And also, there is nothing menacing in those parts of the Caribbean lowlands where the visitor is likely to tread.

THE JUNGLE TRAIN

Any mention of the train ride from San José to Limón requires a preliminary excursion into some Costa Rican history. Primitive trails descended the Atlantic slope to navigable lowland rivers since early in the colonial period, but these were often made impassable by rain, and Costa Rica's limited international trade was channeled through the Pacific port of Puntarenas. As early as 1820, an improved route to the Caribbean was proposed. But no way was found to construct an all-season road, and Costa Rica's ever-expanding coffee exports continued to reach Europe only after a long detour around the tip of South America.

In 1871, the Costa Rican government contracted with Henry Meiggs, an American who had built railroads in the Andes, to construct a line from Limón to San José. The work came under the supervision of a nephew of Meiggs, Minor C. Keith.

Workers were recruited, mostly from New Orleans, and financing was arranged, but the project appeared doomed from the beginning. Floods washed out sections of track almost as soon as they were laid. Nearly 600 of the first 700 workers were soon dead of malaria. The first 25 miles of track cost 4000 lives, mostly new Chinese recruits who succumbed to yellow fever. Keith himself lost three brothers and an uncle, but pushed on nevertheless, contracting workers from Italy and around the Caribbean. Those who survived were mostly West Indian.

Keith's credit was exhausted before the tracks had progressed far, but his men labored on for months without pay, partly out of personal loyalty, partly because there were few alternatives. Finally, Keith sought temporary revenue by planting banana shoots brought from Panama along completed sections of track. Native strains of the fruit already grew in the area, but were inedible, and left to rot. The desperate scheme was successful beyond imagination. Bananas were soon being shipped from Costa Rica, and provided more than ample funds to push on with construction over swamps, rivers and mountains.

A road was opened from San José to the railhead at Carrillo in 1882, allowing the first large-scale movement of people and goods from the highlands to the Caribbean. Landslides, floods, cave-ins and illness continued to plague the builders, but by the end of 1890, the line was open all the way from San José to Limón, a distance of 100 miles.

Meanwhile, Keith continued to expand his banana business. He was granted vast tracts of land and a 99-year lease on the railroad in exchange for completing its construction on his own account. He consolidated his holdings in Costa Rica and elsewhere into the United Fruit Company. His International Railways of Central America constructed lines throughout the isthmus.

With the completion of the railroad, the economy and face of Costa Rica were transformed. Bananas came to be almost

The Train to Limón

as important as coffee to the nation's well-being. Many Jamaican laborers settled along the tracks, taking advantage of land grants under an 1884 law, or went to work on the plantations.

The railroad came under English ownership, and dominated transport in the Caribbean region until the 1970s, when an all-weather road to Limón was completed. With containerization of ocean cargo and the increasing use of trucks, and with buses providing a more rapid passenger service, traffic has declined. Only one passenger train now operates daily in each direction between San José and Limón. The Atlantic railroad was nationalized in 1972, and turned over to JAPDEVA, the official body entrusted with the development of the Atlantic slope.

The train for Limón leaves from Avenida 3, Calle 21, San José. Tickets are sold shortly before departure time. Call 260011 to check the schedule (recent departure time: 10 a.m.). The trip takes about five and a half hours.

The narrow-gauge line uses modern locomotives (an old steam engine sits in front of the station). But the cars are an-

124

tiques, worn though clean, with minimally padded bench seats, painted army-green on the inside, and red, white and blue, the colors of Costa Rica, on the outside. There is usually only one class of service, though tour companies have from time to time added a more comfortable car. One-way fare to Limón is about $4. Try to get a seat on the right side of the train (leaving San José) for better views.

You'll experience part of the atmosphere of Limón as soon as you board the train. Blacks from the lowlands converse with outsiders in Spanish, and with each other in their rhythmic, barely comprehensible English dialect. Occasionally, you may make out a mixed English-Spanish sentence fragment, such as "Bueno, you coming Sunday too?" Vendors stalk the aisles as soon as the train gets moving (always right on time!), offering cold sodas, peanuts, potato and banana chips, and such Costa Rican goodies as empanadas (filled turnovers), enyucados (yucca cakes) and pañuelos ("handkerchiefs," a pastry) that you probably will not have found at restaurants in San José. You need not go hungry, even if you have not packed a hamper.

Immediately out of the station, the train passes by coffee plantings and pastures on undulating terrain backdropped by lush hills. Town after town after small town rolls by, near and in the distance, each dominated by its church. Rivers lined with bamboo thickets flow under the tracks. Coffee mills with concrete drying platforms, factories, grazing sheep, an oil refinery, come into and pass out of view.

An hour out of San José, past Cartago, the valley narrows, and the surrounding mountains become steeper and more dramatic, as the track follows the rocky Reventazón River, become a hillside clinger in stretches, curving back on itself, bridging sudden, sheer-sided canyons. In the distance, the Cachí dam may be seen, and always, the mountainsides densely carpeted with shiny-leafed coffee.

The train makes dozens of stops at apparent nowheres: no houses, no stores, no platforms await, just a few embarking passengers, amid bordering brush and coffee trees. Only when the train moves on do clusters of houses over a rise or down a slope come into view.

Most of the windows in the old cars will be stuck open. Dust will blow in, you will feel the increasing heat as you descend, but neither problem is insufferable. When you lean out, you will alternately brush against the leaves of trees and bushes, and suffer vertigo as the train appears to fly through thin air, on a trestle over an unseen river.

Near Turrialba, the Reventazón widens, as the track descends into lower country. Patches of pasture and sugar cane appear among the coffee forest, become more and more frequent, and eventually dominate, as the steeper slopes disappear. Bare patches of fill, new retaining walls, piles of rock and dirt on both sides of the track, tell of washouts and landslides.

At a distance of approximately 75 kilometers from San José (the track is well marked), coffee has given way altogether, and the land turns truly and tropically lush, the humpbacked hills covered with towering, massively trunked trees. Knowing passengers crane their necks, looking for alligators sunning on favorite rocks in the wider, lazier river. At kilometer 89 is the first of three tunnels on the line, narrow and pitch dark and a source of rollicking, whistling delight to the passengers. Keep your arms and head inside.

The town of Siquirres marks the end of the hills, and the beginning of a totally flat Costa Rica of humidity and lassitude, of ramshackle buildings peeling in the sun. Siquirres is a major railroad yard center, and a junction point for the multiple roads now reaching through the lowlands, sprawling and hot, with many a second story on a building to catch whatever breeze there is.

Past Siquirres is the region first settled by Jamaican railroad and banana workers. Town after town consists of stilt wooden houses along the track, and newer brick and concrete-block houses on the dirt roads leading out to the paved highway. In overgrown yards where a few chickens scratch, and where a causeway provides a dry path when the earth is waterlogged, banana and citrus trees flourish, along with cacao trees, hardly bigger than a man, with red and yellow pods.

More interesting, though, are the people. Most of the railside towns are now well integrated, with as many Costarricense as black residents, and a few Chinese merchants. But the Jamaican flavor stands out. Blacks rock on the porches of their neat houses, women in print shifts, bandannas around their heads, men in shorts and tee-shirts. Public signs in Swampmouth, Bataan and all the other old banana settlements are in Spanish, but English holds its own on noticeboards at Protestant churches, the centers of Jamaican social life.

Nearer to the coast are fields of rice, and, in parts, nothing but bananas as far as the eye can see. Five hours out of San José, after Matina, the track takes a turn southward, and runs through coconut groves along mile after mile of near-deserted beach. The idyll lasts a half-hour, until the oil-storage tanks of Moín come into view. A few minutes later, a shantytown of stilt swamphouses is the first sight of Limón.

On arrival in Limón, you're faced with a few choices. Most obviously, you can head to town (turn right from the station onto the main street, then walk seven blocks to the main square), check into a hotel, and spend a few days exploring the coast to the north or south. Or you can stay over and return by train to San José—the view is different going up. If you're short of time, buses are available for an immediate return to San José.

Travel agencies in San José offer tours that will take you part of the way to Limón on the jungle train, then back to San José by bus.

By Road to Limón

For your return trip from Limón, and on repeat excursions, you'll probably take the highway through Braulio Carrillo National Park. Buses cover the 100 miles from San José in under three hours. The misty environment and the otherworldly vegetation are in many ways just as spectacular as the train ride, though of necessity the trip unfolds at too rapid a pace.

From San José, a divided expressway ascends the slopes of the volcano Barva, into highland tropical forest. Just 21 kilometers out of the capital, now on a two-lane road, you dart out of the Central Valley, into the eerie Zarqui tunnel, unlit but by headlights, the roadway—marked by reflectors along the center line—visible only intermittently through the clouds that roll through from the far end. Beyond is the enchanted high cloud forest of Braulio Carrillo National

Park. The road curves, ascends and drops and ascends again, through near-permanent mist revealing at times moss-, epiphyte- and orchid-laden trees, and shiny-leafed plants at ground level. All vehicles travel cautiously, from the lack of visibility, or from the thin air. About 35 kilometers from San José is a roadside parking area, with lookout point and trail. It's the only access point to the interior of the park along this route.

Fifty kilometers from San José, where the highway comes off the volcano and onto the plain of Guápiles, is the junction for a side road to Puerto Viejo. From this point, the run to Limón is flat and nearly straight.

LIMON

Population: 45,000; Altitude: 3 meters; 168 kilometers from San José.

Limón, Costa Rica's main Caribbean port, opened to banana traffic in 1880, but its place in national history is more venerable. Christopher Columbus landed offshore, at Uvita Island, in 1502. The first Spanish attempts at settlement were made in the area. Intermittently through the colonial period, encounters with the British and Dutch, both commercial and bellicose, took place at Portete, just a few kilometers to the north.

The port city of Limón that grew with the railway was as much a part of the British West Indies as of Costa Rica. Blacks from Jamaica and other islands constituted most of the population, and English was the only language that mattered in business. Immigrant workers kept their British passports, sent their children to school in English, read Jamaican newspapers, and went to the movies to see British films. Limón and the banana lands were separated from Costa Rica not only by language and culture, but also by a law that forbade blacks from crossing the Central Valley or overnighting there.

This separate society began to break down in the 1930s, when the banana industry was uprooted by Panama disease, and relocated to the Pacific lowlands. After the civil war of 1949, blacks were granted full citizenship, and in small numbers began to migrate to the Central Valley. Meanwhile, more and more Costa Ricans of the overcrowded plateau looked for opportunities in the warm country to the east. Most black children were educated in Spanish after 1949, and the use of English has been declining since. Limón today is a mixed Hispanic and Afro-Caribbean city, but more and more, the Hispanic predominates. The local Creole patois, permeated with Spanish words, is the language of the older generation. Blacks are discouraged from using what Hispanic Costa Ricans consider "bad" English, though many can still speak a rather elegant and formal Caribbean dialect. English has no official status, and is studied only in secondary school.

Nevertheless, Afro-Caribbean ways hold on. Columbus Day is celebrated in Limón as it is throughout Latin America, but with a fervor and style that correspond to those of Carnival in the islands. Home cooking, heavy on fish, tripe, rice, coconut, and stews with cow's feet, is less than familiar to other Costa Ricans. Religion is a vibrant part of the lives of the black population, and not the formality that it is to the broad class of Hispanic Costa Ricans.

People rise early in Limón to beat the heat, go about their business, then take a long break until the worst of the sun is gone. Businesses stay open late, and music blares on all streets from record shops, bars and restaurants. The sounds are Latin and Soul, reflecting the population division. Sailors, hangers-on and prostitutes frequent the bars, many of them open 24 hours. The best show in Limón is the street life, the commerce and hustling in the market and open squares, and under the concrete overhangs on all the main streets.

To the visitor, Limón at first glance is probably a disappointment, rich in culture and tradition, but run down. Fruit and sodden garbage sometimes rot in the streets waiting for a tardy pickup, buildings decay in the salt air, ironwork balconies and tin roofs rust away. But appearance is a relative matter. Compared to the towns of the Central Valley, Limón is shabby. Compared to other ports on this coast—Belize City, Puerto Barrios in Guatemala, La Ceiba in Honduras—Limón is pristine with its paved streets, functioning sewers, a clean market. Of teeming tropical ports, it is a good choice for the outsider to sample. But if people-watching in a throb-

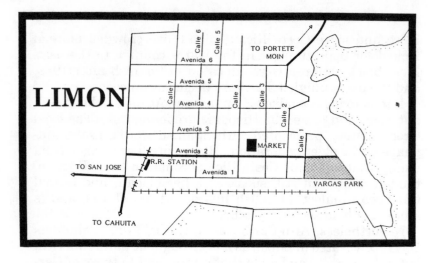

LIMON

bing, hot town is not your cup of tea, move on to the beaches and parks to the north or south.

ORIENTATION

Avenida 2 is Limón's main street, running east from the railway passenger station to Vargas Park, near the waterfront. Avenidas 3, 4, 5, etc. run parallel to Avenida 2, and north of it. (There is no odd-even segregation, as in San José). Calle 1 runs north-south at Vargas Park. The higher-numbered calles are to the west, toward the railroad passenger station. The freight line of the railroad, running to the docks, bounds Limón to the south, along Avenida 1.

Though all streets have numbers, you won't find them posted anywhere. Locals use their own tags—Avenida 2 is the Market Street. Memorize where key points are—the market is along Avenida 2, between Calles 3 and 4—or else ask directions shamelessly.

HOTELS

Note: With the completion of the new highway from San José through Carrillo Park, demand for hotel rooms in Limón and all along the coast exceeds capacity. It isn't a good idea to arrive on a weekend without a reservation. The best hotels are on the northern edge of town, or farther out.

Hotel Maribu Caribe, Portete road, tel. 584543. 14 units. $57 single/$73 double/extra person $13.

The newest hotel on Costa Rica's Caribbean, and certainly the most attractive, on a rise along the water, with commanding views. Guest rooms are in unusual round cottages with high thatched roofs. All are air conditioned. Amenities include a double pool, air conditioning, and television. Restaurant and bar, tour service.

Hotel Acón, Calle 3, Avenida 3, P. O. Box 528-7300, tel. 581010. 39 rooms. $18 single/$24 double.

Best in the center of town, despite plain, bare rooms and washbasins that drain into the showers. Clean and air-conditioned.

Hotel Internacional, Calle 3, Avenida 5, P. O. Box 288-7300, tel. 580434. 20 rooms. $8/$15.

Of recent vintage, a good buy.

Hotel Las Olas, Portete, P. O. Box 701-7300, tel. 581414. 53 rooms. $23/$40, lower rates without air conditioning.

Located a couple of kilometers north of Limón, practically over the water's edge. Attractive rooms, two pools. The views from the restaurant are altogether pleasant. Take a taxi to get here after dark, or the Moín bus during daylight hours.

Hotel Miami, Avenida 2, Calles 4/5, tel. 580490. 32 rooms. $10/$15.

One of the first hotels you come to on the main street, as you walk from the railroad station. Bare rooms, but with air conditioning, one of the better buys.

Hotel Park, Avenida 3, Calles 1/2, tel. 580476. 14 rooms. $11/$13.

Limón's dowager hotel, with restaurant, bar, good view of the port, simple but adequate rooms, and an aura of faded glory. Adequate, if you can do without air conditioning. Rooms without sea view cost less.

Hotel Lincoln, Avenida 5, Calles 2/3, tel.580074. $4 per person.

Plain, fans available.

Hotel Tete, Calle 4, Avenida 3, tel. 581122. 14 rooms. $9/$15.

In the center of the action, opposite Limón's market, but clean.

Hotel Cariari, Calle 2, Avenidas 2/3, tel. 581395. 7 rooms. $3 per person.

Bare, hot. If you can get by the toilet down the hall, the second-floor balcony offers good people-watching opportunities.

There are other cheapies on the same block as the Cariari. Inexpensive lodgings can also be found on Calle 4, opposite the market.

Other lodgings are available around Playa Bonita, five kilometers north of Limón, and in Moín, the terminus of the Tortuguero Canal. These are mentioned below.

FOOD

With the sea nearby, lobster and shrimp cost slightly less in Limón than in San José, so you may be tempted to try them. Another specialty of the town is Jamaican-style cooking, but unfortunately, it's a home phenomenon that only rarely makes its way to restaurant menus. In general, you can eat wholesomely and heartily in Limón, but not exquisitely.

The dining room of the Hotel Acón is air-conditioned and comfortable. The menu has the usual assortment of chicken, beef and fish main courses for $4 to $5, American breakfasts for $3.

If you want something a little more pleasant, with sea views, drive or take a bus or taxi to the Hotel Las Olas, two kilometers north of the center of Limón. Main courses are reasonably priced at $4 and up for versions of tournedos Rossini and entrecôte; shrimp costs as much as in San José, and breakfast starts at $3.

The Internacional, at Calle 3, Avenida 5, opposite the hotel of the same name, offers some inexpensive Chinese food. Across the street, the Tureski restaurant, on the ground floor of the Hotel Internacional, has assorted main courses from $4.50, and tablecloths. La Fuente, Calle 3, Avenidas 3/4, is cleaner than the run of restaurants here. About $5 for a meal. If none of these places suits you, you can get roast chicken to take out, with a stack of tortillas, at Avenida 2, Calles 6/7.

The American Bar is the liveliest place in Limón, an open-to-the-street place at Calle 1 and Avenida 2, opposite Vargas Park. Good for seafood (shrimp $6, lobster $12) and beef ($4) if you like large portions and don't fuss about preparation. Sailors and available women and persons on extended visits and even a few locals hang out here, more for the booze than the food.

Also active is the Springfield, on the northern edge of town. And you'll have no trouble finding additional drinking spots in Limón.

For the cheapest meals, try rubbing elbows with the locals at the eateries inside the market buildings.

TRANSPORTATION

The most famous way to get to Limón is via the train, described above. Departures for San José are currently at 6 a.m. from the passenger station, at Avenida 2, Calle 8. For a shorter (though less interesting) ride on the choo-choo train, there's a departure at 1 p.m. for Guápiles. Faster buses (three hours for the run) leave every hour from 5 a.m. to 7 p.m. from Avenida 3, Calles 19/21, San José. Return buses leave on the same schedule from Avenida 2, Calle 2, Limón. For buses along the coast, look a few pages ahead. There's also an airstrip three kilometers south of town along the sea, with on-again, off-again service. Check with Sansa airlines in San José, tel. 333258.

AROUND LIMON

The favorite place for sitting down in Limón is Vargas Park, a square of jungle at Avenida 2 and Calle 1, facing the sea. Giant hardwoods struggle against the odds with strangler figs, huge palms shoot toward the sky, vines and bromeliads compete for space and moisture, birds dart and flit through the tangle. There are supposed to be monkeys and three-toed sloths up there somewhere in the canopy, and perhaps you'll be luckier than me and spy them.

Across from the park is Limón's perfect tropical-port city hall, with its cream-colored stucco, open arcades and breezeways, balconies, and louvered windows. Limón's older architecture is well suited to the climate. Thick walls moderate the extremes of temperature, concrete overhangs block the sun and keep people dry when it rains, as it does drenchingly often.

The market, on Avenida 2 between Calles 3 and 4, is ever lively, set back in a large building in its own little park. Stop in and admire the papaya and passionfruit, as well as the more mundane but no less impressive one-pound carrots. The streets around the market are Limón's social center, where purveyors of food and games of chance set up shop during the Columbus Day celebrations and for the month preceding Christmas. The Columbus Day "carnival" season features floats, street bands, dancing and masquerades, and everything else that one expects to find in the islands at Mardi Gras.

Along the southern rim of Limón (Avenida 1) are the railroad tracks and the piers where bananas are loaded aboard ship. Despite the long journey to markets all over the world, bananas are delicate. In hot weather, the large leaves of the plant collapse to shelter the fruit. In dry spells, the pores contract to conserve water. Once the stems with their "hands" (rows) of "fingers" (individual fruits) are cut from the plant, natural defenses are gone, and the fruit is rushed from the field to cooled ship's hold in 18 hours. The plants are chopped down after harvest, but new plants grow up from suckers and bear fruit in nine to fourteen months. Watch the banana loading from a distance, if you can and while you can. More and more, the fruit is loaded into cargo containers right after cutting, minimizing damage from excessive handling. With advanced cultivation techniques, Costa Rica's banana fields have the highest yields in Latin America.

It is the Latins in Limón who stay up late and party. The bars open at 8 a.m. and soon people are bending elbows. Blacks, religious Protestants most of them, go family-style to the numerous and substantial churches.

Try to catch and understand snatches of Limón English. Many a word is different from what you know, and the rhythms and speech patterns further obscure what is said.

Most confusing is that many of the words are not English at all, but Spanish, notably numbers. Most of Limón's blacks can also speak a more standard form of English that you'll find intelligible in direct conversation.

Limón is located on a rocky point, and is one of the few places along Costa Rica's Caribbean coast without a beach. There's a government-sponsored pool in town, but most visitors will prefer the nearby beaches.

EXCURSIONS FROM LIMON

Cahuita and Puerto Vargas may be reached on day excursions from Limón. By chartering a canal boat (see below), you can also get to Tortuguero and back in a day. In either case, you're better off to stay at least overnight. If time is limited, arrange a tour to Tortuguero from San José. You can do so in Limón as well, but you won't save any money. The Hotel Las Olas offers a day-long excursion to Tortuguero for $170, including a night's accommodation in Limón. Telephone the hotel at 581414, or call Mawamba boat service at 584915. Similar trips are available through the Hotel Maribu.

North Of Limón

PLAYA BONITA AND PORTETE

Several beaches north of Limón are play areas for people from the area and for weekenders from San José. Playa Bonita is a public park about four kilometers from Limón, with an absolutely idyllic bay, plenty of lush jungle vegetation as a backdrop, and a beach that attracts quite a share of debris. Facilities are limited—a few picnic tables and a children's play area.

Portete, a little cove full of fishing boats, adjoins Playa Bonita to the north. You can sit at one of the many little stands that serve food, and watch as lobster traps are prepared, or just stare at the sea or the jungle and coconut trees. The shore is rocky and littered.

HOTELS

All around Playa Bonita and Portete are a number of beach houses, and a few places offering accommodations to transients. Bare beach *cabinas*, just south of Playa Bonita park, little more than cubicles, are available starting from $9 double. Cabinas Cocorí (tel. 582930) are a slight cut above the others, with cooking facilities. $18 double. The Hotel Matama, recently remodelled (tel. 581123, P. O. Box 686—7300 Limón) rents out eight bungalows in a nicely lush hillside setting, with kids' and adults' pools, and an attractive restaurant. The rate is $23 single/$27 double.

At Moín (see below), the Hostal Moín (tel. 582436), near the port, has 18 bare double rooms for $10 with private bathroom. This is the nearest hotel to the boat for Tortuguero, though the Banana Power disco downstairs might detract from your rest.

The public bus for Playa Bonita, Portete and Moín runs every hour from Calle 4, Avenida 4 in Limón, in front of Radio Casino.

TORTUGUERO CANAL

Moín, seven kilometers from Limón, reached by a spur from the highway or by the coast road from Limón, is hardly a town at all, but rather a transport center. All of Costa Rica's oil supplies are off-loaded here, and stored in huge tanks, and cargo containers are shifted between trucks and ships.

More interestingly, Moín is also the passenger and freight terminal for the Canal de Tortuguero, the 160-kilometer stretch of natural rivers, lagoons and estuaries, and connecting man-made waterways, that runs almost to the Nicaraguan border. The canal is the main "highway" of the northern coastal region, complete with directional signs and branches from the main trunk route. Cargo and passengers move on narrow, tuglike, 30-foot-long launches. Ask permission to enter the compound of JAPDEVA, the government agency in charge of economic development in the area, to take a look at river port operations. Coconuts, bamboo, cacao and bananas are unloaded, and consumer goods, largely bottled sodas, are loaded for the return run. From the terminal, you can see the stately waterway, thick with water lilies, its banks lined with vine-entangled trees, dissolving in the distance into swamps.

To ride on the canal, you have a number of choices, not all of them convenient. JAPDEVA runs a a boat on Thursdays and Saturdays to the village of Tortuguero, and tour boats operate to Tortuguero and the adjacent national park on Fridays and sometimes on other days. There are also cargo boats. See page 139 for details.

However you go along the canal, you will be well rewarded with views of pastel-colored toucans and macaws, monkeys swinging through the trees, sloths hanging from branches, alligators taking the sun, and, perhaps, some of the coatis, jaguars and ocelots that roam the forest. Colonies of mangroves and water hyacinth appear here and there. Scattered along the way are people, too—fishermen and farmers whose dugouts serve all the purposes of pickup trucks elsewhere. Knots of women washing clothes and clusters of thatched huts show that the canal is serving its purpose of bringing settlement to the area. But mostly, the banks remain wild, and the screams of monkeys and whistles of birds predominate over the noises of humans. Riding a canal boat is probably the easiest way that exists of penetrating the lowland tropical rain forest.

TORTUGUERO NATIONAL PARK

Located eighty kilometers north of Limón, Tortuguero National Park is most famed for the nesting sea turtles that give their name to both the park and adjacent town. Every year from June to November, turtles waddle ashore at night, climb past the high-tide line, excavate cavities in the sand and lay their eggs, then crawl off, exhausted.

Only fifty years ago, the waves of turtles were so dense that one turtle would often dig out the eggs of another in the process of making its nest. The eggs were gathered by locals almost as soon as they were deposited, and enjoyed great popularity not only as a food, but because of their alleged aphrodisiac powers. The turtles, too, were often overturned and disemboweled for their meat and shell. Now, depredations by humans have reached such an extent that the survival of some species is in doubt.

Tortuguero is one of the few remaining nesting places of the green Atlantic turtle, a species that reaches a meter in length and 200 kilograms in weight. Green turtle eggs are deposited from August to November every three years. Other species that nest at the beach are the hawksbill, loggerhead, and the huge leatherback, which weighs up to 700 kilograms.

Even with human enemies under control in the park, the turtle eggs, slightly smaller than those of hens, face numerous perils. Raccoons, coatis and coyotes dig them out and eat them up. The hatchlings that emerge two months after laying face a run for the sea made perilous by crabs and lizards, and birds that swoop down and pluck off tasty morsels of leg or head. Only a small fraction of hatchlings reaches the sea, and fewer still make it to adulthood. The odds are being improved somewhat by programs that see to the safe transfer of hatchlings to the water.

Visitors come to Tortuguero to witness the nighttime nesting of the turtles, but the park is also an important conservation area for other plant and animal species, as much of the tropical forest nearby is cut down and otherwise disturbed by humans. Fresh-water turtles, manatees and alligators are found in the park's canals, as well as sport fish, and sharks that reach up to three meters in length. Forest animals include the jaguar, tapir, anteater, ocelot, white-faced, howler and spider monkeys, kinkajou, cougar, collared peccary, white-lipped peccary, and coatimundi. Due to the dense vegetation, you'll probably hear these rather than see them. Over 300 bird species have been reported in the park, including the endangered green macaw, Central American curassow, and yellowtailed oriole.

All of Tortuguero is wet—rainfall averages 5000 millimeters (200 inches) per year—but there are several vegetation zones. Morning glory vines, coconut palms and shrubs characterize the sandy beach area, while other sectors are covered with swampy forest that bridges the waterways. In the forest on higher, less saturated ground, orchids and bromeliads live at all levels and take their nourishment from the air, and "exotic" houseplant species, such as dieffen-bachia, flourish. Tortuga Hill, a 390-foot rise, is the highest point all along the Caribbean coast of Costa Rica.

TRAVELING THE CANAL AND VISITING TORTUGUERO

Getting to Tortuguero is not easy, unless you charter a private plane to the beach landing strip, three miles to the north of the village. From Moín, north of Limón, you can try to board one of the JAPDEVA canal launches heading north on Thursday at 8 a.m. or Saturday at 9 a.m. The trip takes about six hours. Line up at the JAPDEVA ticket window well before scheduled departure time. Phone 581106 to confirm the schedule. Fare is about $4. The boat returns to Moín the next morning.

Cotur, P. O. Box 26-1017, San José 2000, tel. 336579 or 392375, has a three-day, two-night package trip from San José that includes a bus ride to Moín, travel to Tortuguero on the 51-foot canal boat Miss Caribe, all meals, accommodations at the Jungle Lodge, and a half-day tour of the park. This trip would be a bargain even if Tortuguero were an easier place to get to by other means. Departures are usually on Friday, with return on Sunday, but there's also a mid-week trip when demand warrants. Book this trip yourself if you're interested—most hotel travel agencies will steer you to more expensive tours.

Similar trips are offered aboard the Mawamba, which runs twice a week from Limón to Tortuguero. The price is lower on the Mawamba tour if you stay at the basic Sabina's Cabinas. Call 339964 in San José to arrange your travel, or 581564 in Limón. The Mawamba is also available for charter by smaller groups. Costa Rica Expeditions (tel. 239975) operates a day-long flying trip to Tortuguero for about $220 per person. The Río Colorado Lodge (Box 5094, San José, tel. 328610) has a $200 package that includes bus transportation to Moín, a cruise through the canal to Barra del Colorado with a stop at Tortuguero National Park, a night's lodging, and return by air to San José. For slightly less, you can do it all in a day. Note that this tour does not pause at the park in the evening, when turtles nest.

Cargo-and-passenger boats also operate on an irregular basis to Parismina, Tortuguero and Barra del Colorado. Get to Moín early, or go out the day before to try to arrange your

139

trip with one of the boat captains. You might have to sit atop the cargo, and your continuing or return transportation will not be assured. Or ask at the JAPDEVA office for assistance in finding a private speedboat.

A last alternative is to fly from San José to Barra del Colorado, 35 kilometers north of Tortuguero, and hire a boat to the park, a trip of three to four hours.

Traffic on the canal is sparse and irregular, and without advance arrangements through a travel agency, you can't count on anything. When locals can't find a boat, they simply walk along the beach—six hours to Parismina, twelve or more to Tortuguero—and count on friendly dugout owners to take them across intervening estuaries.

ACCOMMODATIONS

Overnight accommodations in Tortuguero are limited, and it's a good idea to reserve in advance; or, given the whimsical nature of transport along the canal, to book your travel and sleeping as part of a single package.

The **Tortuga Lodge**, three kilometers north of Tortuguero, near the airstrip, is a jungle destination in itself, with high thatched roofs, hammocks, parrots, and gardenias and ferns, all straight out of a Dorothy Lamour movie. On a practical level, there are rooms with private bath, meals, and boats for fishing or exploring the waterways of the park, taken mostly as part of tour or fishing packages. The rate for a room alone is $60 single, $72 double. Meals run $7 for breakfast, $10 for lunch or dinner. Contact Costa Rica Expeditions, Calle Central, Avenida 3, San José, tel. 239975 for information.

The **Jungle Lodge** is the newest hotel in Tortuguero, a neat complex of red-roofed pre-fabs in a canal-side clearing, one kilometer from the park. Comfortable but not luxurious—all 14 rooms have fans and private showers. There's a bar and meal service, and fishing and boat rental are available. Contact Cotur (see Miss Caribe, above) if you would like to stay here without a tour. The rate is about $18 single, $30 double.

There are also rooms for rent in the village of Tortuguero, which contains several dozen houses and something like a hundred inhabitants. At Sabina's Cabinas (tel. 718099), the rate is about $4 per person. It's also possible to camp in the park, but the best rain protection is essential.

Inclusive tours generally include a morning's cruise through the canals of the park, during which birds can easily be sighted. For further exploration, dugouts are available for hire in Tortuguero village for about $10 per day. A motorboat with guide, rented at Tortuga Lodge, costs about $30 per hour. And there are assorted guided tours arranged through hotels. If you take a dugout on your own, stay out of the water. Sharks are sighted regularly.

BARRA DEL COLORADO

The Tortuguero Canal terminates at the settlement of Barra del Colorado, which sits astride the mouth of the Colorado River, a delta branch of the San Juan River that borders Nicaragua. Barra prospered in the forties as a lumber center and depot for cargo coming downriver from Nicaragua. But as woodcutting and river trade declined, so did Barra's fortunes. The population is now down to a few hundred, many of Nicaraguan descent.

Barra serves today as a takeoff point for visiting Tortuguero Park, and as a sport fishing center. But it also has its attractions as an out-of-the-way place with a friendly populace, where one can stay on the edge of the wild in relative comfort.

Sansa Airlines operates flights twice weekly between Barra and San José (current departures from San José Tuesday and Thursday at 6 a.m., leaving for San José at 6:45 a.m.). Fare is less than $15. Inexpensive packages including hotel and a cruise along the Tortuguero Canal are sometimes available from the airline. Private boats may be hired for jungle cruises in the vicinity, or for trips to Tortuguero Park. In less troubled times, small cargo boats have operated up the San Juan and Sarapiquí rivers to Puerto Viejo, which is tied by road with San José.

The wide San Juan lies entirely in Nicaragua, but Costa Rica enjoys full rights to use the river. More than a hundred years ago, Cornelius Vanderbilt established a combination riverboat-ferry-stage coach service that used the San Juan as part of a passenger route across Nicaragua, connecting with steamers from both coasts of the States. The service was disrupted during William Walker's takeover in Nicaragua, and as part of the post-war settlement, Costa Rica pushed its border north to the banks of the river. Panama thereafter dominated interoceanic transport, though the San Juan has been proposed from time to time as part of a new canal. The most famous navigators hereabouts nowadays are the sharks that move between Lake Nicaragua, upstream on the San Juan, and the Caribbean. Sharks frequent the coast down to Tortuguero as well, feeding on the abundant fish and making swimming one of the less peaceful diversions available.

ACCOMMODATIONS

Río Colorado Lodge. 12 rooms. $200 per person minimum with meals, use of boats, and guides; or $75 single/$100 double without fishing. San José office: Hotel Corobici, P. O. Box 5094-1000, tel. 328610. U.S. reservations: tel. 800-243-9777.

Simple but comfortable screened cabins, whirlpool, satellite t.v. This is mainly a fishing lodge, but the management also organizes excursions through the Tortuguero Canal and welcomes non-sportsmen to beachcomb and relax on the edge of the jungle. A mini-zoo on the grounds hold animals from the area. Open all year.

FISHING ALONG THE CARIBBEAN

Although remote, the Caribbean coast of Costa Rica is world famous for sport fishing. Tarpon, or *sábalo*, is the most notable (or notorious) species, most easily found in rivers and lagoons from January to June, with March and April the best months (though tarpon habits are unpredictable, and some claim June and July are best). Tarpon generally weigh from 60 to 100 pounds. A world-record 182-pound tarpon was caught from the Tortuga Lodge in 1987.

Second to the tarpon as a sport fish is snook (*róbalo*), generally caught from mid-August to mid-October, and averaging over 25 pounds. Other species are snapper *(pargo)*, *machaca, guapote,* bass, *mojarra*, king mackerel, grouper, catfish, sawfish, and jacks, which generally run under five pounds.

Almost all the fishing along the coast is in fresh-water river estuaries and lagoons, which at times are converted into furious cauldrons of spawning fish. At the right times, not having a good catch is virtually impossible. Fishing in the open waters of the Caribbean is a risky business, due to the unpredictability of winds and storms.

In addition to the Río Colorado Lodge, the following fishing camps are located along the Caribbean:

Parismina Tarpon Rancho, near Parismina (40 kilometers north of Limón). 10 rooms, from approximately $250 per person per day. San José address: P.O. Box 5712. U.S. reservations: tel. 800-531-7232 or 512-492-5517; in San José, tel. 357766; or write P. O. Box 290190, San Antonio, TX 78280.

Located on the edge of Parismina village. Rooms are in wooden cottages. Fishing is from 16-foot aluminum skiffs. Open January to May and August to October. Rate includes open bar, accommodations in San José, and transport to and from lodge.

Isla de Pesca, near Barra del Colorado. 12 units, approximately $200 per day, all-inclusive. Reservations: Fishing Travel, 2525 Nevada Ave. N., Golden Valley, MN 55427, tel. 612-541-1088. In San José: P. O. Box 8-4390, tel. 234560.

Simple A-frame cottages, with full bathrooms. Fishing is from 16-foot skiffs. Rates include the flight from San José to Barra, as well as use of boat and guides, and meals. This hotel also operates a Tortuguero Canal cruise similar to that offered by Río Colorado Lodge.

Tortuga Lodge, mentioned above under Tortuguero. Fishing from a skiff runs $200 per person as a minimum. If you're alone, the price will be about $400 daily for room, meals, boat, guide, and basic fishing equipment.

Casa Mar Fishing Lodge, Barra del Colorado. 12 rooms. $250 per day and up. U.S. reservations: P. O. Drawer 787, Islamorada, FL 33036, tel. 800-327-2880 or 305-664-4615.

Unlike some other fishing lodges, Casa Mar has full-time electricity. Guests stay in screened wooden cottages, each with two rooms. Package rate includes meals, boat, guide service, transport from San José, and bar consumption. Open January through mid-May and September through October.

Contact any of the fishing lodges, or their U.S. representatives, for a fat packet of information that will give you ample details about the quality of cooking, guides, boats, camp furnishings, and fishing grounds, along with ample endorsements, all of which will demonstrate, beyond reasonable doubt, why it is the premier fishing resort on the Caribbean. This is no fish story.

RIVER EXPORATION

Several tour operators offer rafting trips down the lower, wider, slower stretches of the Parismina and Reventazón rivers. Contact Ríos Tropicales or Costa Rica Expeditions (see San José chapter) to arrange travel.

South of Limón

The coast to the south of Limón, as to the north, is a nearly continuous stretch of sandy, idyllic, usually deserted beach. There are a few differences, however. Rainfall is lower to the south, and the terrain is generally better drained. This gives the landscape a less jungly nature, and makes it more habitable. It also makes things easier for the visitor, though you will be inevitably rained upon. Transport to the south is better developed as well. A paved road runs down the coast to Puerto Viejo, a branch road reaches Sixaola on the Panamanian border, and rail lines and spurs serve the banana operations of the area. The region is still sparsely settled, however, with many kilometers between settlements, and few places where a visitor may stop for the night.

South from Limón, the main road generally hugs the coast. Visitors may take a bus and get off at any point that looks attractive for swimming and sunning at deserted beaches. Landward, scrub vegetation alternates with cattle pastures and coconut plantations. About 30 kilometers from Limón, the road starts to run back a couple of kilometers from the sea. A branch road goes up the valley of the Estrella River, where a revival of banana cultivation is under way. Forty-five kilometers from Limón is the town of Cahuita.

CAHUITA NATIONAL PARK

Cahuita National Park has beaches as beautiful as any on the Caribbean, and a few additional distinctions. Just off-shore is a living coral reef, the most accessible in Costa Rica, where brightly colored fish feed and breed. In the marshes and forests of the park, animal and bird life are abundant.

The coral reef, which consists of the remains of small animals called polyps, lies up to half a kilometer from shore, and from one to seven meters under the surface. With diving equipment (bring some if you're interested), you can see the formations—brain, elkhorn, star and dozens of other corals—as well as the fish, sponges, crabs and snails that are attracted to feed and live on the reef. At two points on the reef's western side, cannonballs, anchors, cannon and bricks have been found, giving evidence that a Spanish galleon (or more than one) sank in these waters.

In the reef-protected shallows of Cahuita, sargasso and other grasses flourish, along with conch and ghost crabs. Dead trunks of trees lie just under the water, penetrated by seawood borers, the termites of the sea.

Beyond the reef at the south end of the park, Cahuita's lovely beach, beaten by huge waves, backed by coconut palms, is a nesting site for green, Hawksbill and leatherback turtles. The gentle sweep of the bay is quite unusual on this coast. In some sections, little pools form at low tide, temporarily isolating fish.

Inland, Cahuita's protected area includes extensive areas of marsh. The Perezoso (Sloth) River that flows to the sea in the park is dark brown in color, said to be an effect of the high tannin concentration, which also reputedly keeps a cap on the local mosquito population. The forests are alive with howler monkeys, white-faced monkeys, three-toed sloths, anteaters, and collared peccaries. Raccoons and coatis are often seen along the nature trail, which penetrates the damp world of ferns and bromeliads and huge jungle trees.

The town of Cahuita, at the northern end of the park, has sandy streets, widely separated houses, a friendly assortment of people, and a limited range of hotels and eating places.

ACCOMMODATIONS

Hotel Cahuita, tel. 581515, extension 201. 30 units.

Best of a few small hotels (a relative matter). Friendly management. There are 20 basic rooms, with shared bath, for $5 single, $8 double; and 10 harsh, motel-style rooms off the pleasant courtyard with private bath, for $15 double. Small pool.

Cabinas Vaz, tel.581515, extension 218.

Similar to the Hotel Cahuita, without the arches in the dining area.

The above hotels are right at the entrance to the park.

Surfside Cabinas, tel. 581515, extension 246, are 15 substantial concrete units, a few blocks from the park entrance, on the way to Black Beach (Playa Negra) on the other side of town from the park entrance. The rate is $8 single or double.

Black Beach, a kilometer from the center of Cahuita, is more isolated, not that any part of Cahuita is urban. **Cabinas Black Beach** (extension 251) has just two woodsy units with private baths in a large garden for $14 double. Four more units are being prepared. There are several other cabinas scattered in the palms by Black Beach, but I was told by the Rural Guard that they are not secure.

For those with cars, there are a couple of roadside campsites and hotels on the way to Cahuita. Cabinas Lemar, 26 kilometers from Limón, has a bar and pool, opposite a deserted beach. Five kilometers farther is a campsite.

There are a number of small diners in Cahuita. Cabinas Black Beach serves lasagna, among other items, in a pleasant bar and restaurant. The restaurant at the Hotel Cahuita is popular, with meals for $5 and up. Right next to the entrance to the park, the restaurant under the great thatched roof serves good casados (meat or fish or chicken with rice, beans and cabbage) for $3, and assorted steaks, fish, Italian dishes and yogurt.

Assorted other facilities for visitors: One little house on the main street offers snorkeling tours and trips to other villages, from time to time; another has souvenirs, of a sort. The Hotel Cahuita rents out bikes and snorkeling equipment. There are no banks, no car-rental agencies, no fishing lodges, no restaurants with tablecloths, no significant action. Cahuita is a live-and-let-live place where one can stay for a while without any particular justification. The small population includes Creoles who speak Spanish at the shops and unintelligible English among themselves; Germans, French and Americans on extended stays, spending their days surfing and their nights stringing necklaces; Hispanic Costa Ricans, of course; and the Bribri Indian from the bush of the Talamanca mountains who works at one of the hotels and deals with guests in impeccable Californian.

If you plan to snorkel, you'll find the water clearest from February through April, when it rains the least. The park is usually nearly deserted, except on weekends and at holiday periods, which should be avoided.

The southern entrance to the park is about six kilometers farther on, at Puerto Vargas (Vargas Harbour), which is a bay, not a village. Here the park administration, nature trail and camping facilities are located.

TRANSPORTATION

From San José, comfortable, direct buses for Sixaola (without a stop in Limón) depart from Avenida 11, Calles Central/1, at 6 a.m. and 2:30 p.m., passing both entrances to Cahuita Park. Telephone 210524 to confirm the schedule. The trip through Braulio Carrillo National Park and the humid coastal plain takes about four hours. From Limón, rickety, usually crowded buses leave from Avenida 4, Calles 3/4 at 5 a.m., 10 a.m., 1 p.m. and 4 p.m., arriving at Cahuita in about an hour. Get to the station early to find a seat. Departures from Sixaola for Limón are at 5 a.m., 8 a.m., 10 a.m. and 3 p.m.; for San José at 6 a.m. and 2:30 p.m. These buses pass Cahuita about 25 minutes out of Sixaola.

PUERTO VIEJO

Fifteen kilometers south of Cahuita, Puerto Viejo (Old Harbour) is a mixed Tico, Creole and Indian community, about a kilometer-and-a-half off the paved road. Though larger than Cahuita, Puerto Viejo is hardly bustling. A derelict barge just offshore sprouts a tree. One can easily make a round trip from Limón in a day to enjoy the black sand beaches here.

ACCOMMODATIONS

Facilities at Puerto Viejo are basic and limited. Cabinas Chimuri, in the jungle by the sea, about 400 meters north of where the road meets the beach, has three cubicles in a stilt camp building for $5 single, $8 double. There's a common cooking facility, and shower and outhouse. The owner, who comes from the interior, offers horses for rent, jungle trips, and Indian crafts for sale. The clapboard annex (*anexo*) of the Hotel Maritza, at the edge of town, is the most attractive of lodging places right in Puerto Viejo. The small rooms, upstairs over the eating area, share baths. There's a sea view from the porch. $5 single, $8 double. The Hotel Maritza proper, and Cabinas Ritz, are farther on, and less desirable, with similar rates.

There is one Chinese-seafood eatery, and there are two "discos"—bars with dance areas—called Stanford's and Bambú, just south of the village, by the dump. Activities at Puerto Viejo include listening to reggae music, and watching dugouts being hacked from giant logs.

MANZANILLO, BRIBRI, SIXAOLA

A newly cut dirt road runs through the forest along the sea to Manzanillo, 12 kilometers to the south. The area is hardly populated for now—there are scattered vacation houses, including those of a couple of ex-presidents—and magnificent trees grow right to the edge of the road and arch overhead. Streams are crossed on rattling and somewhat unsure plank bridges. A spur road will eventually loop back to the paved highway. There are plans to develop this area for tourism, so go and see it now, before all the trees are cut down. At Manzanillo, a fishing post of just a few houses,

Cabinas Maxi has basic cubicles. There is an informal car and truck service for passengers. If you're not drivng, take food and camping equipment in case the accommodation at Manzanillo is full.

Bribri, 65 kilometers from Limón, includes in its population a number of Indians, and there are other, more remote Indian centers farther inland.

Sixaola is the crossing point to the isolated northwest region of Panama. No roads continue to the rest of Panama from this area, but flights are available to David, and onward to Panama City.

Up and Down the Pacific

Pacific Costa Rica covers a vast sweep of territory along the wide side of the country, from Nicaragua down to the Panamanian border. Overlooking a complicated, varied terrain are the volcanoes and mountain peaks of the Guanacaste, Tilarán and Talamanca mountain ranges, which largely block the rains that blow across Costa Rica from the Caribbean. Winds blow on shore from the west from May through October, bringing storms to the area, while the rest of the year is dry. But there are exceptions to this general picture. The Guanacaste lowlands of the northeast, hemmed in by coastal mountains, are subject to periodic droughts. In the south, on the other hand, near Golfito, the coastal mountains act as a watershed, and it rains throughout the year. In general, rainfall, humidity and discomfort increase toward the south. The daytime temperature throughout the area is generally in the nineties Fahrenheit (32-37 Centigrade).

The central part of the coastal region is a narrow plain, broken by rivers that drip down over rocky beds from the highlands in the dry season and rush down in torrents during the rainy months. Farther to the north, the plain widens into the savanna of Guanacaste, a former forest area that lost its natural cover as it was turned into farm and grazing land. A rocky fringe borders the sparsely populated Nicoya peninsula, in the north, along the sea. Barely settled at all is the Osa Peninsula, in the southern part of the region.

Travel to the main towns in the northern part of the Pacific coastal region—Puntarenas, Cañas, Liberia—is made easy by an excellent highway and frequent bus service. Most of the main attractions—notably the best beaches—are off this route, however, and are reached by plane, or with difficulty on poor roads.

PUNTARENAS

Population: 39,000; Altitude: 3 meters; 112 kilometers from San José

Puntarenas is one miles-long sandspit (which is what its name means), sticking out into the Gulf of Nicoya, a narrow, muddy estuary on one side, clear water on the other. Opened to shipping in 1814, the port was for many years Costa Rica's only outlet to world commerce. The coffee crop moved down to the coast from the highlands on oxcarts with a legendary breed of driver, rough and ready, but scrupulously honest. Today, the major shipping terminal is nearby at the modern port of Caldera. But Puntarenas is still one of the larger cities in the country. Trains and trucks arrive with goods, and the streets are choked with commerce.

The location of Puntarenas is strategic for the visitor. The ferries that depart from here provide the easiest access to some of the nicer beaches on the Nicoya peninsula. Cruises from the yacht club touch the many islands in the Gulf of Nicoya. Puntarenas is the nearest Pacific point to San José.

Unfortunately, though, much of the city is a dump. I don't mean only that the beach is dirty for its whole great length along the south side of town, though it is. The central part of the city consists of dismal, rotting and rusting, ramshackle structures, cheap flophouses, bar after bar oozing drunks, and streets strewn with garbage and emitting a stench into the humid, dense air that will make you gag.

Not that all of Puntarenas is hard to take. There are some nice residences near the western tip of town, a few good hotels, and a substantial yacht club. The headquarters of the port, at the main pier, are in a lovely old building. Eating in the open-air diners along the beach and mixing with the crowds that come down for the day from San José can be pleasant. But Costa Rica has much nicer seaside places to offer, and you didn't come all the way from home to hang out here.

HOTELS

Because Puntarenas is so accessible from San José, hotels are overpriced for what they offer.

Hotel Tioga, Paseo de los Turistas (Avenida 4, beach side, ten blocks west of the large pier), P. O. Box 96-5400, tel. 610271. 46 rooms. $18 to $27 single/$24 to 37 double.

Nice rooms, many with views to the sea, well-maintained, air-conditioned. Best of the in-town lodgings. There's a pool, and a restaurant offers good fresh fish as well as meat and chicken dishes at $4 to $5 for a main course. Rates include full breakfast in the fourth-floor dining-room-with-a-view. Higher rates are for rooms with hot water and balconies.

Hotel Cayuga, Calle 4, Avenidas Central/1 (one block north of the microwave tower), P. O. Box 306-5400, tel. 610344. 31 rooms. $8/$11.

Located near the center of town, which is unfortunate, because this is the best hotel buy in Puntarenas, clean, modern, with a decent restaurant (main courses $3 to $4) and air conditioning.

Hotel Las Hamacas, Paseo de los Turistas (Avenida 4), Calles 5/7, tel. 610398. 25 rooms. $11/$21.

Quite visible with its compound facing the beach, but a last choice among the centrally located hotels, with hospital-type rooms and no hot water.

Hotel Las Brisas, Calle 29, tel. 612120. 9 rooms, $22-$30/$27-$45.

Of recent construction, near the tip of the peninsula, clean and airy. The higher rates are for balconied rooms with views away from the city, to the mountains of the Nicoya Peninsula and the hilly islands of the gulf. If you arrive on the late ferry and don't want to face Puntarenas, this is a good bet.

Next door to Las Brisas, a new hotel is under construction at the very end of the peninsula.

Various "cabinas" (simple rooms with few facilities) are also available at locations along the beachfront, at prices of about $6 to $8 per person. A half block from the bus station, the Hotel Imperial is a clean old wooden building that faces

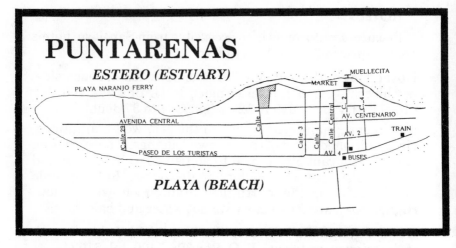

PUNTARENAS

ESTERO (ESTUARY)

PLAYA NARANJO FERRY

MUELLECITA

MARKET

AVENIDA CENTRAL

Calle 1

AV. CENTENARIO

Calle 3

Calle 1

Calle Central

C. 2

C. 4

AV. 2

TRAIN

Calle 29

PASEO DE LOS TURISTAS

AV. 4

BUSES

PLAYA (BEACH)

the water and offers rooms with shared baths for about $5 per person. And there are loads of other cheap hotels. East from the center of town are:

Costa Rica Yacht Club, Calle 74, three kilometers from downtown Puntarenas, tel. 610784 (in San José: P. O. Box 2530, tel. 223818). 28 rooms. $14 to $30 single/$17 to $37 double.

Full docking facilities, with food and fuel supply, as well as a hotel open to non-members. Rooms are comfortable, cabins will sleep up to six in marine-style, tight quarters.

Hotel Porto Bello , Avenida 1, Calles 72/74, P. O. Box 108-5400, tel. 321248, 611322. 34 rooms. $65/$75.

Located a safe few miles from downtown Puntarenas in its own nicely landscaped compound. Attractive Mediterranean-style construction, air-conditioned, t.v. in some rooms, pool. This is one of the nicer hotels in town, but still, Puntarenas is no resort.

Hotel Colonial, adjacent to the Yacht Club, Calle 72, P. O. Box 368-5400, tel. 611833. 56 rooms. $25/$38.

Colonial-style compound, facilities comparable to those at the above two hotels.

Out at the eastern end of Puntarenas, at San Ysidro, are a number of compounds that attract the family trade from

154

San José. One of the better of the lot is Cabinas San Isidro, but these are still barracks-like rows of housekeeping units.

At Barranca:

Hotel Río Mar, tel. 630158. 50 rooms. $11/$15.

A pleasant, older hotel, with a children's pool only, located near Doña Ana beach on the highway south. This is a good stopping place if you're driving and don't want to go into Puntarenas.

RESTAURANTS

You can try the restaurants at the hotels in town, or the sodas near the market, but the most fun, and the freshest fish, are at the open-air eating places along the beach, near the main pier. Otherwise, I think the best downtown food is at the Hotel Cayuga. For pleasant outdoor dining away from the hubbub, and not too far from the terminal of the ferry for Nicoya, go to the Hotel Las Brisas.

TRANSPORTATION

Buses for Puntarenas leave from Calle 12, Avenida 9, San José, every hour from 6 a.m. to 6 p.m. The trip takes about two hours. In Puntarenas, buses for San José leave from Calle 2 and Avenida 4, one block east (toward the mainland) from the main pier.

Trains for Puntarenas leave from the station at Calle 2, Avenida 20, San José, at 6 a.m. and 4 p.m. Take the Paso Ancho bus from the main square to the station. The trip takes four hours, follows a different route from the highway, and is quite scenic. Trains for San José depart from Puntarenas at 6 a.m. and 4 p.m. The terminal is three blocks east of the bus station for San José.

Buses depart for various nearby and distant towns from a shelter along the sea opposite the bus station for San José. The bus for Santa Elena, near Monteverde leaves at 2:15 p.m., for Quepos at 5 a.m. and 2:30 p.m. The bus for Barranca, at the armpit of the peninsula, leaves from the market in Puntarenas.

SWIMMING

Since the beach at Puntarenas isn't inviting, you might want to look for other swimming opportunities. The boats mentioned below will take you to some nice beaches on the Nicoya Peninsula. Nearer to Puntarenas, the best swimming is at Doña Ana beach, a public park with ample shade and picnic areas, out of town on the road to Caldera and points south. The Mata Limón bus from Puntarenas passes the entrance.

BOATS FROM PUNTARENAS

Really, the only reason for a foreign visitor to go to Puntarenas is to leave promptly for one of the nicer places along the coast. Many are accessible by boat, either directly or in combination with car or bus travel.

A passenger and automobile ferry operates daily between Puntarenas and Playa Naranjo, on the Nicoya Peninsula. Departures from Puntarenas are at 7 a.m. and 4 p.m., from the dock at Calle 29 and Avenida 3, on the estuary side near the western end of the peninsula. The ferry leaves Playa Naranjo at 9 a.m. and 6 p.m. Fare is about $1 for passengers. There's an extra daily trip on Thursday, Saturday and Sunday from Puntarenas at 11 a.m., and from Playa Naranjo at 1 p.m. Basic restaurant service is available on board. The crossing takes about one hour. Phone 611069 to confirm schedules.

The Playa Naranjo ferry provides a shortcut to the southern part of the Nicoya peninsula. Buses going to the town of Nicoya meet the ferry, but public transport to other places is hard to find. Playa Naranjo is a dock and little else, but one of the nicer hotels in the peninsula, the Oasis del Pacífico, is just a few hundred meters down the road (see page 194).

A passenger-only boat for Paquera, also in the Nicoya Peninsula, leaves daily at 6 a.m. and 3 p.m. from the broken-down dock ("la muellecita") behind the market in Puntarenas (Calle 2, on the estuary side). Fare is less than a dollar. Buses provide onward transportation from Paquera to Tambor and Cóbano.

On Sundays only, a boat leaves at 9 a.m. for El Coro beach on San Lucas Island, halfway across the gulf. Departure for Puntarenas is at 2 p.m. San Lucas is the site of a prison colony, where inmates to some degree run their own affairs.

The yacht Calypso makes a daily cruise from the yacht club to seven islands in the Gulf of Nicoya. Fare is $65, including overland transportation from San José, or slightly less if you're already in Puntarenas. This is a well-planned, well-run excursion that has been running for years and years. A stop is made at a deserted, palm-shaded beach on Tortuga Island for swimming, snorkelling, beachcombing, and a picnic lunch that includes fresh gulf fish. Book the cruise through any hotel in Puntarenas, or call 333617 in San José, or 610585 in Puntarenas. Longer cruises are also available.

Arrangements may also be made with private boat owners at the docks in Puntarenas to visit the islands in the Gulf of Nicoya. On Chira, the largest, near the northern end of the gulf, cattle are raised and salt is extracted from sea water. Guayabo, Negritos and Los Pájaros islands are biological reserves, noted for their abundance of seabirds. Guayabo is an important nesting site for brown pelicans, and peregrine falcons are known to hibernate there. Cedros and several smaller islands have no restaurants, hotels or any other facilities, and few inhabitants, but are excellent locales for birding, reached by chartered boat or naturalists' tours.

Boats for deep-sea fishing are said to be available in Puntarenas and at Mata Limón, to the south, if you ask around.

Being a place where the sea and boats have always been important, Puntarenas celebrates with particular enthusiasm the festival of the Virgin of the Sea, on the Saturday before or after July 16. Boats are festooned with decorations and pass in review. Dances, parades, beauty contests, fireworks and drunkenness are part of the goings on.

North from Puntarenas
The main coastal highway runs north through the rolling plain inland from Puntarenas, passing through Cañas, and then over flat country to Bagaces and Liberia. None of these

places is of much interest to visitors. But off the road, and accessible from it, are some of the natural wonders for which Costa Rica is known.

MONTEVERDE

High on the ridge above the coastal plain are the town of Santa Elena, and the adjacent farming colony and cloud-forest reserve of Monteverde. Costa Rica is rich in montane tropical rain forest of the type included in the Monteverde reserve—the forest atop the volcano Poás is one example, and is much more accessible. But the slow ascent to Monteverde offers spectacular views, the rolling, pastured countryside is idyllic and even spiritually uplifting, and the reserve is large. The inns in the area invite the visitor to linger and explore the forest, or relax in the fresh mountain air.

The Monteverde farming colony was founded on April 19, 1951, by Quakers from Alabama, some of whom had been imprisoned for refusing to serve in the U.S. armed forces. There were only oxcart trails into the area at the time, and the trucks and tractors of the settlers had to be winched up the mountains. Land was laboriously cleared, and the colony eventually found some prosperity in dairy farming. Monteverde cheeses now have a solid share of the Costa Rican market. Over the years, the settlement changed, as some of the original families moved on, while non-Quakers bought land in the area. Monteverde is now a mixed, largely English-speaking community.

The original settlers set aside 2500 hectares of land to protect native plant life, even as it was being destroyed by clearing in other parts of the colony. A private foundation, the Tropical Science Center, now administers the reserve. Government protection has been afforded to the rare species found at Monteverde, including the golden toad (sapo dorado), which is known to live only in rainpools in the vicinity. The original area of the reserve has been expanded to 10,000 hectares (22,000 acres) by the purchase of adjacent lands, some of which had been farmed but are now being allowed to return to their natural state.

GETTING TO MONTEVERDE

A bus operates to Monteverde from the corner of 14 Calle and 9 Avenida, San José, departing at 2:30 p.m. on Monday, Tuesday and Thursday; and at 6:30 a.m. on Saturday. Fare is about $3. Return buses depart from Monteverde on Tuesday and Thursday at 6:30 a.m. and Friday and Sunday at 3 p.m. Telephone 612659 to verify the schedule.

From Puntarenas, there's a daily bus to Santa Elena, six kilometers from the reserve. Departure from the bus shelter at Calle 2 along the beach is at 2:15 p.m.; from Santa Elena for Puntarenas at 6 a.m. Buses on this route are of the uncomfortable school-bus type that serve the back roads of Costa Rica. To connect with this bus on days when the bus from San José isn't running, take the train from San José (Calle 2, Avenida 20) at 6:30 a.m., or a bus to Puntarenas (Calle 12, Avenida 9), no later than 11 a.m. Better yet, avoid Puntarenas altogether, and take a bus from the Coca-Cola terminal in San José (16 Calle, Avenidas 1/3) heading toward Cañas, Liberia or Peñas Blancas. Leave no later than 11:30 a.m., and ask to be let off at the Lagarto junction, at kilometer post 149. The Santa Elena bus passes this junction at about 3 p.m.

From the junction, it's a two-hour ascent on a bumpy, unpaved road to Santa Elena, with spectacular views, on a clear evening, of the sunset and orange-tinged sky over the Nicoya Peninsula, below and in the distance. When visibility is limited, you'll have to settle for views of the nearby landscape, as it changes from rolling hills covered with citrus and mango trees to steep grazing lands on the slopes of the mountain ridge, patches of oak and evergreen forest, and many a cool, misty valley with scattered clusters of farmhouses.

By automobile, follow the Pan American Highway (Route 1) to the junction at kilometer 149, then the dirt road for 32 kilometers to Santa Elena. This last stretch will usually take at least an hour and a half to cover. During part of the rainy season, it is passable only with four-wheel-drive.

Most travel agencies in San José offer tours to Monteverde. Transportation can be arranged as well through some of the hotels mentioned below.

ACCOMMODATIONS

Santa Elena is a pleasant little town, about 1500 meters above sea level, though the dramatic, broken landscape all around, strong winds, and the cool, misty air make it seem higher. There are numerous bars, and also a few lodging places. A room in the pleasant and simple Pensión Santa Elena costs less than $5 per person. Other establishments charge about the same.

However, if you have the energy to walk after you arrive, probably in the evening, you might as well stay nearer to the reserve. The pensions and hotels mentioned below are located from two to three kilometers uphill from Santa Elena, along or near the road to the reserve. You may be able to pick up a ride from locals, who charge about a dollar for the service. Bear in mind that if you're travelling by bus, you'll probably face an early start on the day you leave. Traffic is sparse, so don't count on being able to hitch a ride after the bus goes.

Hotel de Montaña Monteverde, 12 rooms, $38 to $70 double, meals additional. Tel. 611846. In San José: P. O. Box 70, tel. 333890. U.S. reservations: tel. 800-327-4250.

Located on the east side of the road to the reserve, about two kilometers from Santa Elena, the Hotel de Montaña is cozy and rustic, with hardwood-panelled rooms, and beds covered with thick woolen blankets. There are acres of adjoining farm and woods available to guests for exploration, and spectacular views down toward the Pacific. Horses are available for rent, and boots are lent for hiking through the reserve. Transportation to the hotel may be arranged through the San José telephone number.

Pensión Quetzal, 8 rooms. $19 per person with three meals. Tel. 610955.

This is a comfortable lodge with a homey atmosphere, also heavy on the wood panelling, located about half a kilometer beyond the Hotel de Montaña, and 150 meters back from the road.

Hotel Belmar, tel. 611001. 18 rooms. $35/$40. Tel. 611001.

A four-story chalet-style building which, though not in an indigenous contemporary architectural idiom, suits the high forest surroundings. Beautiful panoramas are afforded from the private balconies, all the way to the Gulf of Nicoya. Attentive service and home-style cooking by the owners. Boots, horseback trips and transportation to the reserve (three kilometers away) are available. They'll also pick you up in San José on request.

Pensión Flor Mar, 6 rooms. $14 per person with three meals. Telephone 611887.

Three kilometers from Santa Elena and three from the reserve, the Flor Mar is a rustic place that reminds me of a summer camp. Basic and friendly. You sleep on bunks, and can have a room all to yourself if they're not too busy. The food is vegetarian and hearty, and they'll pack a lunch to carry to the reserve if you so desire. This is probably the only place in Costa Rica that serves imitation coffee.

Meals without lodging are available at the Hotel de Montaña and the Pensión Flor Mar, at the Sapo Dorado bar and dance hall, and at a couple of diners in Santa Elena.

VISITING THE RESERVE

The Monteverde cloud forest is created by winds, particular temperature and moisture conditions, and mountainous topography, which combine during the dry season to hold a steady cloud cover along the continental divide. During the rainy season, of course, the forest receives its full share of precipitation from storms blowing up from the coast. The rains, and the moisture in the air, nourish trees and plants rooted in the ground, as well as many plants that live at the upper levels of the forest, and take their nutrients directly from the mist and dust that pass through the air. The result is an enchanted, fairy-tale environment, where trees are laden with orchids, bromeliads, mosses and ferns that obscure their branches, where the moisture and mild temperatures and sunlight filtered by the forest canopy encourage the exuberance of begonias, heliconias, philodendron and many other tropical plants in every available space on the ground. Leaves are gigantic, vines penetrate everywhere, flowers blow through the air from the tree canopy. The forest is almost visibly growing and changing, throbbing and vibrating with life at all levels. Hummingbirds feed on nectar, frogs use pools of rainwater trapped in bromeliads to rear their young, worms and tree roots alike mine decaying matter whether it lies on the ground or in the crook of a branch. The air resounds with a crack as an epiphyte-laden branch drops to the ground, to rot and return to life by feeding the creatures and plants all around.

More than 2000 plant species have been catalogued at Monteverde, including more than 500 kinds of trees, 300 orchids, and 200 ferns. Within the 10,000-hectare reserve there is a variety in the forest habitat. Parts are relatively dry, with little undergrowth, others are swampy. There are areas of dwarf trees, and gradations from premontane to rain and cloud forest.

And, of course, there is more to the forest than the trees and lesser plants. Of over 320 bird species, the most notable is the quetzal, with its long arc of tail feathers. It nests in the trunks of dead trees. Other visually spectacular species include the three-wattled bellbird, the great green macaw, the bare-necked umbrellabird, and the ornate hawk-eagle. Assorted trogons in addition to the quetzal inhabit the reserve, along with more than 50 varieties of hummingbird. About 500 kinds of butterfly are found at Monteverde. Among the more than 100 mammalian species are howler, white-faced and spider monkeys, coatis and their cousins, raccoons; and pumas, ocelots, jaguars, tapirs, kinkajous, and, of course, the golden toad, a symbol of the natural treasures that may turn up in protected areas. Some of these may be seen scurrying for cover as you walk through their territory.

There are no specific hours for visiting the Monteverde Reserve. Go as early or late as you like, sign in, and pay your entry fee of about $5 ($3 for students). Give the person at the reception desk an idea of your route so that somebody may look for you if you don't return. On sale at the entrance are bird and plant lists, as well as a guide for the nature trail (which is marked only with numbers).

Camping is permitted near the entrance for a small fee. There are, as well, two cabins well inside the reserve, available for rent. Take along supplies if you would like to use these.

Trails are well marked, and it would be difficult to lose your way. There is some mud (more squishy leaf rot than shoe-sucking ooze) and damp terrain, but thoughtful planners have placed plank bridges and stump steps wherever they are needed. Leon Bean's Maine hunting shoe would be the ideal footwear for a walk in these woods, but otherwise, any sturdy walking shoe and an eye to where you step are all that are needed. Elevations vary from about 1500 to 1700 meters. Most of the steeper grades are near the entrance, so don't be discouraged. You'll be handed a map when you pay your fee. Any of several routes is possible, for walks of a few hours to a few days. While you're supposed to come to look at the forest and animals, the long-distance views are also magnificent, especially from the point called La Ventana (The Window, or Opening). However, you will be very lucky indeed if you see an ocean. This is, after all, a cloud forest, and the clouds are often there.

One last bit of advice before you take off on your walk is to go slowly. Stop every once in a while and take a 360-degree look around at the moss- and bromeliad-laden canopy, and at the lower levels of the forest. If you only walk at a steady pace—in other words, if you hike—your eyes will be necessarily glued to the trail in order to keep your footing, and you'll miss the whole show overhead.

Several individuals offer guided walks in the reserve. Inquire at your hotel. The fee for a morning visit for two is about $40. There are also horseback trips.

Those planning an intensive acquaintance with the reserve can pick up pamphlets about its wildlife (in English and Spanish) at the Tropical Science Center, Calle 1, Avenidas 2/4 (no. 442, P. O. Box 8-3870), San José, tel. 226241. Rustic accommodations in the reserve, meals, and slide shows are available to students by advance arrangement with the Center.

Aside from the reserve, the only site to see in Monteverde is the cheese factory. Visitors may look in on the operations, which are unspectacular. A handicraft cooperative sells woodware and embroidered linen clothing.

The Monteverde community as a whole attracts much curiosity. It is, after all, unusual to find an English-speaking, North American-descended farming colony dispersed over these beautiful mountains. Outsiders are treated courteously, but the local residents would just as well be left to their labors.

From Monteverde, one can descend again to the main highway, and continue by bus or car to the northwest. At kilometer 168 is the junction for a road that goes to the town of Nicoya and the Nicoya peninsula, via a ferry crossing of the Tempisque River. Along the way is Barra Honda National Park, with its many caves (see page 177).

CAÑAS, TILARAN, LAKE ARENAL

At kilometer 188 is the farming center of Cañas (altitude 90 meters). Tilarán (altitude 564 meters), 22 kilometers from Cañas through foothills of the Tilarán range dotted with cylindrical hydroelectric stations, is picturesque, warm, slow-paced, clean, and lightly trafficked, a ringer for a hill town in the Portuguese Algarve.

Four kilometers beyond Tilarán, the road approaches fjord-like Lake Arenal, the perfect Arenal volcano at its south end, islands sprinkling its waters. The lake is said to be good for sport fishing: guapote, a bass-like fish, and machaca populate its waters. Around the lake are the remains of twelve pre-Columbian settlements, which were encountered with the aid of American satellite photographs and radar tracking. They appear to have been incinerated during an eruption of Arenal several thousand years ago, in the manner of Pompey. Much of this archeological curiosity was buried during the construction of the Arenal hydroelectric project and the filling of the lake.

The right fork at the lake approach takes you six kilometers to Tronadora, where there are some basic cabinas with lake access. The main road runs northwest, then circles the waters through the highlands above. There are no shoulders on which to pull off to admire the view, and few access points to the tempting water below. The town of Arenal is 29 kilometers beyond the junction at the lake approach, following the left fork in the road; Fortuna, with a stretch of poor road in between, is 73 kilometers distant, past

Arenal volcano (see page 223). A few buses a day ply this route all the way to Ciudad Quesada (San Carlos).

ACCOMMODATIONS

In and near Cañas:

Hacienda La Pacífica, Cañas, P.O. Box 8-5700, tel. 690050. 28 rooms and cottages. $12 to $20 single/$16 to $30 double/$36 to $43 for four.

Five kilometers north of Cañas, along the highway, the attractive La Pacífica offers three different types of units, ranging from modest to quite comfortable, (though without air conditioning) in cottages widely spaced on shady lawns. La Pacífica is a self-styled *Centro Ecológico* (Ecological Center), a model farm where environmentally sound methods are used to raise cattle and crops. All of the hacienda, covering about 16 square kilometers of cultivated fields, pasture and windbreaks, is open to visitors for exploration, along roads, trails, on foot or on horseback. About two kilometers from the hotel is the dairy; five kilometers away is the hundred-year-old ranch house. Near the guest accommodations, trees in groves are handily labelled—tamarind, cocobolo, hog plum, and many others. Swimming is available in both a pool and a lake. Birds squawk, goats whinny, and roosters crow. It's all quite lovely. But also, trucks roar and an occasional small plane drones. But for the latter noises, I could recommend La Pacífica as a vacation destination in itself. Stop by for lunch, at the very least. The food is good—mixed grills, chops and cordon bleu for $4 and up—served in a pavilion bordered by cages of macaws, a fish pond, and leafy plants and ferns. From August until December, rates drop by 20%. The National Parks Service has an office at La Pacífica.

Right in Cañas. Cabinas Corobicí, six blocks east of the highway, is basic but friendly, with rooms for about $4 per person.

In Tilarán:

Cabinas El Sueño, tel. 695347. About $6 per person.

A block from the square, and pleasant enough.

165

The **Hotel Central**, tel. 695363, two blocks from the park, is less attractive, at about $3 per person. There are others in the same price range.

BUSES

Buses for Cañas depart five times daily from Calle 16, Avenidas 1/3, San José. Buses for Tilarán leave from Calle 12, Avenidas 7/9, San José, at 7 a.m. and 12:45, 3:45 and 6:30 p.m. Buses for San José depart Tilarán at 7 and 7:45 a.m. and 2 and 5 p.m. The trip takes about three hours. From Tilarán, there are buses for Arenal, across the lake, at 10 a.m. and 4 p.m., and for San Carlos (Ciudad Quesada) at 7 a.m. and 1 p.m.

Back on the Interamerican Highway, at Bagaces (kilometer 215), is the junction for the Miralvalles thermoelectric generating project, 27 kilometers to the northeast.

PALO VERDE

Southwest of Cañas, near the mouth of the Tempisque River, is Palo Verde National Park, a reserve of seasonally dry tropical forest, which once covered much of this area. There are hiking trails and observation points. Inquire at the National Parks Service in San José before visiting.

Less developed for visitors is the adjacent wetland Lomas Barbudal Biological Reserve, a refuge for migrating waterfowl, including herons, egrets, ducks and grebes. The station for the reserve is six kilometers from the kilometer 221 marker on the Interamerican Highway. At the mouth of the Tempisque River is the Rafael Lucas Rodríguez Caballero Wildlife Refuge (Refugio de Vida Silvestre), which encompasses a variety of habitats ranging from dry forest to marsh to lagoons to pasture and evergreen groves, where peccaries, deer, white-faced monkeys, waterfowl and crocodiles may be observed, among others. For information about the wildlife refuge, contact the Wildlife Department (Departamento de Vida Silvestre) of the Ministry of Agriculture, Calle 17, Avenidas Central/2, San José, tel. 219533. In the refuge is the Palo Verde Field Station of the Organization for Tropical Studies, where research facilities are available and outside visitors may stay for about $50 per person, including meals, if space is available. Contact the Organization for Tropical Studies, P. O. Box 676, 2050 San Pedro, tel. 252218. (As you can tell from this flurry of names and places, conserving the wonders of nature can get to be a complex matter.)

LIBERIA

Population: 17,000; Altitude: 150 meters (492 feet);
236 kilometers from San José.

Liberia, the major city of northwestern Costa Rica, is a bustling place with wide, clean streets, relatively good accommodations, and a pleasant, dry climate. All lowland towns should be like Liberia. Strangely, modern Liberia has one of the relatively few surviving colonial churches, La Agonía. But this dates from a period when the area was part of Nicaragua, then a more prosperous and populated colony than Costa Rica.

Liberia is the capital of Guanacaste, a province with a separate tradition and a separate history from the rest of Costa Rica. By Spanish fiat, the area was detached from Nicaragua in 1814 in order to give Costa Rica a population sufficient for representation in the Cortes (parliament) at Cadiz. A vote in Nicoya in 1820 confirmed the transfer, at a time when Nicaragua was racked by civil wars. That early exercise in self-determination is celebrated on July 25 every year. Nicaragua for many years protested the loss of the territory, but finally gave up its claims in the Cañas-Jérez treaty of 1858.

The province takes its name from the *guanacaste* (earpod) tree that provides shade on vast, flat grasslands. In a country short on folklore, Guanacaste provides tradition and color for all of Costa Rica. The *punto guanacasteco* is the national dance. Music played on the marimba, a xylophone-type instrument used by pre-Columbian Indians of Guanacaste, with sounding boxes made from wood or gourds, arouses nostalgic feelings in San José, though it has no roots there.

The culture of Guanacaste is largely Mestizo, or mixed Indian and Spanish. The Chorotega Indians of this area had

167

strong ties to the peoples to the north, in Mexico and coastal Central America, before the arrival of the Spanish. Even today, there are pockets of Chorotega life in the Nicoya peninsula, where old farming practices, such as the use of the digging stick, and traditional forms of burnished pottery are maintained. Mostly, however, the Chorotega heritage may be seen in Guanacastecan faces that are browner than those in other parts of Costa Rica.

Large areas of drought-prone Guanacaste have been made productive for rice and cotton cultivation with the construction of irrigation systems. A sparse population produces surpluses of fruit, corn and beans as well. But for most Costa Ricans, Guanacaste signifies vast herds of cattle munching away on the grasslands. The folkloric figures par excellence of the area are Costa Rica's poor man's cowboys, mounted on horses with elaborately decorated saddles, and *boyeros*, tenders of oxen.

ACCOMMODATIONS

Hotel El Bramadero, P. O. Box 70-5000, tel. 660371. 24 rooms, $10 single/$15 double.

A modest motel with rooms arranged around a courtyard, the Bramadero has seen better days. Air-conditioned, but no hot water. Swimming pool sometimes filled. Large pavilion restaurant. Located at the turn from the highway into town.

Nuevo Hotel Boyeros, P.O. Box 85, tel. 660722. 62 rooms. $16/$25.

Also located at the turn into town. Modern, with air conditioning, pools for kids and adults, and attractive leafy landscaping. Bands sometimes perform on weekends—inquire beforehand if you need a good night's sleep.

Hotel La Siesta, Calle 4, Avenidas 4/6, P. O. Box 15-5000, tel. 660678. 25 rooms, $12/$20.

Clean hotel, with small pool and air conditioning, and inexpensive restaurant; nearest to the bus station (from the Central Park, walk one block toward the highway on Avenida Central, then two blocks to the left).

Hotel Las Espuelas, P. O. Box 88-5000, tel. 660144. 39 rooms. $28/$34.

Best in the area, a hacienda-style building with palm-shaded grounds, courtyard filled with birds and flowers, a good, reasonably priced restaurant with kids' menu, quiet central air conditioning (highly unusual), and pool. Located on the highway, about a kilometer south of the turn into town.

Hotel El Sitio, (P. O. Box 471-1000 San José), tel. 661211. 52 rooms. $15/$30.

On the road toward Nicoya, an airy, open, modern ranch-style complex, air conditioned. Two pools, simple dining.

Hotel La Ronda, tel. 660700. 21 rooms. $7/$12.

Located on the highway near the above hotel. Pool and air conditioning, modest rooms.

For cheaper, no-frills lodging, the Hotel Oriental, half a block in from the highway, near the Hotel Bramadero, has doubles for about $5, with shared bath.

All of the above have restaurants and bars. The Pokopí restaurant, opposite the Hotel El Sitio on the Nicoya road, is a small steak and seafood house, with such items as chicken in wine sauce, pepper sirloin tips, and the unexpected sea bass à la Goldberg (in white sauce with mushrooms), for $4 and up. Not bad. In addition, a few Chinese restaurants in the downtown area—Chung San, Canton and Pekín—serve inexpensive meals.

TRANSPORTATION

Buses for Liberia leave from 14 Calle, Avenidas 1/3, San José, every day at 7, 9 and 11:30 a.m., and 1, 4, 6 and 8 p.m. Most are modern units, and cover the route in about four hours. There are additional buses from Avenida 3, Calles 18/20. Buses for San José leave Liberia at 4:30, 6 and 7:30 a.m. and 2, 4 and 6 p.m.

Liberia is the transportation crossroads of northwestern Costa Rica. From the terminal next to the square, buses leave for Peñas Blancas and the border of Nicaragua approximately every two hours, starting at 9 a.m. These will drop you on the road to Santa Rosa National Park. A bus for El Coco beach leaves at 8 a.m.; for Playa Hermosa and Playa

Panamá at 11:30 a.m. and 5:30 p.m. Slow buses to Santa Cruz and Nicoya leave every one to two hours throughout the day. Current schedules are clearly posted. Buses from San José to these localities also pass through town.

The Liberia airport is located about 10 kilometers out, on the road to Nicoya. Currently, there is no scheduled service.

RINCON DE LA VIEJA NATIONAL PARK

The Rincón de la Vieja volcano, one of five in the Guanacaste range, lies northeast of Liberia, and rises to an altitude of 1895 meters (6216 feet). Slopes steaming with mud pots, hot springs and geysers; heavy rainfall and resultant lush vegetation; abundant mammalian wildlife (white-faced monkeys, collared peccaries, and especially coatimundis) and a variety of birds all create a rare combination of sights and experiences for the visitor to the volcano and the surrounding forest.

The ascent of Rincón de la Vieja is completed in two stages. First comes a walk of two to three hours from park headquarters to the Las Pailas area, where mud bubbles and shoots into the air. From there, the climb to the summit takes six to seven hours. Severe winds, suddenly dropping temperatures, fog, rain, and loose, rocky volcanic debris underfoot can make the going difficult and the rewards elusive. A morning ascent during the driest months (December to May) is recommended for the best views at the summit. But even if the peak is obscured, the clouds may blow away if you sit and wait.

You can drive to the park entrance, 27 kilometers from Liberia, or hike, which is somewhat of a ritual among Costa Rican outdoor enthusiasts. There are no regular buses, but the park service in San José might be able to help with transportation if it already has a vehicle going out. Contact the park service in any case before visiting.

Camping is permitted, and is recommended in order to get an early start toward the summit from the mudpot area.

SANTA ROSA NATIONAL PARK

Located 36 kilometers north of Liberia, Santa Rosa National Park was established in 1971 as a historical monument. The natural treasures of the park, which were originally included only incidentally, are now the main attraction for the foreign visitor.

The Santa Rosa hacienda was the scene of one of Costa Rica's most glorious military episodes—an episode that lasted the approximately fourteen minutes it took for a Costa Rican force to defeat the invading army of William Walker on March 20, 1856. Walker's army—and much of the opposing Costa Rican army as well—was finished off not long afterward in a cholera epidemic. The original great house of the Santa Rosa hacienda still stands as a monument to the Costa Rican victory. Santa Rosa's location near the Nicaraguan border made it the scene of later intrigues and battles as well, most notably during a 1955 invasion by political exiles.

Among the many natural features of the park are the only protected area of deciduous dry tropical forest from Mexico to Colombia; and Nancite beach, where hundreds of thousands of Pacific Ridley turtles nest from August until December every year.

VISITING SANTA ROSA

The junction for the access road to Santa Rosa is at kilometer 269 on the Interamerican Highway. If you're not driving, you'll have to hitch or, more likely, walk the seven kilometers from the highway to the hacienda building and administration center. Buses leave Liberia for La Cruz every two hours or so during the day, passing the junction. From San José, buses for La Cruz depart from the Coca-Cola terminal (Avenida 3, Calle 16), at 4:45 a.m., 7:45 a.m. and 4:15 p.m. Time to the junction is about five hours. Telephone 217202 to confirm schedules.

Partly because of its historical importance, the park is quite well run, and is one of the most visited in the national park system. Best time to visit Santa Rosa is in the dry season, when thirsty animals congregate around the permanent water holes and streams, making for easy viewing.

During the rainy season, when few visitors appear, markers along the nature trail may be down.

Facilities at or near the park center include a historical museum in the old great house of the hacienda, seven kilometers from the Interamerican Highway, and a nature trail nearby. The campsite, about a kilometer away, back toward the park entry, then down a side road, near the administration building, is basic, with showers and latrines, as well as many picnic tables. It's muddy in the rainy season (when I have spotted snakes), and there are no shelters. There's a small fee to camp, in addition to the admission fee to the park.

The *casona*, or great house of the Santa Rosa hacienda, is a large, whitewashed building with aged tile roof and wooden verandas. Part of the casona may date from the colonial period, though the age of the building is indeterminate. Houses of this sort were continually repaired, remodeled and expanded during their useful lives. The stone corrals around the house are almost certainly a few hundred years old, and were in use until the hacienda was nationalized. Great wooden mortars and pestles lie in the shade of overhangs of the old house. In the clearing in front of the casona is a huge guanacaste tree, which witnessed past battles.

Along the kilometer-long nature trail, signs point out features of plants, such as seasonal loss of leaves, which are adapted to the scarcity of water for much of the year; rock formations; and plants that survive the periodic fires of the dry lands. Typical dry-forest vegetation includes oaks, wild cherry, mahogany and the calabash, or gourd tree, the acacia bush, the ficus or *amate* tree, and the gumbo limbo, also called the naked Indian from the rich, reddish-brown color of its bark. Less exotic, "decorative" vegetation is also present, such as the hibiscus.

At the waterholes in the park, during the dry season, one can sit at a prudent and non-interfering distance and watch raccoons, coatis, spider monkeys, tapirs, agoutis, deer and assorted birds take their turns at the trough. Other wildlife that is more or less easily spotted in the dry season includes white-faced and howler monkeys, ocelots, jaguars, coyotes, armadillos, iguanas, collared and white-lipped peccaries, and rabbits. As well, more than 250 bird species have been recorded.

Much of the savanna of the central part of Santa Rosa was created through clearing of the native forest. The grass periodically burns off, either through accidental fires or controlled fires set by park personnel. Efforts are being made to regenerate the forest in these areas. Typically for Costa Rica, there are several habitats in the park beside seasonally dry forest. Moister areas contain abundant hardwoods that never lose their leaves. Gallery forest sweeps over the park's waterways. Near the coast are mangrove swamps, with dense populations of crabs, and high, sandy beach.

Nancite beach is one of two known nesting areas in Central America for the Pacific Ridley sea turtle. During the rainy season, the turtles crawl up onto the beach, first by the dozens, then the hundreds, then the thousands, to shove each other aside like so many commuters fighting for space, dig nests, and lay eggs before departing for the open sea. Green and leatherback turtles nest at the beach as well, but in smaller numbers than the Ridleys. With humans and other predators scooping up the eggs when park employees aren't looking, and vultures and frigate birds diving down for bits of hatchlings, less than one percent of the eggs make it to the sea as young turtles. Crabs and sharks lie in wait to further deplete their numbers.

Access to Nancite is controlled, in order to protect the turtle eggs. Inquire at park headquarters before heading for the beach, by trail or in a four-wheel-drive vehicle.

Naranjo, a larger beach than Nancite, is an excellent locale for bird watching. Cuajiniquil Canyon, at the northern edge of the park, contains a series of waterfalls, as well as numerous palms and ferns in its moist environment. Platanar Lake, covering a hectare, is four kilometers north of the great house and administrative area, and attracts varied waterfowl as well as mammals during the dry season.

North of the main section of Santa Rosa Park is the Murciélago addition, a rugged, seaside strip of scrub forest and rocky outcrops where jaguars and mountain lions roam. The park land was expropriated by the Costa Rican government from former Nicaraguan president Anastasio Somoza. Access is via the Pan American Highway to Cuajiniquil, the turnoff for which is 30 kilometers north of the junction for the main section of Santa Rosa Park. The Murciélago addition entrance is eight kilometers from Cuajiniquil. Buses operate at 5 a.m. and noon from La Cruz, 20 kilometers from the Nicaraguan border on the Pan American Highway, to Cuajiniquil. No facilities for visitors are available.

Peñas Blancas, 311 kilometers (194 miles) from San José on the Pan American Highway, is the small town located on the border with Nicaragua. If you plan to visit Nicaragua, it's advisable to first obtain a visa in San José. Latest currency regulations require visitors to exchange a set amount of dollars at the official rate when entering. Nicaraguan currency is available at a substantial discount at some banks in San José.

The border is open from 6:30 a.m. to 11 a.m., 12:30 p.m. to 5:30 p.m., and 6:30 p.m. to 10 p.m. Buses operate between Peñas Blancas and Liberia approximately every two hours. A bus operates to the border at 7:45 a.m. from Calle 16, Avenidas 3/5, San José, and there are other buses from San José to Managua (see page 72).

THE NICOYA PENINSULA

The Nicoya Peninsula is separated from the rest of Costa Rica by the Gulf of Nicoya, as well as by Indian heritage and colonial history as a part of Nicaragua. Sparsely populated, with poor roads, Nicoya enjoys a relatively dry climate, due to the barrier of hills and low mountains along the coast. Those same mountains create a series of sun-drenched beaches with rugged, dramatic backdrops (more on these later). Inland are some of the oldest towns in Costa Rica, as well as the mountain-trimmed plains where cowboys rope stray horses and calves (often right on the road you're trying to negotiate), and fields of sorghum, sugarcane and irrigated rice ripen in the sun. In parts of Nicoya, as in few other areas of Costa Rica, steep hillside plots of corn are laboriously cultivated with hand tools, using methods that have not changed in hundreds of years.

There are several routes into Nicoya: by ferry from Puntarenas to Playa Naranjo or Paquera; by the road that branches from the Pan American Highway at kilometer 168,

174

with a ferry crossing at the Tempisque River; and by the main highway south from Liberia to Belén, Santa Cruz and the town of Nicoya.

SANTA CRUZ

Population approximately 6000; 56 kilometers from Liberia

Santa Cruz is a sleepy, clean, pleasant, sunny and hot town, with a ruinous bell tower surviving from a colonial church. Several stores here sell pottery made in Nicoya's particular style, brown-colored and often with tripod bases, much of it made by Chorotega Indians in Guaitil, a craft center near Santa Bárbara, about ten kilometers to the east. The town comes alive for its annual fiesta, culminating on January 15.

For most visitors, Santa Cruz is a stopping point on the way to some of the Pacific beaches.

HOTELS

Hotel Diriá, tel. 680080 (P.O. Box 4211, San José). 28 rooms. $15 single/$18 double.

A roadside establishment on the edge of town, unprepossessing on the outside, but nicer inside, with functional, air-conditioned rooms arranged around a courtyard, garden and pools. The dance hall next door might not be an advantage on weekends.

Hotel Sharatoga, tel. 680011 (P. O. Box 33, San José, tel. 336664). 40 rooms. $15/$21.

A lesser hotel, located a few blocks in from the highway, half a block from the square. Air-conditioned rooms, mini-swimming pool, restaurant, and sparsely furnished rooms. This is a family-style hotel, in the Costa Rican sense. A marimba band plays on weekends.

FOOD

There are several Chinese restaurants, those saviors of the traveler's stomach in Costa Rica, and assorted places for snacks. Best-known for home cooking, though, is Coopetortilla, housed in a cavernous tin shed three blocks south of the

175

church on the square. Casados, gallo pinto, and tortillas cooked over wood fires are served for just a couple of dollars.

TRANSPORTATION

A bus leaves at 3:30 p.m. for Tamarindo. Buses for Paraíso, four kilometers from Junquillal beach, leave at 10:15 a.m. and 2:30 p.m. from the bus stop two blocks west of and one block north of the church. From San José, buses for Santa Cruz leave from Avenida 3, Calles 18/20, at 7:30 a.m. and 2, 4 and 5:30 p.m. Return buses are at 4:30, 6:30 and 8:30 a.m. and 1:30 p.m. Telephone Tralapa, 217202, to confirm the schedule. The Alfaro company (Calle 16, Avenidas 3/5, San José) has additional service. And there are hourly buses to and from Liberia.

NICOYA

Population approximately 10,000; 78 kilometers from Liberia

Nicoya, the major town of the peninsula, is a commercial and cattle center, its single point of interest being an attractive, whitewashed, tin-roofed colonial church, one of the oldest in Costa Rica.

ACCOMMODATIONS

Hotel Curimé, P. O. Box 51, tel. 685238. 20 rooms. $12 single/$24 double.

Half a kilometer south of the main square, just off the Sámara road, the Curimé is a large, palm-shaded and altogether pleasant compound of hacienda-style bungalows, each with twin beds. Pool and children's play areas, restaurant. It would be worth walking down this way, even if you arrive by bus.

In town, lodging places include the plain and adequate Hotel Las Tinajas (tel. 685081, $6 single/$9 double); and the Hotel Jenny, a block south of the square (tel. 685245, $12/$16 in air-conditioned concrete rooms). And there are several lesser places.

Several Chinese restaurants on the square serve square meals for $4 to $6.

Buses leave for Nicoya from Calle 16, Avenidas 3/5, San José, at 6:30, 8, and 10 a.m., noon, and 1:30, 2:30, 3 and 5 p.m. Buses for San José leave from the Nicoya bus station, south of the square, at 5, 6:30, 7:30 and 9:30 a.m., and noon and 2:30 p.m. The trip takes five hours. Buses depart from Nicoya for Playa Naranjo at 5 a.m. and 1 p.m., meeting the ferry for Puntarenas.; to Nosara beach at 1 p.m. (5 a.m. in the rainy season); and to Sámara and Carrillo beaches at 3 p.m., on Saturday and Sunday at 8 a.m.

BARRA HONDA NATIONAL PARK

About 14 kilometers northeast of Nicoya, off the road that leads to the Tempisque River and the Pan American Highway, is Barra Honda National Park, with its extensive limestone caverns, and peaks offering long-distance views out over the Gulf of Nicoya.

Barra Honda mountain, once thought to be a volcano, rises 300 meters above the surrounding plain, and is pocked by holes where the roofs of underlying caves have collapsed. The caves were formed—and are still being formed—by the rapid erosion and chemical decomposition of layers of limestone sediment that once lay on the bed of a prehistoric sea. A geological fault line runs roughly along the nearby Tempisque River, and the former seabed was steadily lifted as the Nicoya Peninsula slid alongside the mainland.

There are more than two dozen caves in Barra Honda, some of them still unexplored. Most are entered by vertical drops, and the difficulty of entrance may account for their excellent state of preservation. Various caves have stalactites, stalagmites, "soda straws," cave grapes, "popcorn," "fried eggs," and numerous other formations. Pozo Hediondo, once thought to be a crater, reeks with bat guano, though the bat population of the other caves is low. Other denizens of the dark are rats, insects, birds, and blind fish. Nicoa cave contains skeletal human remains, some grotesquely meshed with stalagmites or covered with layers of calcium carbonate. Visitors may enter the caves with the permission and supervision of park rangers.

Facilities at Barra Honda Park include trails, latrines, drinking water, and a campsite. The bluffs are high, and will require quite a lot of exertion to ascend. Park headquarters are in the town of Barra Honda, four kilometers west of the highway from Nicoya to the Tempisque River. It's another six kilometers to the center of the park.

Alfaro buses depart at 2:30 p.m. from Calle 16, Avenidas 3/5, San José for Hojancha, passing the turn for Barra Honda at dusk in the dry season. More feasibly, travel first to the town of Nicoya, then take a morning bus heading by the turnoff for the park, 15 kilometers from Nicoya.

Vehicles cross the Tempisque River on the direct road from Nicoya to San José on a ferry, a barge-and-tug arrangement. Service is continuous, from 6 a.m. to 6 p.m., and the crossing takes only ten minutes, but space is limited to about ten vehicles, and the ferry might make several trips until you get aboard. Fare is about $3 for a car. Snack stands will feed you while you wait.

East from the town of Nicoya, the main highway runs for 75 kilometers (the last 40 unpaved) to the ferry slip at Playa Naranjo (see page 194), through sugarcane and rice fields, and pastures broken by clumps of trees, and bordered by windbreaks. The plain is edged by mountains and random, lumpy hills, but at a few high spots along the way, tantalizing glimpses of the Gulf of Nicoya are available. The distance is covered in four hours by slow (and dusty) bus, in half that time by car.

BEACHES, BEACHES, BEACHES

First, the good news. Along the coast of the Nicoya Peninsula are dozens of beaches, each set in its own sweep of bay, bordered by rocky promontories and hills and coconut palms and lush tropical foliage, drenched in sun, with views to glittering blue sea broken here and there by huge rocks and by islets. Some of the beaches are virtually deserted, others have luxury hotels where most of one's needs are anticipated and attended. Commercial exploitation is limited. There are no coral jewelry salesmen to hound sunbathers, nor noisy discos, nor beachwear shops, and rarely are there crowds.

Now, the bad news (or hard facts). The nicest beaches in Nicoya are difficult to reach. Most of the roads to the coast are dusty and rutted, or muddy and occasionally impassable, depending on the time of year. Buses reach most of the coastal villages only once a day, after crunching, thumping, seemingly interminable (but only 30-kilometer-long) rides and numerous river fordings from Santa Cruz or Nicoya, and deliver passengers with a new coat of fine, reddish-brown grit. A few beaches are served by bus with less than daily frequency, and some not at all. Getting from one beach to another is often difficult, if not impossible. The motto of public transportation in Nicoya might as well be "you can't get there from here."

The alternative to bus travel is to rent a car (an expensive proposition in Costa Rica), and brave the roads on your own. If you can find your way, that is. Some roads shown on maps of Nicoya exist only in the minds of hopeful cartographers.

Beyond the problems of getting to them, Costa Rica's Pacific beaches have far fewer facilities than one might expect from the publicity about them. There are only a few hundred first-class rooms in the hundreds of kilometers of coastline from the Nicaraguan border to Panama. Most of the remaining accommodations are *cabinas*, budget-priced rooms with cold water only. There is hardly anything in the middle range.

Restaurants at the beaches are few and offer little variety, while food at the hotels—with notable exceptions—is not what one expects at a resort. There is little opportunity for shopping and browsing, nor, in most cases, are there car-rental agencies, dive shops, or many of the amenities one associates with a beach resort. Food stocks in stores—where there are stores—are limited to a few basics.

But the bad news may also be good news. So many of the Nicoya beaches are nearly deserted and unspoiled precisely because they are hard to reach. If your intention really is to swim and take the sun and read and enjoy some special company without any distractions, then there are few better places to go than the less accessible beaches of Nicoya. As overnight destinations during a week of hopping around Costa Rica, forget them. But for a few days at a time at least, most are fairly wonderful.

To make your beach excursion easier, consider renting a car, even if you normally use public transportation. Fill up on gas at every opportunity—filling stations are sparse. Or else hire a taxi to take you, say, from the town of Nicoya or Santa Cruz to one of the beaches. This will cost $25 or so—not excessive for two people or more—and save much time as well as personal wear and tear. Some beach hotels and travel agencies will also make transportation arrangements.

Consider carefully where you will stay. If you're going at a leisurely pace, you can always book into one of the cabinas and switch the next morning. But if you've invested a certain amount of money in a short vacation, many of the available accommodations just won't fill the bill, especially when the rain is pouring down and the streets have turned to mud.

Call ahead, when you can, to reserve a room, and to allow your hosts to lay in supplies—a difficult task at beaches. Reservations are essential on weekends. You could well arrive after a difficult trip, only to find that all the cabinas have been taken by hordes of local *excursionistas* travelling on chartered buses. Reconfirm bus departure times at the tourist office in San José. If you're backpacking and camping out—tempting on deserted stretches of coast—take supplies from San José or some other large town. If there are children in your group, take a variety of snacks (a good idea for adults, too). And take a supply of cash—you won't find any banks to exchange travelers checks. Try to avoid arriving after dark. In general, don't count on finding anything out there that you haven't been told is there.

Here's a rundown of some of the beach resorts on the Nicoya coast, from north to south.

PLAYAS DEL COCO

The beach here is in a dramatic setting on a large horseshoe bay with great rocks offshore, sailboats gliding around, and dozens of fishing boats tied up or on their way in to or out from shore. But this is one of the Pacific points most easily reached from San José, and it shows. The little town and the central part of the beach are dirty, though there's less litter the farther you walk from the center.

ACCOMMODATIONS

Hotel Flor de Itabo, tel. 670003, P. O. Box 32. 23 rooms, 5 suites. $46 single/$52 double, slightly less in low season.

This attractive hotel, well managed by European owners, is not on the beach—in this case an advantage. The large, beamed, tile-floored restaurant (reasonably priced) looks out through archways to the huge adults' pool and children's pool, lawns shaded by coconut palms, and jungly gardens beyond. Rooms are comfortable, with carved hardwood bedsteads, air conditioning, and satellite television. Suites have cooking facilities. Boats are available for deep-sea fishing and, unusually for Pacific coastal hotels, river fishing as well. And horseback riding and trips to Rincón de la Vieja are offered. It's all quite nice if your stay will be centered on your hotel. But consider: if you have to go a kilometer from the beach to find pleasant surroundings, is this where you want to be?

At the beach, accommodations are of the popular sort, without hot water, and with neighbors close on. The Hotel Casino Playas del Coco offers the best of the available cabina-type rooms with sea view and private bath for $9 single, $15 double. If you're stuck in back, the rate is slightly lower. The price drops from July through November. There are similar places to stay, such as Cabinas El Coco next door, and Cabinas Luna Tica, to the left as you face the beach; and lesser ones, with prices down to $5 per person, or $3 in the rainy season, none of which I can particularly recommend. Private houses toward the ends of the beach are rented out from time to time.

Assorted stands sell fried fish, and there are several bars. For a good meal, try the Hotel Flor de Itabo.

Various hotels and shops rent fishing gear and boats.

TRANSPORTATION

A bus leaves Liberia for Coco at 8 a.m., and returns from Coco to Liberia at 3 p.m. Service is more frequent in the dry season. One bus a day leaves from Calle 12, Avenida 9, San José, at 10 a.m. for El Coco, and there's a departure for San

José at 9:15 a.m. The trip takes just under five hours. To drive to Playa Hermosa or Playa del Coco, take the main Nicoya highway from Liberia and turn off at the Tamarindo restaurant, 20 kilometers from Liberia. El Coco is 15 kilometers onward.

North of Playas del Coco

PLAYA HERMOSA

Hermosa is a more serene place than El Coco, with a few houses scattered along the low ridge that backs the water.

ACCOMMODATIONS

Cabinas Playa Hermosa, tel. 670136. 20 units. $14 single/$24 double.

This is a compound pleasantly landscaped with cactus, giant aloe and hibiscus, at the end of a winding 500-meter spur road. All rooms, in whitewashed brick buildings that bear a patina of age, have fans and private bath. The beach in front is the most attractive in the area. The restaurant serves up a decent meal, with main courses, such as a native-style combination plate, from $3. Quiet, compared to the honky-tonk style of hotels at El Coco, with no shops, outside restaurants or diversions other than those at the hotel, not that you need them. The owner is a transplanted Oregonian.

There are also some cheaper and far less attractive cabinas nearby.

Condovac La Costa, tel.670267 (P.O. Box 55-1001, San José). 100 units, $70 single/$80 double. U.S. reservations 305-588-8541.

Three kilometers on from Cabinas Playa Hermosa, a vacation village of cottages arranged in camp-style rows on a hillside. Amenities and activities include water-skiing, fishing facilities, sailing, a nice sandy beach, pool, air conditioning, tennis, and cooking facilities. These are time-sharing units, and they're sometimes advertised in San José newspapers at discounted rates. Unfortunately, you can't look around and decide whether you want to stay, except at a price. There's a hefty charge just to go through the gate.

TRANSPORTATION

A bus for Playa Hermosa and Playa Panamá leaves from Calle 12, Avenidas 5/7, San José, at 3:30 p.m. Departure from Playa Panamá is at 6:30 a.m. There are also daily buses from Liberia, about 35 kilometers away, at 11:30 a.m. and 5 p.m. Return buses pass at about 6 a.m. and 4 p.m. Or take a bus to El Coco, then a taxi for seven kilometers to Playa Hermosa. If driving, turn off the road to El Coco at the Condovac sign, about ten kilometers from the Tamarindo restaurant. The branch road to Playa Hermosa, and five kilometers onward to Playa Panamá, is unpaved.

PLAYA PANAMA

Two kilometers past Condovac, Playa Panamá is a sweep of beach that looks out on the great sheltered Gulf of Papagallo, almost surrounded by green carpeted hills. Deserted but for a few shacks, it must be something like the Acapulco of 70 years ago. And another Acapulco is what it might one day become, for there are ambitious and controversial plans to establish a vacation city here. For now, most residents have been moved out, and you can arrive under your own steam, with supplies, and swim and picnic in magnificent solitude . . . for how long, I don't know.

South of El Coco

PLAYA OCOTAL

Three kilometers south of El Coco, Ocotal is reached by a rutted, boulder-strewn road. But there are rewards, if you're interested in a secluded hotel, deep-sea fishing, or diving.

Hotel El Ocotal, tel. 670230 (P.O. Box 1013, 1002 San José, tel. 224259). 8 cottages. $70 single/$85 double.

The cottages here are in a bare but dramatic clifftop setting overlooking the beach. Facilities include tennis courts, pool, riding horses, and equipment for fishing and water skiing. Deep-sea fishing programs, using 20- and 30-foot boats, are available at $200 to $250 per person per day.

Bahía Pez Vela, tel. 670129, P. O. Box 7758 San José; or c/o World Wide Sportsman, P. O. Drawer 787, Islamorada, FL

33036, tel. 800-327-2880 or 305-664-4615. Fishing packages from about $275 per day.

First of the west-coast fishing resorts in Costa Rica, renovated as of a few years ago.

Diving Safaris, based at Ocotal, runs scuba trips for about $50 per day, including tanks, weights, guide and boat. Make arrangements at the Hotel Ocotal; or write to P.O. Box 425, Zapote, San José (tel. 240033) or 7210 Jordan Ave., Suite C-37, Canoga Park, CA 91303, tel. 818-713-1508.

At Belén, 40 kilometers from Liberia on the main Nicoya highway, a branch road heads for the sea at Brasilito, 32 kilometers away, and onward to the beaches of Flamingo and Potrero, to the north. The first 25 kilometers of the road, to Huacas, are paved, and the rest are in fairly good shape as far as Brasilito. Follow the Playa Flamingo signs if you're driving.

BRASILITO

The road reaches the water at Brasilito, where a wide, sandy beach lines a typical horseshoe bay. There are some basic, cheap cabinas here for overnight stays, at about $5 per person, and a couple of fish restaurants. Six kilometers to the south is Conchal, a beach where there are currently no facilities for visitors.

Hotel Hacienda Las Palmas, tel. 680573, P. O. Box 10-5150 Santa Cruz.

A kilometer past Brasilito, and another kilometer along a side road, this hotel is atop a hillock in a large estate. The buildings are plantation-style, with tile roofs, and the public areas have soaring ceilings. Las Palmas is billed as a fishing lodge, though the boats are parked a couple of kilometers away at the Flamingo marina. But never mind. The pool is large, and the sea views from the terraces are excellent. The restaurant is fairly pricey, but so are most things in this area.

PLAYA FLAMINGO

Four kilometers onward from the turn for Las Palmas is Flamingo Beach, a stunning horseshoe of white sand in the web of a hand-shaped promontory, bordered by cliffs and a prominent hill.

What really distinguishes Flamingo is what man has added to nature: a full-service marina which, though small, is the most complete in the region.

For all the money that has been poured into the attractive facilities at Flamingo, there's no town, and little shade. If you're not into fishing, sunbathing and real-estate pitches, and don't have a car to circulate to other locales, Flamingo can get old rather quickly.

Hotel Playa Flamingo, tel. 680444 (P. O. Box 692-4050 Alajuela, tel. 391584). 90 rooms and 32 suites. $70/$80. Suites from $125 double, $170 for four. U.S. reservations: tel. 800-327-9408.

This hotel is all first-class. Rooms are large and comfortable, air-conditioned, with television, and most have terraces looking right out over the sand and water. Between the main section of the hotel and the hilltop suites (which are somewhat drably furnished, but have complete kitchens and two bedrooms), there are three pools, including one for children. The restaurant is attractive, with no surprises on the menu (assorted spaghetti, brochettes, stroganoff, about $9 for a main course, $17 for shrimp, a few kids' choices). Car rentals, casino. Private bus service is provided three times weekly from San José for $25.

FACILITIES

Just down the road from the Hotel Playa Flamingo is Marie's Restaurant, an attractive, informal, open-air bistro. Complete breakfasts are served for $2.50 to $4, as well as lasagne, cordon bleu and seafood items for $5 and up, tacos and sandwiches for less.

A few basic food items are available at the Marina Trading Post, as well as information about privately owned beach and hillside houses, which sleep from six to ten persons and rent for $80 to $250 per night. Catamaran rentals can be arranged there as well.

An airstrip is planned for Flamingo, but for now, the hotel picks up passengers at Tamarindo.

PLAYA POTRERO

Around the sweep of bay from Flamingo is:

Bahía Flamingo, P.O. Box 45-5051 Santa Cruz, tel. 680976. $50 to $60 double.

These are recently remodelled housekeeping cottages, with two double beds and kitchenettes, right on the beach in an attractive, tree-shaded compound with a small pool. Helpful American owner. A Hobie Cat is available for rent, and deep-sea fishing charters can be arranged. If you plan to use the cooking facilities, bring your groceries from San José, or stop in Brasilito.

Cabinas Cristina, 200 meters back from the beach in a pasture, has three basic housekeeping units with cooktop and refrigerator for $21 double. Telephone 680997.

There's also a simple eatery in the area of these lodging places, but no other facilities. The village of Playa Potrero— a soccer field, general store and several houses—is three kilometers onward.

Sunset House Inn is a hillside bed-and-breakfast house overlooking and set back from the sea, 2.5 kilometers past the Bahía Flamingo, and up from the road. Best if you have a car to get to beach and villages. Phone 680933 to make sure someone's in, and to get the rates.

A poor dirt road, passable with a four-wheel-drive vehicle in the rainy season, winds up into the hills beyond the village of Playa Potrero and down to solitary Playa Pan de Azúcar (Sugar Beach).

Hotel Sugar Beach, tel. 680959 (P. O. Box 66-5150 Santa Cruz). 10 rooms. $25 to $30 double. U.S. contact: tel. 213-935-3918.

This hotel's brochure calls its beach the most beautiful in Costa Rica. With a gentle hillside and gray sand, trees growing down almost to the water, and streams meandering through, I can't take issue with the claim. Four rooms are in an elevated round house, the others in ranch units with front porches facing the bay and offshore islands. All are air-conditioned. Food is served under a great rotunda, and is reasonably priced, even shrimp Breakfast $2 to $3, main courses at lunch and dinner from $3. A pet iguana scurries around the grounds, and monkeys and macaws share the hillside with guests. Horses are available, and a dive shop is planned. There's nobody out here but you and the people at the hotel. With advance notice, you can arrange a pickup at Tamarindo airstrip, or at Perla's Cantina in Playa Potrero, where the bus from Santa Cruz ends its run.

TRANSPORTATION

Buses for Brasilito, Flamingo and Potrero leave daily from Santa Cruz at 4:20 and 10:30 a.m., and 2:30 p.m. Return buses from Potrero depart at 5:30 and 6 a.m. and 5 p.m. The run to Potrero takes about two hours. Verify this schedule at the tourist office before leaving San José. In the dry season, direct service may be available from San José. Inquire at Tralapa, Calle 14, Avenidas 1/3, San José. By air, fly to Tamarindo, then take a taxi, if you haven't arranged to be picked up by your hotel.

FISHING

Deep-sea fishing is available from Flamingo Bay Pacific Charters (tel. 314055 in San José; or 121 Nurmi Drive, Fort Lauderdale, FL 33301, tel. 800-654-8006 or 305-987-5860); and Tom Bradwell (tel. 680942, P.O.Box 109, Santa Cruz); or through Hotel Hacienda Las Palmas (tel. 680932, or 305-462-7029 in Florida). Boat rates are anywhere from $250 to $1000 per day.

PLAYA TAMARINDO

Tamarindo is a wide, mostly empty beach curving around a miles-long bay, with rocks and little sandy islands offshore. Pelicans float overhead and dive into the waters, skiffs bob up and down in the gentle surf. The setting is nearly perfect. And yet, many who know the Nicoya beaches say that Tamarindo is spoiled. Which is a measure of what some of the other beaches are like.

There is something of a village at Tamarindo, with a few houses spread out along the last stretch of road, and a couple of hotels. More development is on the way—the subdividers have arrived, and billboards advertise house lots for sale. For now, though, things are fairly peaceful. The tamarinds that give the beach its name are the trees with the dangling seed pods, and fingery, brush-like leaves.

ACCOMMODATIONS

Hotel Tamarindo Diriá, tel. 680474 (P. O. Box 4211, tel. 330530 in San José). 60 rooms, $62 single/$68 double ($51/$57 May-June and August-November).

A pleasant motel with rooms nicely furnished in Spanish-colonial style, grounds landscaped with lush tropical trees, and a pool. Moderately priced restaurant—$5 for filet mignon, and a few unusual plates such as paella, and lemon chicken. Air conditioned, televisions with satellite programming in all rooms. Water skiing and fishing are available.

Cabinas Zullymar, tel. 264732. 19 rooms. $11 single/$15 double.

At the end of the road, cold-water rooms with private bath, around a shady courtyard. Curiosities in an otherwise simple place are the hardwood doors carved with pre-Columbian motifs. The owner is a character. Across the road from the Zullymar is its Bar El Tercer Mundo (Third-World Bar), worth a visit for the name alone. Good, plain food is served, mostly beef and fish, at $4 to $5 for a main course.

Cabinas Pozo Azul, tel. 680147. 17 units. $22 per cabina, $15 in the low season (June, and August through November).

Despite the "cabina" tag, these are housekeeping units, with refrigerator and stove, on a hillock at the entry to town. They're relatively new, and air-conditioned, and there's a large pool. Standard units have two beds, larger ones have three beds and a separate kitchen, and go for $30 in the high season. A good buy.

There are several lesser accommodations, such as the Hotel Doly, which has cubby-hole rooms for about $6 per person—but it's on the water.

Johan's Belgian Bakery is a surprise eating spot, with fresh croissants, rye bread, sandwiches, cookies and gourmet pizza to eat in or take out. You can have a light meal, accompanied with fresh juice, in the shady compound in back, overlooking a tidal inlet, for just a couple of dollars. Hours are 6 a.m. to 5:30 p.m.

TRANSPORTATION

If you're driving from San José, the preferred route to Tamarindo is via the road that forks from the main Nicoya highway at Belén. Continue through Huacas (instead of turning for Flamingo) to the junction for the dirt road to Tamarindo. Total distance is 38 kilometers from Belén. Tamarindo can also be reached by road from Santa Cruz, paved for 18 kilometers to the village of 27 de Abril, then typically potholed for another 15 kilometers.

A direct bus for Tamarindo leaves from Calle 16, Avenidas 3/5, San José, daily at 3:30 p.m. The trip takes about five hours. The return bus leaves at 5:45 a.m., on Sundays and holidays at 1:45 p.m. From Santa Cruz, a bus for Tamarindo leaves the main square at 3:30 p.m. The Hotel Tamarindo Diriá has a direct air-conditioned bus three times a week for $40 round trip (versus $6 for the public bus). There is air service from San José as well, on Sansa airlines, on Monday, Wednesday and Friday at noon. Fare is about $15. Sansa has a two-night package trip to Tamarindo for about $80

Fishing at Tamarindo, and windsurfing and water skiing and swamp trips, are available from Papagayo Excursions, tel. 680859. Prices start at $200 per day. Their trips can be booked at the Hotel Tamarindo Diriá gift shop.

PLAYA JUNQUILLAL

Hardly anybody lives here. The beach is empty, clean and beautiful, on a two-kilometer-wide bay trimmed by rocky outcrops at either end, bordered by a wide strip of tall grass. Like a number of other Nicoya beaches, Junquillal is a favorite nesting site for sea turtles during the rainy season.

Villa Serena, tel. 680737, P. O. Box 17-5150, Santa Cruz. 7 rooms. $100 per couple with meals, slightly less in the rainy season. If rooms are available, singles are accommodated for $60.

Not right on the beach, but an intimate estate a few steps away, with large, comfortable rooms. Everything is in good taste. Facilities include a video cassette player and library, riding horses, sauna and game room. All rooms have terraces facing the ocean. Children not allowed. Say the owners (one of whom is always on-site): "Ours is a small hotel where a stay is more like a visit to a friend's house than to an indifferent hotel. People who don't enjoy Villa Serena don't enjoy anything and should not travel, period."

Hotel Antumalal, tel. 680506, P. O. Box 49-5150 Santa Cruz. 20 cottages. $80 single/$100 double with meals.

A tasteful cluster of colonial-style buildings on a hill overlooking the sea. Pool with bar, tennis court, lovely thatched dining pavilion. Friendly management. The food is good. Located about 500 meters beyond Villa Serena.

Buses leave Santa Cruz at 10:15 a.m. and 2:30 p.m. for Paraíso, four kilometers from Junquillal. You'll probably take a taxi to Junquillal from Santa Cruz, or from the Tamarindo airport. The road from Santa Cruz, 34 kilometers away, is paved for 18 kilometers to the village of 27 de Abril.

Beaches South of Nicoya
An unpaved road runs up and down from Nicoya, through pastures and occasional corn fields closed off by wire strung to living *poro* fenceposts, south to the Pacific at Sámara. The route is scenic, but barely passable toward the end of the rainy season, when trucks carrying the rice harvest from the interior of the peninsula churn up the road.

SAMARA AND CARRILLO

Sámara has a long, gray beach, wide at low tide, littered with driftwood, bordered by promontories. Islands and rocks break the waves along the long entrance to the bay, making this beach relatively safe for swimming.

There are numerous vacation homes in the area, but Sámara is also something of a fishing and farming village. On a morning stroll, you might see a pig being carved up, agricultural laborers on their way to their duties, boats being prepared for the day's passage.

Aside from the hotel situation, which is not good, Sámara has more facilities than other villages on the Nicoya coast. There's even a well-stocked (especially with liquor) convenience store. More Development, with a big D, is in progress. The road to Cangreja, the adjacent settlement across the river, has been cut by the construction of an airstrip, forcing a long detour, and bulldozers are pulverizing a large swatch of village for a new resort. Things might have settled down by the time you arrive.

ACCOMMODATIONS

Hotel Brisas del Pacífico, tel. 680876 (P. O. Box 709-3000 Heredia). 12 rooms. $36 single/$45 double.

About one kilometer south of the village, on a hillside overlooking the sea. Pool, and nicely landscaped grounds. Altogether attractive. But the folks here tried to charge me for a double when I arrived alone, and they might do the same to you.

In town, there are assorted basic cabinas, most of them dismal and lacking more than one sheet on the bed. Los Almendros, at the center, might be okay but for the late night disco. You get a private bath here for $8, $5 in the mud season. At other lodging places in Sámara, and nearby at Cangreja (adjacent by walking through the river, or a ride around the airstrip), there's sometimes a long walk to the john. Rates are slightly lower than at Los Almendros.

In Carrillo, an attractive beach southeast of Sámara, there are also basic cabinas, and the substantial Cabinas Guanamar (tel. 536133), $75 for large units that sleep six.

TRANSPORTATION

Access to Sámara is by a dirt road from Nicoya, about 36 kilometers away. A bus leaves for Sámara at noon from Calle 16, Avenidas 3/5, San José, and departs Sámara at 4 a.m. Buses leave Nicoya for Sámara and Carrillo at 3 p.m., on Saturday and Sunday at 8 a.m. Return is at 6 a.m., at about 1 p.m. on weekends. Sansa airlines operates flights from San José three times a week, currently on Monday, Wednesday and Friday in the early afternoon. Fare is about $15. Sansa's package trips to Sámara, including three nights in a hotel and all meals, cost about $90.

PLAYA NOSARA

Nosara is the favorite of many retired foreigners who have settled down to life by the sea. It's not that the beach is superior to those elsewhere on the peninsula (although it's nice), only that hustlers of building lots staked out land here first and did a better job of selling in San José. Land sales to foreigners constitute one of the more visible economic activities in parts of Nicoya, and the visitor to Costa Rica is sure to come across some compatriot who is harvesting basketsful of cash at least in his dreams in the land business. (There are also the coconut business, the mango business, the shrimp business, the jojoba business, the macadamia business and others in which your buddies from home will deal you in on "secure" future profits for a substantial investment now, but those are other stories.) Various hotels in Nicoya exist at least partly to encourage the romance between visitor and house lot (or condominium, or time-sharing unit). There is no reason to get a creepy feeling about real estate activities in Nosara or elsewhere—the climate, the views and much else are attractive. But one should bear in mind that promised amenities, such as electricity, running water, transportation and shopping, might not materialize during your lifetime.

Ostional National Wildlife Refuge, near Nosara, is noted for a long beach where sea turtles nest. There's also an extensive marsh where the Nosara River meets the sea, good for birding.

Hotel Playa Nosara, P. O. Box 4-5233, tel. 680495. 16 rooms. $21-30 single/$27-$36 double.

Bar, restaurant.

TRANSPORTATION

The road to Nosara, 55 kilometers from Nicoya, forks from the Sámara road about five kilometers before Sámara. In the dry season, it's a pleasant jungly drive along a route canopied by tall trees decked with drooping vines and air plants. In the rainy season, it's not always passable. Buses run once a day from Nicoya at 1 p.m., and from Nosara for Nicoya at 6 a.m. In the rainy season, departure from Nicoya is at 5 a.m., from Nosara at noon. The ride takes two hours in the dry season, up to four hours or even longer in the rainy season.

At the very end of the Nicoya Peninsula are the Cabo Blanco reserve, and the beaches of Montezuma and Tambor, all reached most easily by ferry from Puntarenas, and bus.

CABO BLANCO ABSOLUTE NATURE RESERVE

Located at the southeastern point of the Nicoya Peninsula, the Cabo Blanco reserve is not as absolute as its name implies. Visitors are allowed in to watch the birds (especially pelicans, frigate birds and various others that frequent the shore), as well as howler monkeys, porcupines, abundant crabs, and the creatures that become trapped in tidal pools. The woods here in the rainiest part of Nicoya are classified as moist tropical forest, and have many more evergreens than those in the northern part of the peninsula. The shoreline is rocky, and beaches are therefore few and small. Off the very tip of the peninsula is Cabo Blanco island, a rock that is white with encrusted guano during the dry season.

Access to the reserve is only by car or on foot. Get in touch with the National Park Service before going.

MONTEZUMA

Isolation and tranquility are features at this end-of-the-road beach, reached by car from Playa Naranjo, or bus from the Paquera ferry landing to Cóbano, then a taxi for four kilometers to Montezuma. The little Hotel Montezuma (tel. 611122) is a pleasant stopping-point, with modest facilities and modest tariffs (about $12 double with fan, private bath). There are various cabinas with rooms for $5 to $15 double. El Cocozuma Retreat has private ocean-front bungalows at $23 single, $34 double. Phone the town bar, at 612472, to be assured of a place. In the U.S., contact Joe Zimmerman, 7380 W. 15 Ct., Hialeah, FL 33014, tel. 305-822-0173. Within a half hour's walk of Montezuma is a 30-meter-high waterfall.

TAMBOR

Tambor is another favorite place of retired foreigners, given its relative proximity to San José. Access is by car from Playa Naranjo, or bus from Paquera (where the passenger boat from Puntarenas lands), or small plane. The attractive Hotel La Hacienda (tel. 612980, P.O. Box 398-2050 San Pedro) has 20 small rooms going for $25 single/$40 double. There's a pool and tennis court. The Hotel Dos Lagartos (tel. 611122, ext. 236) has rooms at $10 single/$15 double.

PLAYA NARANJO

There's no beach here, despite the name of the town ("Orange Tree Beach"). In fact, there's hardly a town at all, only a ferry slip. There are, however, very attractive accommodations at the Hotel Oasis del Pacífico, 500 meters down the road from the dock.

TRANSPORTATION

The ferry leaves Playa Naranjo for Puntarenas at 9 a.m. and 6 p.m., and at 1 p.m. on Thursday, Saturday and Sunday. Sailings from Puntarenas are at 7 a.m. and 4 p.m. (and 11 a.m. on Thursdays and weekends). Phone 611069 to check schedules. The crossing takes a little over an hour. Buses for Nicoya, 75 kilometers, four hours and various river fordings away, meet the ferry.

ACCOMMODATIONS

Hotel Oasis del Pacífico, tel. 611555. 36 rooms. $34 single/$47 double. U.S. Reservations: tel. 800-344-6342 or 818-843-1226. P. O. Box 200, Puntarenas.

This is a beautiful complex of air-conditioned cottages on lush, landscaped grounds, one of the nicest hotels in the Nicoya peninsula, as well as one of the most accessible. Extensive facilities include tennis courts, adult and children's pool, a wide stretch of private beach (unfortunately, it's pebbly), riding horses, and a large restaurant-bar with good, low-priced food—lately with some Cajun items. Views over the peaceful Gulf of Nicoya are magnificent, and management is quite friendly. Yachts are welcome, and non-guests may use all facilities for a daily charge of about $2. Rates drop by about a third in the rainy season.

Hotel de Paso, tel. 612610 (P. O. Box 232-2120 San José). 13 rooms. $9-$13/$12-$18.

More modest than the Oasis. Rooms have private baths.

Other beaches are plentiful all around the rim of Nicoya, some with basic lodging, some accessible only by seasonally passable dirt roads, some uninhabited but for wild creatures. Go and find them!

THE SOUTH COAST

The southern Pacific beaches of Costa Rica are every bit as inviting and pleasing to the eye as those along the Nicoya Peninsula, though they differ in character. Most are more open and sweeping and exposed, with fewer bordering outcrops of rocks. The farther south you go, the more humid and rainy is the climate, and the more lush and exuberant the vegetation that runs up to the sand. The mugginess is always relieved and attenuated, however, by breezes blowing off the water.

There is one fact about the southern beaches that is often not mentioned in polite company: they are dangerous for swimming. Large volumes of water flow toward shore across a deceptively smooth, broad front of waves, then recede in fast-flowing, unpredictable streams. These rip currents drive bathers out to sea from waist-high waters, and cause drownings on a regular basis. Those who suddenly find themselves far from shore should swim across the current to escape its pull, then head on in. If you are not a good swimmer. stay close to shore.

Beach hotels are concentrated at Jacó and at Manuel Antonio (near Quepos), but there are numerous little-frequented beaches as well where cabinas and similar basic accommodations are available. You can poke around and explore for some of these paradisiacal hideaways if you decide to rent a car in San José. By bus, such meanderings would be more difficult. There is only infrequent service along the road south of Jacó, the humidity is uncomfortably high just inland from the coast, the lesser beaches would have to be reached by jaunts of a kilometer or two along side roads, and you'll find it difficult to move on if you don't like what you see (or the facilities that you don't see) at the water's edge.

To reach the south coast by car from San José, follow the turnoff to Atenas from the highway to Puntarenas. After a potholed, winding stretch, the road is generally good past Orotina. The asphalt ends just before Quepos. Beyond Quepos, the road is poor, with limited bus service.

South from Puntarenas

The new road from Puntarenas south toward Orotina is a well-surfaced, controlled-access, two-lane-wide, California-standard coastal highway.

Mata de Limón, one of the first towns out of Puntarenas, is a picturesque gathering of vacation houses around a mangrove inlet. There are some eating places, and it's pleasant to observe the birds, and stroll across the footbridge. The train from San José stops here. You could get off, look around, and continue by local bus to Puntarenas.

Caldera, a few kilometers on, is a modern container port, through which much of Costa Rica's Pacific commerce now moves. Beyond it, the highway continues through the coastal foothills roughly following the railroad line. Near Orotina, it joins the road from San José via Atenas.

CARARA BIOLOGICAL RESERVE

Carara is a tropical forest area in the central Pacific coastal region. All around are fields devoted to pasture and rice cultivation. But most of Carara Biological Reserve was virgin forest when its 2100 hectares (4700 acres) were separated by the government from an agrarian settlement project in 1978.

The climate along the coast just south of Puntarenas is relatively dry and hot; farther on, rainfall is heavier. Carara is in a transitional area, and with its varied elevations (the entry is at 700 meters, but most of Carara is higher), contains a variety of vegetation types, from cool evergreens to

196

the broad-leafed, vine- and epiphyte-laden trees that are the kings of everyone's imagined jungle. There are rushing streams and sedentary lagoons, and even some archeological remains from pre-Columbian times. The undergrowth is relatively less dense and tangled than in other forests, so getting around and seeing the vegetation and wildlife is slightly easier. Resident birds at Carara include macaws, vultures, ducks, guans and toucans. Jaguars, ocelots and margays are occasionally spotted. More common are monkeys (squirrel, white-faced, howler and spider), sloths, coatis, agoutis and crocodiles, blue morpho butterflies, and assorted ants.

VISITING CARARA

The administration center for Carara is just off the highway, past the bridge over the Tárcoles River on the way down from San José. There's a small admission charge. An unposted nature trail—a muddy path—is all the access that most casual visitors will have. Rubber boots would be the gear in the rainy season. Grades are mild. The reserve is a wonderland of tall trees, vines and shiny-leafed plants, shared with troops of leaf-cutter ants. But the sense of isolation is diminished somewhat by the nearby roar of traffic.

For a more intensive acquaintance with Carara Reserve, you'll have to come on a guided tour arranged through one of the agencies mentioned in the San José chapter. Buses for Jacó and Quepos pass the entrance, and on a weekday, when these are not crowded, you can get off for a visit, then hop on another bus to continue your journey.

Tárcoles, past Carara, is a sleepy village one kilometer off the highway, where it begins to run close to the sea. There's a rocky beach, exuberant vegetation, and some attractive tidal inlets; but mostly, Tárcoles is undeveloped for tourism. About 600 yards past the village center is the basic Hotel El Parque, where rooms are available for $8 or so for anywhere from one to four persons.

Herradura, farther down the coast and four kilometers off the road, features an attractive private campsite with showers and cooksites. The charge is about $2 per person. There are also some inexpensive cabinas. Otherwise, development is limited here, too. A cattle corral occupies the

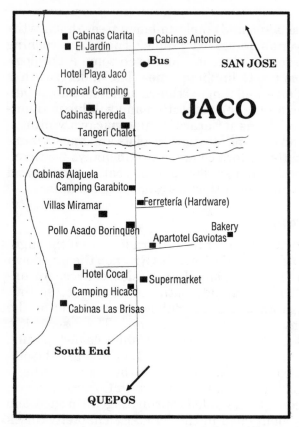

prime piece of real estate, and the wide curve of driftwood-littered beach is lined by palms, a few vacation houses, and pastures. Best to drop by if travelling by car, or if you have plenty of time.

PLAYA JACO

Jacó has what other beach places in Costa Rica are missing: streets, and life. It is a pleasant community, where you can stroll and look in stores, shop for groceries, choose from a selection of restaurants and snack bars, and buy a souvenir at some place other than the captive boutique of your hotel. Vacation houses are scattered on coconut-palm-shaded lots, surrounded by wild grass and carefully manicured gardens. Accommodations range from basic to expensive, and there are definitely places in between. There's also a certain measure of Tico tackiness—Foxy's Disco dominates the entry road. All of which is not to say that Jacó is cosmopolitan. Rice fields still reach most of the long length of the main street that loops off the highway.

Jacó is the nearest of the beach resorts to San José (if you don't count Puntarenas), three hours away by public bus, less by car, or a half-hour hop by chartered plane. The beach at Jacó is typical of this section of coast—wide, long, curving to promontories, littered with driftwood, palm-fringed in parts, vegetation creeping over some small dunes. There is also a certain accumulation of trash—diapers, bottles, juice cartons—in the most frequented sections, but the beach is large enough that most of it is inoffensive.

HOTELS

El Jardín, tel. 643050. 10 rooms. $17 single/$23 double.

Rooms—small but attractive, with varnished woodwork, desks, stuccoed walls and tiled floors, and fans—are set in a compact, nicely landscaped compound with a pool. French-speaking owners. Continue along the entry road to Jacó, without turning onto the main street, and you'll end up at El Jardín.

Hotel Jacó Beach, tel. 643032. (P. O. Box 962-1000 San José). 104 rooms and suites. $48 single/$59 double. Reservations: tel. 324811 (San José), 800-327-9408, 305-588-8541 (U.S.A.).

The main hotel building, a newer building and cottages are spread out on extensive grounds—kids have lots of space to run around. Rooms are large, and all are air-conditioned. Amenities include a pool for adults and one for kids, tennis courts, casino, travel service, pool tables, and other games. The disco can be noisy. Most of the facilities are showing signs of wear. Food choices are *extremely* limited. Transportation arrangements can be made through the Hotel Irazú in San José.

Hotel Cocal, tel. 643067. 9 rooms. $28/$33.

Low-slung, Spanish-style, with most rooms off arched passageways around the two pools in the courtyard. A few rooms face the water. Very attractive dining area overlooking the beach. Reserve through Hotel Galilea in San José.

Tangerí Chalet, tel. 643001 or 420977, P.O. Box 622-4050 Alajuela. 10 units. $160 for two nights on a weekend, $66 per night mid-week.

These are attractive cottages, set well apart from each other in manicured grounds. Each unit sleeps six, and there's a pool.

Apartotel Gaviotas, tel. 643092. 12 units. $30/$45, $54 triple ($18/$30 May-June, August-November).

These new, modern suites with cooking facilities sleep up to six persons on a combination of beds and sofa-beds. Small pool.

Marparaíso Hotel and Club, P. O. Box 6699, San José, tel. 216544

In a residential area next to the roads department depot, down at the southeast end of town. The beach is nice, anyway. Mostly a club for Ticos. Children's and adult pools.

Villas Miramar, tel. 643003. 9 units.

Colonial-style cottages with kitchenettes on extensive grounds. A one-bedroom unit rents for $37 and sleeps three. Two-bedroom units for six go for $52. Good value.

Cheap Lodging
The run of cabinas is generally better than elsewhere along the coast. Cabinas Clarita, next to El Jardín, has rooms for $8 single/$12 double with private bath, and also lockers and showers available for day trippers. At Cabinas Las Brisas, Bill, the owner, welcomes surfers. The 10 seafront units, varying from bare to comfortable, go for $12 to $21 double. Try to get a room in the roundhouse. And there are assorted other rooms in Jacó for $8 or less single. In some of the cabinas, you'll get a cooktop. Tropical Camping is an extensive, coconut-palm-shaded area (watch where you pitch your tent), with basic sanitary facilities. Dry season only, $2 per person. There's another camping site down near the Marparaíso Hotel.

RESTAURANTS

El Jardín. What you get here is Tico food—a pile of cabbage, a mound of rice—with something French in between. The something French is quite good—dorado armoricain (in lobster sauce), kebabs, beef in delicate sauces—but the salads are just plain. Where are *les crudités*? $5 and up for a main course. There's a good selection of liquor at the bar. The sea-view terrace is the best area, with heavy chairs, and lamps fashioned from baskets. Good for a lightning show in the rainy season. Inside, the heavy beams are hung with macramé planters. At the hotel of the same name.

Pollo Asado Borinquen—Puerto Rican Roast Chicken— serves chicken off the spit, simply and deliciously, at $6 for a whole bird, less for portions. Dutch owned, of course.

And there are many, many other eateries, mostly burger and snack joints, and seafood restaurants, which are inexpensive for fish, not so for shrimp.

TRANSPORTATION

Bus departures from the Coca-Cola station, Calle 16, Avenida 1/3, San José, are at 7:30 a.m. and 3:30 p.m.; from Jacó at 5 a.m. and 3 p.m. The Jacó Beach Hotel runs its own bus for groups. Chartered small planes use the airstrip alongside the entry road.

AND . . .

Bicycles are rented at the hardware store . . . not a bad idea in this spread-out town. A bank is available for changing travellers checks. Stores include a "supermarket" (a large convenience store), and a bakery.

Esterillos Este, down the coast from Jacó, has a long, deserted, open beach—beautiful, but not terribly safe for swimming.

Hotel El Delfín, Playa Esterillos, tel. 711640, P. O. Box 2260, San José. $45 single/$65 double.

Located at the end of the dirt (or mud) spur from the coastal highway. Pool.

There are also some cabinas on the way to the Delfín, but nothing much else out here.

Past Esterillos, the coastal highway passes through mile after mile of what were once neatly laid-out banana plantations, with clusters of precise two-story worker housing. These have now been supplanted by equally neat plantations of oil palms. All this order is near the town called—what else?—La Palma. Outside of the plantations, tropical exuberance and disorder are more evident. Brown rivers ooze through mangrove and mud flats, and are negotiated by narrow, planked trestles. The broad- and shiny-leafed plants characteristic of the humid tropics grow to ferocious dimensions. Towns are littered and ramshackle, and are few and far between. Iguanas dart across the road, and snakes slither out of the bushes. Sweat lubricates everything. The landscape is fascinating to look at, but there are few attractive stopping places, until the area of Quepos.

The coastal highway is currently paved to just past Parrita. The gravel surface beyond is well maintained to Quepos.

QUEPOS

Population: approximately 8000; 144 kilometers
from San José.

Once a banana shipping center, Quepos saw its fortunes decline with those of the plantations nearby. The town is now languid and shabby, with a strip of dingy sand. Who would guess that the nicest beaches in Costa Rica are just over the ridge? Read on.

MANUEL ANTONIO NATIONAL PARK

Seven kilometers beyond Quepos are the perfect beaches of Manuel Antonio National Park, each an arc of sand curving around a bay strewn with islands of rock, and shaded by green bordering forests. All are backdropped by dramatic cliffs. Manuel Antonio beach is one of the few places in Costa Rica where unspoiled primary forest grows right to the high-tide mark, allowing visitors to bathe at times in the shade.

South Espadilla is the northernmost of the park's beaches, followed by calmer Manuel Antonio beach, offshore of which

202

are some coral spots. Third Beach has tidal pools where brightly colored fish and eels are temporarily stranded. Last is Puerto Escondido, access to which is made difficult by the bordering rocky promontory.

Some of the most frequently observed animals at Manuel Antonio are marmosets—the smallest of Costa Rican monkeys—white-faced and howler monkeys, raccoons, pacas, opossums, and two-and three-toed sloths. Easily sighted seabirds includes frigate birds, pelicans, terns, and brown boobies. A network of trails winds along the sea, and all through the forest.

ACCOMMODATIONS

While Manuel Antonio itself was rescued from developers, in 1972, a variety of facilities crowds the edge of the park and continues up the bordering ridge, making this the easiest national park at which to stay.

Above the park
Not being right at beach level isn't necessarily a disadvantage: views are better from high up, a public bus passes regularly, and most hotels provide a shuttle service. Each of these hotels has its individual character, is of manageable size, and provides a pleasant environment for relaxation and amusement.

Hotel Plinio, P. O. Box 71, tel. 770055. 6 rooms. $27/$37, or $14/$27 May through June and August through November.

The Plinio is a roadhouse built into a hillside, with extensive woodwork, high thatched roof, and great balconies hung with hammocks—it looks like a big tree dwelling. Friendly owners, and good food. An especially good value in the off season. Rooms are near the popular bar and restaurant, but this is not a raucous all-night place. Good for singles. The rate includes a buffet breakfast. One kilometer out of Quepos.

Hotel La Mariposa, tel. 770355, P.O. Box 4, Quepos. 10 rooms. $115 single/$150 double/$260 for four. U.S. reservations: tel. 800-223-6510. Canada: 800-268-0424.

The Mariposa is one of the more tasteful hotels in Costa Rica, an intimate, luxury establishment in a dramatic clifftop set-

ting. Each Mediterranean-style cottage is on two levels, with separate bedroom, beamed ceilings, deck, and unusual bathroom with interior garden. The views to the horseshoe beaches below and islets offshore are spectacular. Service is somewhat parental. Rates include light breakfast and dinner. Children and credit cards are not accepted. Horses and boat tours are available. Three-and-a-half kilometers out of Quepos.

Hotel Divisamar, tel. 770371. P. O. Box 82. 21 rooms. $45 double with fan, $56 double with air conditioning.

Pleasant rooms overlooking a small valley. Nice touches include Delft-style tiles, and central hot water (most hotels here have only one lukewarm tap). Some rooms air-conditioned. Restaurant with essential, reasonably priced menu, pool, protected parking, small library. Airport pickup on request. Family-managed, eager to please. No credit cards. Located across from the Mariposa. A trail leads down to the beach, or you can get a lift from the owners.

El Colibrí, P. O. Box 94, tel. 770432. 8 rooms. $40/$45, $56 for four, or $23/$29 during low season.

Gilles and Pierre offer good taste in their compound—rooms with tiled floors, varnished beams, louvered doors. The hilltop Mediterranean-style units, back from the road, across the gardens (where something is always in bloom) are the nicest, with porches and hammocks. Sea views are good from the second floor of the main building. One charming little guest unit has the bedroom on a screened upper level. A pool is under construction. Children under ten should look elsewhere. 4.2 kilometers from Quepos.

La Quinta, P.O. Box 76, tel. 770434. 5 units. $35 to $45 double.

This is an intimate hilltop resort, with extensive grounds and magnificent sea views, a somewhat less pretentious version of the Mariposa, which sends its overflow here. Mediterranean-style cottages all have three beds, tiled showers, terra cotta floors. The personable owners, a French-Hungarian couple, are on-site to see to guests' needs. Pool. Breakfast and beverages available. 4.5 kilometers from Quepos. (The owners and I buy our sheets at the same store. They can explain.)

Hotel Arboleda, tel. 770414 (351169 in San José). 30 units. $40/$45 ($27/$35 in the low season).

This hotel occupies its own section of rain forest, extending down to the water. Twelve hillside stone cottages with whitewashed interiors have basic beds, but are otherwise attractive, with decorations of Mexican tiles, and terraces. The 18 units at beach level are generally more comfortable, even if they offer less breathtaking views. The snack bar is up near the road level; a restaurant at the beach operates in the dry season only. Airport pickup, horses available. Five kilometers out of Quepos.

Apartotel Karahé, P. O. Box 100, Quepos, tel. 770170. 9 units. $44 daily.

Pleasant, rock-walled cottages, each accommodating three persons, with refrigerators but no cooking facilities. Good sea views. Airport pickup. The restaurant, on a huge porch, serves chops and chicken cooked in the open, at $7 or so for a main course. On the hillside just before the beach, seven kilometers from Quepos.

At the beach

Starting where the road comes down to the beach (and where the bus leaves passengers), there is a series of cabinas, basic, cold-water units with few services. You might think it would be to your advantage to stay nearer the entrance to the park. But the noise levels, lack of security at some hotels, harsh concrete rooms and suspicious disposal systems could change your mind. All the cabinas, spread among the palms, are close enough to each other that you can look them over before selecting one to settle into for a while. All are likely to be full or nearly full on weekends, and deserted on weekdays.

Those cabinas nearest the bus stop go for $5 per person, sometimes more, sometimes less, depending on the season. The more substantial Cabinas Manuel Antonio and Hotel Manuel Antonio (separate establishments) are 200 meters farther along, toward the park entrance. The former has five rooms above a restaurant, the latter 18 basic rooms near the water's edge.

The best accommodations in this area are on a road that winds back from the beach. Cabinas Espadilla has 20 units with cooking areas for $15 single/$18 double, $24/$27 with a separate kitchen. The rate drops substantially during the rainy season, except in July. The Vela Bar (tel. 770413) has attractive rooms for $19/$30, $10 additional with air conditioning. And Los Almendros rents motel-style units on attractive grounds for $22 for one to three persons. Nearby, the self-styled Costa Linda "Youth Hostel" is a dive.

One other place with cheap concrete rooms, Cabinas Pedro Miguel, is located a kilometer out of Quepos. $5 per person.

Back in Quepos, there are several modest hotels where you can get a room if everything on the way to the park is filled. The Hotel Viña del Mar looks out on the muddy beach, which is the best view downtown. $15 and up for a double. The places back toward the bus station all charge less, and give you less.

FOOD

The Hotel Plinio, one kilometer out of Quepos, has a bar and restaurant with good German and Italian food. The bread is home-baked, the salads are crisp, and I can recommend the lasagne. $5 and up for a main course. If you're not staying at the Plinio, it's worthwhile to go over for a drink and a meal.

The Barba Roja bar, opposite the Divisamar, commands the same magnificent sea and cliff views available from the Hotel Mariposa. There are assorted daily specials for $5 to $10, burgers for a couple of dollars, and rock music.

Of several eateries at beach level, the most popular is the large, open-air Mar y Sombra, located where the road from Quepos meets the beach. A whole fried fish goes for $4 and up, depending on the size, and there are huge tropical fruit plates, as well as the usual rice-and-bean combos, and beef and pork main courses for $3 to $5.

TRANSPORTATION

Direct buses for Manuel Antonio depart from the Coca-Cola terminal in San José (Calle 16, Avenidas 1/3) at 6 a.m., noon and 6 p.m., and leave Manuel Antonio for San José at 6 a.m., noon and 5 p.m. Slower buses that terminate in Quepos depart at 7 and 10 a.m. and 2 and 4 p.m.; return buses at 5 and 8 a.m., and 2 and 4 p.m. The trip on the direct bus takes more than four hours, and can be nausea-inducing on the run down to the coast. On weekends, it's best to buy your ticket in advance at the bus company office inside the Coca-Cola market.

A local bus for Manuel Antonio departs about every two hours from the bus stop in Quepos.

Buses leave for Puntarenas at 4:30 a.m. and 3 p.m. Buses for Dominical depart at 5 a.m. and 1:30 p.m.

Sansa, the domestic airline, has a morning flight from San José to Quepos, daily except Sunday. In the dry season, there's an extra flight in the afternoon. As on all domestic flights, fares are quite low—currently about $10 one way.

Sansa also has inexpensive packages including hotels and some meals: $30 for a one-night stay, $65 for two nights.

VISITING THE PARK

Despite the sometimes frenzied activity at Espadilla beach, things turn peaceful as soon as you cross a stream (wading in the rainy season) and enter the park. Visiting hours are from 8 a.m. to 4 p.m.

Take a good look at the map posted at the entrance, and plan your route—trails are not well-marked. Take note of the illustrated signs warning of the *manzanillo de playa*, a tree with poisonous, apple-like fruits, and sap that irritates the skin.

The trails at Manuel Antonio wind through the forest, up to clifftops, and down to beaches—depending on which nomenclature you use, there are from three to five beaches, those farthest from the entrance being usually deserted. But their availability for swimming depends on the time of day— at high tide, they simply disappear, and you have to get up and hike.

Along the trails, bromeliads decorate tree limbs, and the leaf rubbish underfoot is teeming with life. Crabs scurry when you take a step. Iguanas scramble from your presence. White-faced monkeys go about their business, having seen the likes of you before.

Whatever your sightings of these, or of parrots, squirrels, iguanas, coatis, agoutis, or, more rarely, peccaries, you are sure to run into several pairs of *amantes costarricenses*. Be discreet.

AROUND MANUEL ANTONIO AND QUEPOS

The variety of inexpensive accommodations at beach level at Manuel Antonio attracts a lively, mostly young crowd. Many of the visitors are foreigners on extended travels. The beach is known as a good place to hang out for a while, trade information, recoup, and re-group.

The concentration of facilities and beauty also make this an event center. A three-day Festival of the Sea takes place in January. Surfing contests, rock concerts and conventions are scheduled at other times. You'll want to check what's on tap (the tourist office in San José will probably know) in order to get in on the action, or avoid it, depending on your sensitivities.

I am told by a reliable source that the mayor of Quepos took considerable offense when, in an earlier edition, I called his city "squalid, rotting, and garbage-strewn." The lack of attention to public decoration was laid to slow adjustment to self-management of affairs, following the reduction of banana company operations. Quepos is still far from pristine—"charmingly scuzzy" is what one American magazine writer called it—but it is not squalid, nor is it garbage-strewn these days.

Some of Manuel Antonio's touristic development has spilled down into town, in the form of a few shops and services for tourists. One beachwear outlet, La Buena Nota, at the entrance to Quepos, has used books, and owners who are said to be helpful to disoriented tourists. Among other facilities are a bank, and, at the highway junction, a gas station.

Sportfishing Quepos offers deep sea fishing. Telephone 201115 for information in San José, or 770505 in Quepos, or write to P. O. Box 115-1150 La Uruca. Rates start at about $350 for two persons for a full day of fishing in blue water 20 minutes from shore. Longer fishing or naturalist trips are available to Drake Bay on the Osa Peninsula, Corcovado National Park, and Caño Island. Fishing charters may be available from other operators as well. Inquire at La Buena Nota.

Surfboards are available for rent at the beach outside Manuel Antonio park—you don't have to bring your own.

If you continue straight after entering Quepos, past the left turn for Manuel Antonio, and go down toward the docks, then take a half left, you can climb the hill to the old banana company residential compound, a suburb of pleasant, uniform, tan clapboard bungalows with red tin roofs, set behind fences on well-manicured grounds shaded by huge palms. There are sport and community centers, including one of the largest swimming pools around (with one of the largest cracks), and views that rival those available from the resort hotels of the area. The houses are owned by Standard Fruit, and populated by Costa Rican managers, not gringos. It's all quite a contrast to the town below. By the way, the roads are private, and you're not supposed to enter the compound, but foreigners who can't read the signs are not chased away.

One goal of day-trippers from Manuel Antonio is Isla de Damas, which, despite the name, is no island, but a peninsula, ten kilometers up the coast from Quepos. The floating restaurant-bar Tortuga weighs anchor at noon, and serves a lunch of fresh fish while cruising through jungle-lined channels. To get aboard, turn off the coastal highway at the Pepsi-Tortuga sign. The estuary is one kilometer onward. Little motorboats will take you out to the Tortuga. This is a beautiful, fascinating area, off the usual visitors' track, with secluded vacation homes and fishermen's shacks along the water. You can get here by taxi, or Erick at the Hotel Divisamar will put a group together for a trip in his van.

South of Quepos

During the rainy season, inquire about road conditions before traveling south from Quepos (if the highway hasn't been paved by the time you visit). As you proceed—by car, or, more certainly, by bus—the ridge of the continental divide in the Talamanca Mountains, with the highest peaks in Costa Rica, watches over from just thirty kilometers inland. Higher rainfall is evidenced by broader leaves, more gigantic plants, and swollen rivers. The vast palm plantation continues. Huge oil processing plants send up a burned-sweet smell. Every small plantation town has its bus shelters, church, company stores, rows of neat, identical housing (some models quite above the usual local standard), cantina, and Alcoholics Anonymous chapter, with its sign prominently posted.

DOMINICAL

About 50 kilometers south of Quepos is Dominical, a beautiful beach with basic accommodations. A few kilometers beyond the village is the cliff-top, American-owned Hotel-Cabinas Punta Dominical, with clean, pleasant rooms at $12 single/$18 double, and a restaurant. Phone 255328 to reserve, or write to P.O. Box 176, San Isidro del General.

Buses for Dominical leave from Quepos at 5 a.m. and 1:30 p.m. In the opposite direction, buses pass at 9 a.m. and 3:30 p.m.

DOWN TOWARD PANAMA

The southern Pacific slope of Costa was, until the 1950s, isolated from the rest of the country. No highway crossed the Talamanca mountain range from the Central Valley, and all communication with the region was by a roundabout coastal land route that was mostly untraveled. What population there was concentrated in the banana regions around Golfito, which were tied by narrow-gauge railroad with Panama, and by steamship with the banana-consuming world.

With improved highway links, the inland valley of the General River has become one of the fastest-growing areas of Costa Rica. Many farmers have migrated to this frontier region from the overcrowded lands of the Central Valley, with the encouragement and assistance of the government. The warm climate suits the valley to sugarcane and corn production, as well as cattle grazing.

The Pan American Highway runs south from San José, up into the Talamanca range and along the continental divide. The trip this way is an ear-popping ascent through apple country and moss- and epiphyte-laden forest, past swatches of mountain made bare by landslides, up to the windblown landscape of stunted bushes, struggling tufts of grass and feather-duster vegetation of the frigid tropics, known as *paramo*.

The highest point on the whole Pan American Highway, 3355 meters above sea level, is near Cerro Buena Vista (Good-View Peak), also known, less optimistically, as Cerro de la Muerte (Peak of Death). Both names are apt. When clouds are not clinging to the heights, the ride along the ridge affords views down to both the Pacific Ocean and the Caribbean. The second, more common name derives from the frigid climate, said to have killed many an oxcart driver.

At kilometer 80 on the Pan American highway is the junction for the road to San Gerardo de Dota and Finca Zacatales, the ranch and trout-fishing camp of the Chacón family. Most fishing camps in Costa Rica are on the coasts, this being the notable exception. Package day trips, including meals, equipment and guides, are available through San José travel agencies for about $65. The overnight rate, if you're on your own, is only about $7 per person, or $20 with meals. Telephone 711732 to reserve, and to arrange to be met at the highway junction. You needn't come here just to fish. The ranch is in the cool country, above 8000 feet, and if you've been to the peak of Irazú volcano, the vegetation along the Savegre River will look familiar: leafy trees decorated with orchids and bromeliads, and firs. Though not as dramatic as the scenery along the strenuous route to the top of Chirripó, there is some of the same feeling in the air. Birders take note: according to some biologists, the concentration of quetzals in this area is the greatest in the world.

SAN ISIDRO DE EL GENERAL

Population: Approximately 32,000; Altitude: 760 meters; 136 kilometers from San José.

San Isidro is the major town of the south, a transportation and farming center at the head of the valley of the General River. The area always had a scattered Indian population, but San Isidro was founded only in 1897.

There's nothing of historic interest in San Isidro—most of the town was built in the last thirty years, after the opening of the Pan American Highway. But the place is pleasant enough. A grotesque pink-and-white concrete cathedral overlooks a neat park of large palms. The views upward, to the Talamanca mountains, are impressive. And there are quite decent, and decently priced, hotels and restaurants for the visitor who is passing through on the way to the beach, a national park, to Panama, or to a rafting excursion on the General River. An annual cattle show and fair takes place at the beginning of February.

ACCOMMODATIONS

The best lodging in the area is at the 60-room Hotel del Sur (tel. 710233), outside of the city on the highway south, at Palmares. The rate is $10 to $15 single, $12 to $18 double, and there is a pool. In San Isidro itself, the Hotel Amaneli (tel. 710352, 40 rooms, $6 per person) is the tan concrete structure that you first see when you come down the mountain from San José. It's clean enough, and rooms have private bath. Nearby is the brand-spanking-new Hotel Iguazú (tel. 712571, 21 rooms, $6 per person). With private bath, and located just a block from the square, it's a good deal. Right on the square is the Hotel Chirripó (tel. 710529, 40 rooms, $10 double with shared bath,). All of the in-town hotels are more for travelling businessmen than vacationers, but they're quite adequate.

The restaurant of the Hotel Chirripó is a delightful Tico *terrasse* facing the square, excellent for watching town life pass by. There are sandwiches and breakfast combinations, and full meals for $4 and up. The menu includes "Chateu Brian" and "Gordon Blue." It's not really Brian or Gordon, but it's decent provincial bar food.

TRANSPORTATION

Buses and microbuses for San Isidro depart from Calle 16, Avenidas 1/3, San José, every hour from 4:30 a.m. to 5:30 p.m. Three companies on the same block alternate departures. The schedule in reverse is the same. The trip takes about three hours.

CHIRRIPO NATIONAL PARK

Northeast of San Isidro, in the Talamanca mountains, is Chirripó National Park, which includes Cerro Chirripó, at 3820 meters (12,530 feet) the highest mountain peak in Costa Rica. The habitat of the park ranges from rocky, frigid heights and glacial lakes to the stunted, windblown paramo of the harsh altitudes of the tropics, to oak and evergreen forest, highland meadows, and cloud forest. Wildlife at Chirripó is not as varied as at some of the lowland reserves, but includes pumas, mountain goats, rabbits, and tapirs, among others. Quetzals can be sighted at lower altitudes.

There are several trails to Chirripó peak. The ascent generally takes two days. The usual route is through El Termómetro ("The Thermometer"), a climb where the visitor measures if he has what it takes to continue; then up cliffs and across valleys and plains to Valle de los Crestones, where shelters are available, with wood stoves and basic washing facilities.

With an early start on the second day, a climber can beat the clouds to the peak of Chirripó, four kilometers distant. Those who make it to the top are rewarded with views not only of two oceans, but of the chain of mountain and volcanic peaks marching to the northwest toward San José, and valleys and lakes along the way. An alternate way down, on the third day, is by way of Sabana de los Leones, with its concentration of birds and cold streams.

Access to Chirripó Park is via bus at 5 a.m. or 2 p.m. from San Isidro to the village of San Gerardo de Rivas, where park headquarters are located, or by four-wheel-drive vehicle through San Gerardo de Rivas to the park entrance, which is 15 kilometers from San Isidro. Before going to the park, verify current conditions and bus schedules with the National Park Service in San José. February, March and April are the best months for a visit, with the least rainfall. December and January are also relatively dry, but colder. Water, warm clothing, and hiking boots are requisites—this is not a park for casual drop-ins. Horses are available to assist hikers with their gear.

LA AMISTAD INTERNATIONAL PARK

La Amistad International Park stretches onward into Panama—an expression of hope for the future, since there is a certain amount of tension along the border. With the establishment of this huge park, adjacent to Chirripó, Costa Rica doubled its protected lands. Most of La Amistad remains unexplored, and there are hardly any services for visitors.

The Helechales ("Fern") section of the park is reached through Buenos Aires and Potrero Grande, east of San Isidro del General. The Escuadra section is north of San Vito de Java (see below). Inquire about current conditions at the park service in San José, which will provide current bus schedules from San Isidro.

After traversing the General Valley, the Pan American Highway follows the valley of the Río Grande de Terraba, down into sweltering lowlands. Around the town of Boruca is an area populated by indigenous peoples whose ancestors were relocated, under Spanish orders, from the slopes of the Talamanca range. A mission was set up here in 1626. One of the most notable Boruca activities was their practice of birth control, through means unknown to outsiders. The traditional fiesta of the Borucas is celebrated on February 8.

Farther along the road is Palmar Sur (232 kilometers from San José, one Sansa flight daily except Sunday), known for *las bolas grandes,* the nearly perfectly spherical stone balls, ranging up to 2.5 meters in diameter, found on banana lands in the nearby Diquis Valley. Among the mysteries of the bolas: they are made of granite, but there is no naturally occurring granite nearby; it is harder to carve larger spheres accurately, yet the larger ones are more perfect than smaller ones; few stone balls are nearly equal in size, which indicates that a template was probably not used in their manufacture; no datable artifacts have been discovered with the stone balls, which makes analysis and interpretation difficult. One suggestion is that the balls were used as burial-ground markers, but there is little credible evidence to support this idea. Stone balls from the area may be seen in the plaza of Palmar Sur, as well as at the national museum and in Carrillo Park in San José.

THE OSA PENINSULA

The Osa Peninsula, south of the Diquis Valley, is a wild area virtually devoid of roads. Only light planes, and boats running between Puerto Jiménez and Golfito, provide communication with the outside world.

Osa is a fabled area where a rough-and-ready breed of solitary prospectors until a few years ago panned the streams and tunneled the hills for gold. These men from many countries stayed in the wild for months, crossing paths with monkeys, snakes and mountain lions, and, more recently, teams of workers for large mining companies, equipped with heavy machinery.

CORCOVADO NATIONAL PARK

Corcovado National Park, in the southern part of Osa, includes vast stretches of the only virgin rain forest in Central

America. Among the natural treasures of Corcovado are trees of 500 species (including one kapok, or silk-cotton, that is said to be the largest tree in Costa Rica); numerous endangered mammals, among them cougars, jaguars, ocelots, margays, jaguarundis and brocket deer; eagles and macaws; assorted monkeys; snakes; tapirs; and peccaries, which may be the most destructive and dangerous species in the park. Vegetation zones range from mountain rain forest down to beach, and fresh-water and mangrove swamps.

VISITING CORCOVADO AND THE OSA PENINSULA

You don't just drop into Corcovado. With its remote location, Corcovado attracts mainly scientific researchers, and visitors on all-inclusive packages with boats, buses and ox-carts organized beforehand. There are extensive trails along the beach and in the forested interior, however, as well as campsites. You can do Corcovado on your own if you're prepared with camping equipment, rain protection, high boots, snakebite kit, food, water containers and purification means, and repellent against the sandflies that infest the beaches.

The park service offers these on-your-own route suggestions: by chartered plane to the airstrip at park headquarters; by Sansa airlines to Golfito, then by Aeronaves plane from Golfito to Puerto Jiménez (at 6:30 a.m. and 2 p.m.), then by bus at 5:30 a.m. to La Palma, then on foot for three-and-a-half hours to the Los Patos guard station at the eastern section of park, then by trail four hours to Sirena station, then by trail through Playa Madrigal to the campsite at La Leona station, then a day's hike back to Puerto Jiménez; by Tracopa bus from San José (Avenida 18, Calles 2/4) to Golfito, then boat at 1 p.m. to Puerto Jiménez, continuing as above. And there are several variants on these routes—did I mention the one that involves a boat along the Sierpe River? The park service can tell you about it.

ACCOMMODATIONS

Marenco "Biological Station" is a hilltop lodge at the northern limit of the park, with its own airstrip and boat dock, and swath of Osa landscape that includes coastal swamp, beach and trails. There are four bunk beds to a room, and shared baths. This hotel is used mainly by tour groups, and is slow to answer individual inquiries (to P.O. Box 4025, San José, tel. 211594).

Farther from the park, accommodations are available at Las Ventanas de Osa, a remote, cliff-top, rain-forest lodge at the northwest edge of the Peninsula, named for the "windows" formed by waves beating against seaside cliffs. Facilities are limited, but include a swimming pool, and room for 14 in several buildings. Meals are catered by a chef from San José. The lodge sponsors one-week and two-week stays for $1295 or $2590 per person, including air transport from San José, meals, and guided birding and beach trips. Rates are lower for groups. For information, contact Natural History Tours, Box 1089, Lake Helen, Florida 32744, tel. 904-228-3356.

Phantom Isle Lodge, tel. 257682 in San José. U.S.reservations: Phantom Isle Tours, Box 559, Manvel, TX 77578, tel. 713-489-9156. In Canada: tel. 416-479-2600. Packages from $125 per day.

This lodge of simple cottages with high-peaked thatched roofs is set among the palms at the edge of Drake Bay. Virtually *everything*—river trips, guided birding, scuba diving, river fishing, transport from San José, even gold panning—is included in the package price, the exception being an extra charge for deep-sea fishing. Sir Francis Drake once had a camp on these shores, and Spanish pieces of eight are said to wash up with some frequency. Sea turtles nest on the beach in June and July, and whales may be spotted offshore in December.

Caño Island, 20 kilometers off the Osa Peninsula, was once used as a burial ground by coastal tribes. Numerous artifacts have been found, most notably small stone spheres. The variety of materials used in other objects suggests that long-distance maritime trade flourished before the Spaniards arrived. Caño Island, with its high forest, is now a biological reserve.

Coco Island, cliff-bordered and of volcanic origin, lies 500 kilometers southwest of the Costa Rican mainland. Abundant rainfall made Coco a watering place for ships in the colonial period. During the independence upheavals in Spanish America, the aristocracy of Peru entrusted its treasures to Captain James Thompson, who absconded and reputedly buried his loot on Coco Island. Treasure-seekers have periodically sought the cache, but all deny success (at least publicly). Coco Island is now a national park and is the home of three species of bird—the Coco Island finch, the Coco Island cuckoo, and Ridgeway's papamoscas—found nowhere else, as well as the chupapiedra (rock-sucker), a fish with a sucking disk that allows it to ascend waterfalls.

GOLFITO

Golfito, on the Golfo Dulce (Sweet Gulf), is the last major town in the south, an old banana port surrounded by lands that receive abundant rainfall all year. The plug was pulled on Golfito in 1985, when United Fruit abandoned its banana operations in the face of labor unrest and rising taxes. Tourism and a fishing industry are slowly developing, but the town remains in economic distress.

ACCOMMODATIONS

Hotel Costa Rica Surf, P. O. Box 7, tel. 750034. $15 single/$22 double. U.S. reservations: tel. 314-756-2722.
Restaurant, fishing charters available.

Las Gaviotas, at Playa Tortuga, has air-conditioned rooms for $15 to $25, single or double. **Cabinas Playa Tortuga**, tel. 750062, in a nicely landscaped compound, has rooms for $10/$14, and cabinas for $23.

TRANSPORTATION

The Tracopa company, Avenida 18, Calles 2/4, San José, tel. 237685, runs three daily buses to Golfito. Other buses pass the junction for Golfito on the Pan American Highway. Flights to Golfito, departing from San José every morning except Sunday, provide a relatively inexpensive shortcut on the route to Panama. The fare is about $15.

Near Golfito:

Golfito Sailfish Rancho. 10 rooms. About $275 per day. San José address: P.O. Box 5712, tel. 357766. U.S. reservations: P. O. Box 290190, San Antonio, TX 78280, tel. 800-531-7232 or 512-492-5517;

This is a new operation owned by the same people as Parismina Tarpon Rancho, and the policies are similar: open bar, meals and laundry included in the package.

From Ciudad Neily, 17 kilometers from the border, a branch road leads up into the mountains to San Vito de Java, settled by Italian immigrants. Coffee is grown in the region. The Hotel Pitier (tel. 773006) has rooms with private bath for about $5 per person. Buses for San Vito leave from Avenida 7, Calles 12/14, San José, at 5:45 a.m., 7:45 a.m. and 2 p.m.

The **Wilson Botanical Garden** is six kilometers south of San Vito de Java. Now owned by the Organization for Tropical Studies, which also operates La Selva and several other research stations in Costa Rica, the garden was started by Robert Wilson in 1962, with the purchase of the Las Cruces plantation .

Eight hectares of the 140-hectare site are planted gardens, linked by paths and trails, and most of the rest is premontane rain forest. Orchids, bromeliads, ferns and conifers are particularly evident in the planted areas. Over 200 bird species have been listed. The gardens are largely used for research and teaching, but visitors with an interest in natural history are welcome. The fee for a day visit is $12; or $25 for a room overnight, and $15 for three meals. Call the San José office of the Organization for Tropical Studies, at 252218, to confirm rates, and reserve.

Paso Canoas, 347 kilometers from San José, is the town on the border with Panama. Stores do a flourishing business with cross-border shoppers, but accommodations in the area are overpriced. Travelers should plan to get to Paso Canoas early in the day in order to be able to move on. A daily Sansa flights operates from San José to Coto 47, not far away. Tracopa, Avenida 18, Calles 2/4, San José, tel. 237685, has four buses a day to the border, and other companies have service right to Panama City (see page 72).

Around the Volcanoes

or

All of Costa Rica in One Day

North of San José, over and beyond the volcanoes Irazú and Poás, is an area that includes gently rolling pastured hillsides often shrouded in fog; high montane tropical forest barely touched by human settlement and exploitation; hot springs gurgling up from the interior of the earth; jungle dripping with heat and wet; homesteads hacked out of the forest by modern pioneers; and banana lands that have been cultivated for more than 100 years. All this is within just 60 kilometers of San José in a straight line. But until recently, mountains, rivers, jungle, and traditional trade routes that ran elsewhere, kept most of this triangle off the beaten track for visitors and Costa Ricans alike. Now, with the completion of a few strategic stretches of highway and dirt road, it's possible to make a circular trip through this varied area in a matter of hours, even by bus. But for the lack of beaches, it's almost like seeing all of Costa Rica and every era of its development in just one day.

The route described below takes you clockwise from San José. But this is just one possible itinerary. You can spin off from San Carlos toward the northwest, past the sparking volcano Arenal, and down to the Pacific coastal lowlands; take a shortcut northward over the saddle between Poás and Irazú volcanoes; or continue to Limón instead of returning to your starting point.

By bus or car from San José, head to the west, along the Cañas and Soto expressways, in the direction of Puntarenas. The old Pan American Highway, parallel to the newer road, passes through the towns of Alajuela, Grecia and Sarchí (see page 115). At Naranjo, a branch road turns northward, up and out of the Central Valley, across the relatively low stretch of hills between the Tilarán and Central volcanic mountain ranges.

ZARCERO

Two-and-a-half hours from San José by bus, Zarcero has a cottage-style church, and a main square adorned with hedges trimmed into fanciful shapes of animals, curiosities that you can see from the bus as you pass through.

SAN CARLOS

About 48 kilometers north of Naranjo, and 95 kilometers from San José, is Ciudad Quesada (which most Costa Ricans call San Carlos), a bustling trading center for the surrounding prosperous area of meat and dairy production. San Carlos in itself does not count as a tourist attraction. But it's on the way to everywhere, and getting here, on a winding road through fog-shrouded, pastured hills, is a scenic meander. From the attractive, treed main square, you can see the countryside on most sides.

ACCOMMODATIONS

The Hotel Central (tel. 460766, 49 rooms, $10/$15 with private bath), on the square, is a concrete, unadorned building with plain rooms that will do for the night. And there are other, lesser hostelries.

BUSES

Buses for Zarcero and San Carlos leave hourly, or more frequently, from the Coca-Cola station, Calle 16, Avenidas 1/3, San José.

From San Carlos, you can go on by bus toward Arenal volcano, around Lake Arenal; deep into the low-lying tropical forest north of Poás and Irazú volcanoes, and back to San

José through Braulio Carrillo National Park; or even to remote Los Chiles, near the Nicaraguan border at the eastern end of Lake Nicaragua. Some schedules, as recently posted: to Tilarán, near the Pan American Highway, via Arenal, on Lake Arenal, and Fortuna, at 6:30 a.m. and 3 p.m.; to Arenal, about every two hours from 5:30 a.m. to 1:30 p.m.; to Fortuna at 9 a.m. and 1:30 p.m.; to Río Frío, north of the volcanoes of the Central Valley, about every two hours from 6 a.m. to 5:30 p.m.

West of San Carlos
Beyond San Carlos, a road runs to Fortuna, near the Arenal volcano, over the Tilarán range to Arenal lake and dam, and down to the Pan American Highway at Cañas. Currently, a stretch of road past Fortuna is unpaved, and passable during the rainy season only by bus or in a four-wheel-drive vehicle.

ARENAL VOLCANO

Mount Arenal (1633 meters), which overlooks much of the San Carlos plain and the northern Pacific lowlands, has the distinction of being the volcano in Costa Rica that most *looks* like a volcano, with its distinctive conical shape. It also acts like one, having erupted spectacularly in 1968 and spewed ashes over a wide area. The glow of the active crater may often be seen at night.

Arenal is too hot and dangerous to climb. Several people who have attempted to do so in recent years, including at least one tourist, have been killed. But there is no peril in observing the fireworks from a safe vantage point in the valley below, or even hiking on the *lower* part of the slopes.

Fortuna is the town nearest to Arenal volcano, with basic rooms available at the Hotel Central for about $3 per person. At Tabacón, about five kilometers beyond Fortuna, there's a bathing area with pools fed by hot springs.

Several travel agencies in San José operate day-long volcano-watching excursions to Arenal, with stops in Sarchí and at hot springs.

Continuing Around the Volcanoes
The paved road that runs east from San Carlos gradually descends through an area combed with hot springs. At Agua

223

Caliente de San Carlos, nine kilometers away and just north of the highway (look for the large white gates), is the El Tucano Country Club. The complex includes attractively landscaped grounds, as well as forest, all traversed by a river of warm mineral water. Saunas, thermal baths, tennis courts, three swimming pools, whirlpools and restaurants are open to the public in general for an entry fee of about $1. The food here is comparable in price and variety to what you'll find at a downtown San José hotel—sandwiches for $2, pastas, chicken or fish for $5 and up, shrimp for much more. A hotel is under construction. Currently, the restaurant is closed on Mondays. Call 461822 for more information.

From Agua Caliente, the paved road continues over hill and down dale, gradually heading into lower country. Each town is a cluster of clapboard or tongue-and-groove houses, on concrete foundations, with red tin roofs, modest and neat. There are a couple of more substantial dwellings with carport, and, in the case of Venecia, a sprawling, tan, tin-sided church with red roof, surrounded by well-kept gardens.

About five kilometers to the north of Venecia are the ruins of Cutris, a pre-Columbian city that shows signs of having been well ordered, with wide streets. The road from Venecia comes to within two kilometers of the site, which has not been restored and has no visitors' facilities.

Past Río Cuarto, at San Miguel, the road from San Carlos joins another road from San José via Heredia, through the saddle between the Barva and Poás volcanoes. Along the way are the dramatic La Paz falls, at Vara Blanca, just after the Poás turnoff.

Gradually, to the north of San Miguel, the towns become less neat, with much recent, ramshackle construction right along the road, and vigorous, disorderly vegetation. The wrinkles of the land become fewer, and finally fade, and groves of orange trees appear among the flat pastures. Barva volcano, often shrouded in mist or downpours, looms to the south.

This is the San Carlos plain which, despite its proximity to the Central Valley, is a frontier area, where a waterlogged terrain and assorted pests and illnesses until recently obstructed settlement. Even now, hardly a road penetrates the jungle, and rivers are still important transport routes.

The San Juan River forms the northern border of the region with Nicaragua, but it is hardly a barrier. People and goods circulate freely and without formality between the two countries along the many waterways, much to the consternation of political authorities. And in troubled recent times, some of the movement has been far from innocent.

Between La Virgen and Chilamate, near the farthest point that you can go from San José on this road, is Selva Verde Lodge, a rustic guest house on a farm. Telephone 716459, or 800-451-7111 in the United States, if you want to stay out here—it's certainly off the usual tourist track. The rate is about $15 single/$25 double.

PUERTO VIEJO

Seventy kilometers from San Carlos or Heredia, Puerto Viejo was, until a few years ago, the end of the road, from where one traveled onward only by light cargo boat on the Sarapiquí River, toward the San Juan River and Barra del Colorado on the Caribbean. A road extension now provides a way through to the south and east, though you might still be able to negotiate your way aboard a river boat, and make a round trip back to San José via the Tortuguero reserve and Limón. Patience and a flexible schedule would be absolute requirements for such a journey, as floods and fancy play havoc with promised departures. A surer way to float the river is on a rafting excursion organized in San José. These are occasionally scheduled, or you can have one done to order.

Only the most basic of accommodations are available at Puerto Viejo: Cabinas La Paz, and Cabinas Monteverde, which is slightly better than the former, though you're best not to stay in these places at all.

TRANSPORTATION

Buses operate to Puerto Viejo from Calle 12, Avenida 9, San José, daily at 9 a.m. and 4 p.m. Return trips are at 4 a.m. and 2 p.m.

Just south of Puerto Viejo is La Selva Biological Station, operated by the Organization for Tropical Studies, which takes in 1457 hectares (3711 acres) of lowland rain forest, most of it never disturbed by agriculture. The research center is reached by river from Puerto Viejo, or by road and footbridge. Unlike other parks and sanctuaries, La Selva is reserved mainly for scientific investigation. Its natural diversity is notable even in Costa Rica, with 1800 different plant species, of the 8000 in the country.

Most parts of La Selva can be reached by an extensive, well-marked trail system, along which trees are labeled. An arboretum holds most native species—over a thousand.

Living facilities range from bunkrooms to rooms for two with shared bath. Researchers whose work is approved by the Organization for Tropical Studies are given priority, and a daily rate for accommodations of $25 to $35. Outsiders, whether on their own or in tour groups, pay about $75 a day. For information or reservations, contact the Organization for Tropical Studies at P.O. Box 676, 2050 San Pedro, Costa Rica, tel. 252218, or P. O. Box DM, Duke Station, Durham, NC 27706, U.S.A., tel. 919-684-5774. Dial 718527 to reach La Selva directly. The station provides round-trip transportation three times a week from San José, and several daily trips into Puerto Viejo.

Past Puerto Viejo, a bumpy dirt road, best negotiated in a four-wheel-drive vehicle or on a bus, heads southeast around Barva volcano, crossing streams on plank bridges. Though only recently cut through the forest, much of the land to both sides is already cleared in a rather untidy fashion. Cattle are grazing, and corn is growing. You see signs at intermittent mud tracks that lead to clusters of shacks, announcing that so and so many farmers have benefitted from a distribution of land. And you understand the pressure to provide landless people with the means to make their own living, and the political payoffs therefrom, which in no way compare to the domestic benefits available from a policy of conserving the rain forest for future generations.

At one point along the road, there is an outpost of the Comando Atlántico del Batallón Relámpago (Atlantic Commando of the Lightning Battalion), in helmets and camouflage fatigues, ready to control any subversive activities in this strategic area. Pinch yourself, and remember that these are

226

not soldiers—more blur of the distinction between army and civil guard.

Near Las Horquetas:

Rara Avis, P. O. Box 8105, 1000 San José, tel. 530844. U.S. reservations: tel. 800-255-2508.

Rara Avis was established on the site of a former prison colony to demonstrate that standing rain forest can be profitable when used for tourism, managed lumbering, and research. Major activities for visitors to the 1500-acre reserve are birding, swimming in jungle streams and at the base of a towering waterfall, and guided hikes to see exotic species of plants and animals. Several scientific investigations are usually going on, one currently using a makeshift tramway to travel in the jungle canopy. The rate for accommodations is about $35 per person, including meals, in the rustic "El Plástico" lodge, a former prison barracks, with four to six bunk beds per room. The more comfortable Waterfall Lodge has eight rooms, each with a balcony and private bath, going for $75 single, $100 double, again with meals. There are additional charges for transport to the lodge (in taxi, tractor-drawn cart, or on horseback from Las Horquetas) and guide service. The lodges are about 15 kilometers from Las Horquetas via a rutted track paved, in parts, with tree trunks. It's essential to make arrangements before visiting.

RIO FRIO

Southeast of Puerto Viejo, Río Frío is another small settlement, with basic accommodations, and a Chinese restaurant (not at all bad, surprisingly). If you come this way from San Carlos by bus, you'll have an hour to stroll around, and examine town life: the latest Mexican soap operas, baseball, and news from Chicago brought to local eateries through satellite television; shop attendants engaging more in conversation than commerce; strangers on their way to scientific investigations; tractors pulling carts of produce along muddy lanes.

Buses leave Río Frío for San José at 5:30 and 9 a.m. and 3 p.m. From San José, buses leave at 9 a.m. and 1 and 4 p.m., from Calle 12, Avenida 9.

Beyond Río Frío are more dirt roads—and train tracks! Suddenly, you are no longer on the frontier, but in the former jungle penetrated by the railroad before it reached San José. There are great banana processing plants, with signs urging Standard Fruit workers to more productivity; banana tramways making their way through the vast banana fields, on bamboo supports; and papaya plantations. Places have names like Finca Seis, Finca Siete, Finca Ocho (Farm Six, Farm Seven, Farm Eight—romantic) and general-issue tan concrete-block housing. Where the banana plants do not come up to and lean into the road, eerie, tall, ferny bamboo stands lie to either side. Bananas on tramways and railroads have an easier go of it than people: it is easy to lose your way in this world until itself, where one rutted, narrow, bumpy road branches from another much like it, without any signs.

The twelve kilometers from Río Frío to the junction with the paved highway to San José take nearly an hour to negotiate. Then it's an easy ride back to the capital, through the high rain forest of Carrillo Park (see page 108), or to Limón on the Caribbean coast.

Travel Information

GETTING TO COSTA RICA

BY AIR

From the United States, San José is served directly by LACSA, the Costa Rican airline (from Miami, New York and Los Angeles), and Eastern Air Lines and Pan American from Miami. With a change of plane, you can also travel on TAN-SAHSA airlines from Houston, New Orleans or Miami, or on Mexicana from Los Angeles.

Various airlines also fly to San José from all the Central American capitals. LACSA operates flights from San Juan, Puerto Rico, by way of Colombia and Panama. And there are flights to the Colombian island of San Andrés, and weekly service by KLM from Europe.

Fares. Currently, a one-way ticket from Miami to San José costs about $225. A round-trip economy excursion ticket costs about $360. From New York or Los Angeles, round-trip fare is about $600. But these figures are just starting points in the complicated world of airline fares.

There are several possible strategies to improve on the basic price. Midweek fares and low-season travel are sometimes a better deal.

Consider stopovers. On TAN-SAHSA, for the same price as a direct ticket from Miami to San José, you can stop over in Belize, for a visit to the offshore cayes and the archeological sites, or in San Pedro Sula, for an excursion to the Bay Islands. TAN-SAHSA has excursion fares from most large American cities, in conjunction with other airlines. For information, dial 800-327-1225 or 305-526-4300. On Lacsa (tel. 800-225-2272), you can stop in Guatemala if you're travelling from New York, or in Mexico City or Guatemala on the way from Los Angeles.

Or, buy a package that includes hotel accommodations, and get your ticket at a reduced price. If your local travel agent doesn't have anything to offer, take a look at the list of travel agents a few pages ahead. You needn't limit yourself to pre-arranged packages. You can even take advantage of package fares by booking budget accommodations for only part of your stay. You might have to contact the hotel first and ask for its itinerary number, to hand on to your travel agent.

Shop around among travel agents. Some are more adept than others at structuring lower fares.

Charter flights from Canada are operated by Fiesta Holidays in Toronto and Go Travel in Montreal during the winter months. One-week flight-and-hotel packages are available for as little as $600 (Canadian funds). Currently, very few charters operate from the States.

Remember that you may have to show an onward or return ticket to satisfy the immigration authorities in San José.

Tickets purchased in Costa Rica are subject to a 10 percent sales tax, and in most cases must be paid for in dollars.

DRIVING

The shortest highway distance from Brownsville, Texas, to San José, Costa Rica, is about 2250 miles. For the vast majority of travelers, who have limited vacation time, it's simply not worthwhile to consider driving, with six borders to cross, difficult mountain roads, and fears of political turmoil and breakdowns en route.

However . . . if you're going south for the winter, if you're planning to spend time elsewhere in Central America as well, if you're camping, if you happen to be continuing onward to South America, or if your vehicle is simply indispensable, driving may be indicated. Rest assured that getting to Costa Rica is eminently possible.

Your major requirement is a vehicle in good shape. Have it checked out, tuned up and greased before you leave home.

Replace cracked or withering belts and hoses, bald tires and rusting brake lines. If you're planning extensive travel off the main roads, consider taking a couple of spare tires, a gasoline can, water for you and the radiator, points, plugs, electrical tape, belts, wire, and basic tools. Otherwise, there's no reason to prepare for a safari, and the family sedan will serve you well. Be prepared to disconnect your catalytic converter south of Mexico, where unleaded gasoline is not available.

Avoid extra fees by crossing borders during regular business hours, generally from 8 a.m. to noon and from 2 p.m. to 6 p.m. It's prudent to travel during daylight hours only, to avoid stray animals and inebriated humans. Fill your tank whenever you can—gas stations can be few and far between. Plan your route to avoid transiting El Salvador—a direct crossing from Guatemala to Honduras is possible.

Essential documents for entry to any Central American country are your driver's license, vehicle registration, and passport with visa. Liability insurance is available in each country you cross. Coverage for damage to your own vehicle may not be available.

Vehicle permits for Costa Rica are issued at the border, are valid for 30 days, and *may not be renewed.* Drivers wishing to stay longer must take their vehicles out of the country for two days.

Maps of Mexico and Central America are available from your local automobile club.

BUS

The disadvantages of bus travel all the way to Costa Rica are obvious—long hours in a sitting position, inconvenient connections, border delays, and much else. You can, however, see much along the way, and the price is right. Total fare from the U.S. border to Costa Rica is well under $100, and this can be reduced by using less comfortable, slower, second-class local buses. Overland travel will require that you pick up visas in advance for all the countries you'll be transiting.

Some specifics: First-class buses, similar to those used by Greyhound, operate from all U.S. border points to Mexico City, a trip of from 10 hours to two days, depending on your crossing point. Buses of the Cristóbal Colón line depart Mexico City at least twice daily for the Guatemalan border, sixteen hours away, connecting with buses for Guatemala City. From there, the Tica Bus line provides through service to Costa Rica, or you can take Galgos and connect with various other first-class lines. The trip through Mexico may be shortened by following the Gulf coast route from eastern Texas, avoiding Mexico City.

TRAVEL AGENCIES

Your regular travel agent might not be familiar with Costa Rica. Here is a *partial* list of companies that specialize in travel to Costa Rica in one way or another, or that run tours to Costa Rica with some frequency in collaboration with operators in San José.

Agencies with general knowledge of Costa Rica

These companies can sell you air tickets, and to some degree arrange individual travel in Costa Rica. Most other agencies will handle set tour packages.

Americas Tours and Travel, 1218 Third Ave., Seattle, WA 98101, tel.800-553-2513.

Costa Rica Travel, 732 W. Fullerton Parkway, Chicago, IL 60614.

Odyssey Costa Rica, 3350 Wilshire Blvd., Suite 347, Los Angeles, CA 90010, tel. 800-548-6554 or 213-383-9226

Nature and Wildlife Travel, and General Interest Tours

There's some overlap here, as most general tours to Costa Rica include nature-oriented excursions. This is a small selection from many agencies.

Adventure Outback, 3158 Maple Dr., Atlanta, GA 30305, tel. 800-633-6292.

Natural History Tours, P. O. Box 1089, Lake Helen, FL 32744-1089, tel. 904-228-3356.

Extraordinary Expeditions, 1793 Via Rancho, San Lorenzo, CA 94580, tel. 415-276-1569.

International Expeditions, 1776 Independence Ct., Birmingham, AL 35216, tel. 800-633-4734.

Mountain Travel, 1398 Solano Ave., Albany, CA 94706.

Oceanic Society Expeditions, Fort Mason Center, Building E, San Francisco, CA 94123, tel. 415-441-1106.

PCI Tours, 8405 N.W. 53 St., Miami, FL, tel. 800-255-2508.

Overseas Adventure Travel, 349 Broadway, Cambridge, MA 02139, tel. 617-876-0533.

Preferred Travel Service of St. Paul, Robert at 4th St., St. Paul, MN 55101, tel. 612-224-7655.

Quester's Tours and Travel, 257 Park Ave. So., New York, NY 10010.

Special Expeditions, 720 Fifth Avenue, New York, NY 10019, tel. 800-762-0003.

Costa Rica Travel, 544 Fraser Ave., Ottawa, Ontario K2A 2R4.

Rafting

Mariah Wilderness Expeditions, P.O. Box 248, Point Richmond, CA 94807, tel. 800-4-MARIAH or 415-233-2303.

Baja Expeditions, 2625 Garnet Ave., San Diego, CA 92109, tel. 800-843-6967 or 619-581-3311.

Canoandes Expeditions, 310 Madison Ave., New York, NY 10017.

Fishing

PanAngling Travel, 180 N. Michigan Ave., Chicago, IL 60601.

Dockside Fishing and Hunting, 7720 Zimpel St., New Orleans, LA 70118.

World Wide Sportsman, P. O. Drawer 787, Islamorada, FL 33036, tel. 800-327-2880 or 305-664-8833.

Parismina Tarpon Rancho, P. O. Box 290190, San Antonio, TX 78280, tel. 800-531-7232.

Phantom Isle, Box 559, Manvel, TX 77578, tel. 713-489-9156.

Diving

See and Sea Travel, 50 Francisco St., San Francisco, Ca 94133.

Diving Safaris, 7210 Jordan Ave., Canoga Park, CA 91303.

Horseback Riding
FITS Equestrian Tours, 2011 Alamo Pintura Rd., Solvang, CA 93462

If none of the above give you satisfaction or meet your price criterion, take a look at the travel agencies listed in the San José chapter of this book. Most have personnel who can speak some English. A telephone call or two to reserve day trips could be well worth the cost.

ENTERING COSTA RICA

First, a caution. It's always a good idea to re-check entry requirements, with either a Costa Rican consulate or a reliable travel agent, before you leave home. Call the Costa Rican Tourist Board (see page 272) for the location of the nearest consulate. Recent regulations:

Citizens of the United States must have a tourist card or a passport and visa to enter Costa Rica.

Tourist cards are issued at the check-in counter by airlines serving Costa Rica, as well as by Costa Rican consulates, upon presentation of a birth certificate, passport, or other substantial identification. Tourist cards cost $2 and are valid for 30 days. Monthly extensions to up to six months from date of entry may be obtained at the immigration department in San José (see below).

Visas are issued at no charge by Costa Rican consulates. Visa holders also must apply for permission to stay in Costa Rica for more than 30 days. Visas are required for overland travel to Costa Rica.

Canadians may enter Costa Rica with only a passport when travelling on a charter flight directly from Canada. Some airlines, for their own protection, may insist that Canadians purchase tourist cards when making connections in the States. In either case, entry is authorized initially for 30 days.

Travelers from countries of Western Europe can also enter Costa Rica with a passport and no visa, as can citizens of Colombia, Panama, Yugoslavia, Argentina, Japan, Brazil and Romania.

Travelers from most other countries, and all business travelers, must have a passport and visa. Check with your airline or a Costa Rican consulate for requirements.

All tourists may be required to demonstrate their financial resources upon arrival, as well as show a return or onward ticket.

Note that Costa Rican immigration officials are sensitive to appearance, both at entry points and at headquarters in San José. A sprucing-up will help your case.

Land borders are officially open from 6:30 a.m. to 10 p.m., with breaks from 11 a.m. to 12:30 p.m. and from 5:30 p.m. to 6:30 p.m.

EXTENDING YOUR STAY

To stay in Costa Rica beyond the period initially authorized (usually 30 days), you must exit the privileged world of the casual visitor. Changing regulations, whim and lineups can take a heavy toll on your time and patience.

If you are even thinking about staying longer than thirty days, it would be a good idea to get in touch with a Costa Rican consulate before you leave home, and review current regulations regarding travel with children, tests for AIDS, financial means, and anything else you or they can think of.

Permission to extend your stay must be requested from the immigration department (Migración), Calle 21, Avenidas 6/8, San José. Take three passport-sized photos (there are handy photo shops nearby), and be prepared to show several hundred dollars in travelers checks and your ticket home. There are modest fees to pay as well. Revenue stamps to attach to your application can be bought at a booth on the street outside. The extension takes several days to process.

If you overstay your tourist card or visa without first getting an extension, you'll have to pay a fine at immigration before you can leave the country.

Longer stays, student visas, residencies and special situations usually require the intervention of a lawyer, and extensive paperwork that can take months or even years to complete. Really, it's an endorsement of the country, or a demonstration of masochism, that so many hang in there.

CUSTOMS

Visitors are allowed to enter Costa Rica with any used personal possessions that they will reasonably need, including sporting equipment. Items unfamiliar to customs inspectors, including medical items, could be taxed heavily. The exemption for new merchandise is $100 of customs duty. New merchandise may include up to three liters of liquor, one pound of tobacco, and six rolls of film.

RETURNING HOME

U.S. Customs allows an exemption of $400 per person in goods, including one quart of liquor and 200 cigarettes. Canadian residents may use their once-yearly $300 exemption, or their $100 quarterly exemption for goods brought home, with a limit of 1.1 liters of liquor and 200 cigarettes.

Costa Rica prohibits the export of pre-Columbian artifacts. In practice, there is a black market in these items, and there is limited official concern for pieces of little artistic value. One should be careful, however, not least because many artifacts are phony. Items made from protected species, such as turtles and alligators, could also get you into hot water, or at least be confiscated.

GETTING AROUND

BY AIR

Costa Rica's domestic airline, Sansa, operates flights to a number of outlying towns from Juan Santamaría International Airport. Fares are a bargain: $20 or less to any point with scheduled service. And you only have to check in at Sansa's San José office. The airline takes you out to the airport in its own van. Sansa even has a bargain-priced tour operation (see page 84).

Sansa's flights save a lot of the wear and tear involved in overland travel. Even if you like to see things at ground level, they provide an easy lift back to San José. The only drawbacks are insufficient flights to a limited number of destinations, and, occasionally, separation of passengers from their luggage.

Latest destinations and flight frequencies are: to Quepos, Golfito, Coto 47 and Palmar, six times weekly; to Tamarindo and Sámara, three times weekly; to Barra del Colorado, twice weekly.

Recent schedules are given in coverage of towns in this book. For latest schedules and fares, contact the Sansa office at Calle 24, between Paseo Colón and Avenida 1, San José, tel. 333258.

Charter flights in small planes are also available from Tobías Bolaños airport (just west of San José) to places without regularly scheduled service, such as Tortuguero National Park. Arrange such flights through travel agencies, or directly through the companies listed in the yellow pages under "Aviación."

BY BUS

There are several tiers of bus service in Costa Rica. Depending on where you are in the country and how far you're going, getting around by bus can be pleasant and comfortable, tolerable, or—if you're not prepared—an ordeal.

Service between towns in the Central Valley is provided by large buses similar to those used on the city lines in San José. These generally have padded seats, which are closer together than those in comparable American buses, but comfortable enough for the distances involved.

Fares on suburban routes are generally fixed, no matter how far you travel. Fare cards are usually posted near the driver's seat.

Buses in the Central Valley may be boarded either at their terminals, or at bus stops, which are marked either by shelters, rectangular signs, or short yellow lines painted along the edge of the road. Pay the driver, choose a seat, and enjoy the sights along the way.

Buses operating on the major highways between San José and the far points of the country are roughly comparable to Greyhound buses in the United States. They may be older, and lack air conditioning and lavatories, but they are generally well-cared-for, and mechanically sound.

Drivers of long-distance buses try to maintain the maximum legal speed, even on winding roads. Bus crews are ready for such side effects as nausea with plastic bags (comforting). Prepare yourself with motion sickness pills if you're susceptible.

Tickets for long-distance buses may be purchased in advance, and this is recommended for weekend travel. If you try to board a long-distance bus along its route, it might or might not stop—there's no fixed rule. Try to select a waiting place where the driver will see you well in advance and have a chance to slow down. Ask a handy local for advice.

Buses operating in rural areas outside the Central Valley are of an entirely different breed. Most are similar to American school buses. Some in fact *are* old school buses, right down to the yellow paint. (Old school buses never die. They just go to Central America.) Seats are stiff, with minimal padding, designed for small people traveling short distances.

Rural buses stop frequently to let out and pick up passengers, as well as chickens, cardboard boxes full of merchandise, and whatever else has to move. Add poor roads and steep grades, and a trip of fifty kilometers could take a couple of hours. Many a passenger has to stand in a crowded aisle, for there is often no other way to go.

Country people in Costa Rica are used to conditions on buses, and may even doze off, despite the bouncing and shaking and cramped quarters. Without precautions, however, the visitor may find rural bus trips excruciating. Some tips for enjoying, or at least surviving, your trip:

Look for a place where you can stretch your legs. The seat behind the driver is usually best. If it's not available, try an aisle seat, even if this costs you some views. Get to the bus terminal early to be sure of getting a seat at all.

Sit toward the front of the bus—the shaking is always worse at the rear.

By all means, go to the bathroom before you get on the bus (nobody else will tell you this), and don't drink too much coffee or any other liquid before you set out.

Rural buses will generally stop anyplace you flag them down. Pay the driver or his helper, and call out "*¡parada!*" to get the bus to stop.

Fares on all buses in Costa Rica are low, generally less than two cents (U.S.) per kilometer.

AUTOMOBILE

Driving your own car makes a small country significantly smaller—but not without a price. Gasoline prices and car rental rates (see below) are about twice those in the United States.

In the Central Valley, expressways connect the major towns. Roads are well marked with standard rectangular signs. In the center of any town, signs point the way toward the next towns in all directions, and usually indicate distances. Hazard signs use easily understood symbols.

Main routes outside the Central Valley are also well marked, but secondary roads are not. Navigation is made even more difficult by the lack of accurate, up-to-date road maps. Ask directions at junctions if you have any doubts. Gasoline stations (*bombas*) are sparse, so fill up before turning off any main route. While you're at it, inquire about road conditions ahead, especially in the rainy season, and interpret the response with caution. Costa Ricans will usually tell you that a road is passable. Gringos will say that you can't make it after a heavy rain, what with swollen rivers and mud up to your axles. The truth lies somewhere in between, and depends on what you're driving.

Off the paved roads, and sometimes on them, much of your attention is devoted to dodging potholes, or it should be. Conditions are generally worst toward the end of the rainy season. Many roads are graded but once a year. Consider December 1 as the end of mud season for driving the dirt roads of Costa Rica.

Costa Rica's mountain roads are probably more winding than any you're used to. Beep your horn at curves and drive at moderate speeds. The driver going up a hill has the right of way, so be prepared to pull over or back up on narrow stretches.

Other assorted hazards include herds of cattle in the road, driven by cowboys on horses or bicycles; slow-moving trucks; and drunks in the right of way.

The speed limit on the open road is 75 kilometers (47 miles) an hour, and it's seriously enforced, in an attempt to cut down the accident rate. I got my first speeding ticket ever in Costa Rica—the radar clocked me at a blazing 91 kilometers per hour on the flat, straight highway from Limón to San José. You can also get a ticket for not using your seat belt. The worst part is waiting in line at a bank to pay the fine—and pay you must, or risk being turned back at the airport.

Be sure to stop at roadside checkpoints if you're flagged down. It's usually nothing sinister. The police might be looking for contraband turtle eggs, not firearms.

Many auto parts are hard to obtain outside of San José. Try to have your car serviced and repairs made in the capital or nearby. Parts for some makes of car are simply not stocked in Costa Rica, but drivers of most Japanese and smaller American cars should have no problems in this regard.

Car Rental: The smallest cars—the Subaru Justy or equivalent—rent for about $21 daily plus 21 cents per kilometer, or $48 at the unlimited mileage rate with a minimum rental of three days, including insurance. These vehicles are comfortable only for two adults, and are worse than useless on many unpaved roads during the rainy season. A compact car that will fit four adults goes for about $52 per day, or $56 with automatic transmission, while a four-wheel drive vehicle—almost essential for the Nicoya Peninsula, or a trip to Monteverde—comes in at $64 a day. Add in gasoline—roughly $8 for 200 kilometers of driving in a Justy, $20 or more in a Jeep.

Lower rates are sometimes offered when you reserve in advance. I did this once through Budget, though upon arrival I encountered mysterious service charges (I refused to pay), bait-and-switch insurance sales ("your mandatory insurance provides no protection, sir"), and much wasted time—on my meter—while we attempted to come to a consensus about pre-existing damage. But I'm told that similar tactics are used by other companies. In any case, you probably won't get a price break at the moment of renting, so it doesn't hurt to call around before you leave home. Inquire too if your own insurance policy or one that comes with your credit card will cover damage to a rented car in Costa Rica. If so, try to get a statement to that effect in writing.

240

TAXIS

It doesn't occur to most people, but taxis are a very practical way to get around the countryside in Costa Rica. Current official rates are about 70 cents for the first kilometer, 25 cents for each additional kilometer, and $3 per hour of waiting time. For trips over 12 kilometers, the driver is allowed to negotiate the charge. At the official rate, a 120-kilometer round trip from San José to Poás volcano should run less than $30, including a couple of hours of waiting. Even if you're charged more, the cost should compare favorably to that of renting a car. In addition, you'll be able to look around instead of keeping your eyes glued to the road, and can direct the driver to slow down or stop where you please.

Travel by taxi is not without its problems. Many drivers are used to overcharging tourists, sometimes by claiming that their meters don't work. Look for a driver who will agree to charge the legal rates (which your hotel can confirm), or at least not too much more.

For long-distance travel, of course, you'll want to use airplanes or comfortable buses. But taxis are a good bet for going those last few kilometers in rural areas. In the Nicoya Peninsula and other areas with poor roads, taxis are usually Jeeps or similar vehicles well suited to local conditions.

TRAINS

Costa Rica's "jungle train," from San José to Limón, is world-famous. A passenger-and-cargo line also runs from the capital to Puntarenas. See pages 80 and 122-127 for details.

BICYCLE

Bicycle tours within Costa Rica's national parks are offered by the Horizontes travel agency in San José. The company supplies mountain bikes, though according to experienced cycle tourist and author J. P. Panet, riding a bike other than your own can be a painful experience.

TOURS AND PACKAGES

Descriptions of the tours that you may book when in Costa Rica are given in the coverage of San José in this book.

Packages of hotel, meal and tour arrangements that you arrange when you buy your airplane ticket vary from three-night plans that cover only your hotel and a city tour of San José, for $50 per person, to complete arrangements for a week or more of hotels, meals, excursions to the coasts, volcano trips, and/or fishing. Low-priced packages allow you to take advantage of cheaper fares. The more complete packages, of course, spare you much planning and attention to details, and running around during what is supposed to be your vacation. They might save you a few dollars as well.

Packages are best booked through a travel agent. If yours is not familiar with Costa Rica, request information from the Costa Rica Tourist Board (see page 272) or LACSA Airlines (tel. 800-225-2272). For special-interest programs, such as rafting, birding or horseback-riding, contact one of the agencies listed earlier in this chapter, or in the coverage of San José (page 82).

ASSORTED PRACTICAL INFORMATION

BUSINESS HOURS

Businesses generally open at 8:30 or 9 a.m., close for a couple of hours starting at 11:30 a.m. or noon, then open for the afternoon from 1:30 or 2 p.m. until 6 p.m. On Saturdays, many businesses are open in the morning only. Continuous hours, without the midday break, are becoming more common at the larger stores in San José. In the hotter lowlands along the Atlantic and Pacific, stores open earlier, and the midday break is longer. You'll soon get used to doing your shopping before or after the break, or rest (*descanso*), which, by the way, is rarely called a siesta.

During December, as Christmas bonuses are spent, normal hours are abandoned, and many stores remain open throughout the day, and even on Sunday morning.

BUREAUCRACY

(This comes first alphabetically, but I didn't want to start this section on an unpleasant note.)

All countries have their problems—natural disasters, human rights violations, racial tensions, refugees, whatever. Costa Rica has its bureaucracy. When you put it in perspective, it seems a minor matter. To deal with it, however, is deadly.

Costa Ricans are used to runarounds and frustrations in government and commerce. Processing insurance claims, obtaining non-emergency health care, and receiving payments for officially marketed crops all can involve inexplicable delays. Seekers of licenses must peck patiently at the roosts of officialdom. Labor inspectors, hotel inspectors, transport inspectors, tax inspectors meticulously go through their motions. Queues as orderly as any in London form at bus stops, government offices, and even at the entrances to supermarkets. Standing in line is an honorable profession and source of employment in Costa Rica. Many businesses have one or more *mensajeros* (messengers) for this purpose. Their badge of office is a motorcycle helmet.

Visitors may think they are exempt from engagement with the domestic bureaucratic mentality, and in most cases they are. Some exposure, however, is inevitable. See "Money and Banking," below, for an example.

CALENDARS

Some Costa Rican holidays, such as Christmas and Easter, will be known to most visitors. But you can't be expected to be aware of a favorite saint's special day. Take a quick look at the list of public holidays below. If any occur while you're in Costa Rica, don't plan to get anything done on that day except relaxing.

January 1	New Year's Day
March 19	Day of St. Joseph (San José)
Moveable	Holy Thursday
Moveable	Good Friday (Many businesses close all Holy Week)
April 11	Battle of Rivas
May 1	Labor Day
Moveable	Corpus Christi
June 29	Day of Saints Peter and Paul
July 25	Annexation of Guanacaste
August 2	Day of Our Lady of the Angels (specially celebrated in Cartago)
August 15	Assumption Day
September 15	Independence Day
October 12	Columbus Day (*Día de la Raza*)
December 8	Immaculate Conception
December 24, 25	Christmas Eve and Christmas
December 31	New Year's Eve

In addition to the above, all towns celebrate the feast day of their patron saint—San Marcos (St. Mark) on April 25, Santiago (St. James the Apostle) on July 25, etc. Images of the patron saint are borne from the town church in processions, but most of the celebrants' efforts go into the parades of masked figures, raffles, bingo, dances, banquets, drinking and benign bullfights that make these occasions breaks from the humdrum round of chores. And the Christmas-New Year season is a time of extended street celebration everywhere, especially in San José.

CHILDREN

Costa Rica is one of the more benign countries to which you can take children. Health and sanitary standards are acceptable, there are sights and activities for kids as well as grown-ups, and few people give you funny looks if you take children to restaurants, museums, or anywhere else.

Children need their own identification for immigration purposes. If there is any chance that you and your child will stay over 30 days, contact a Costa Rican consulate about applicable regulations and procedures, before you leave home.

Special health concerns for children are few. If you're going to spend time at the beach, make sure that your child gets plenty to drink, and limit exposure to the sun. In general, follow the same precautions for children as for adults (see a few pages ahead).

Pack clothing items similar to those for adults. As well, take a few books and toys (the latter are expensive locally), including a pail and shovel for the beach. Take baby wipes for quick cleanups.

For babies, take changing supplies and bottle-feeding equipment, if needed. Disposable diapers are available in Costa Rica, but cost double what they do in the States, so you might want to pack these, too. A stroller is useful in the cities, a cloth carrier at the beach. Cribs are available in most of the better hotels and you should be able to improvise in the few cases where you won't find them.

Gerber baby foods (instant cereals and strained vegetables and meat) are manufactured in Costa Rica, and are sold in pharmacies and supermarkets in San José and the larger towns. Other readily available food items for babies include canned condensed milk, canned fruit juice, cheeses, fruits, and powdered formulas.

With kids in tow, you'll spend considerable time in your hotel room. Be more selective than you might otherwise be. A television in the room and a swimming pool are attractive amenities for the kids, even if you don't need them for yourself.

Hotels in Costa Rica rarely charge for children up to three years old. Older children will pay a small extra-bed charge, or half the adult rate if meals are included.

CLIMATE

Despite tropical latitudes, climate in Costa Rica varies from near-frigid to humid and sweltering, according to the influence of mountain barriers, altitude and prevailing winds.

The highland climate of the major cities—San José, Cartago, Heredia and Alajuela—is often called "eternal spring," a term that is not used merely to attract tourists. Temperatures are in the low seventies Fahrenheit (about 22 Centigrade) during the day throughout the year. High mountains and volcanoes to the north of San José block the clouds that blow in from the Atlantic, and it rains only from April to November or December, when winds are from the Pacific. But a long rainy day is a rarity in the Central Valley. Mornings are generally clear, followed by a few hours of heavy downpour in the afternoon. Sometimes the rain can last into the night. Clouds hold in the heat of the day, and nights are generally warm. The rainy season is called *invierno* (winter), even though Costa Rica is in the northern hemisphere. In the dry times, or *verano* (summer), days are uniformly warm and sunny. Nights are clear, and the temperature may sometimes drop into the fifties (about 10 Centigrade).

Down toward the Pacific coast, the climate is hotter. In Puntarenas, daytime temperatures are in the nineties (above 32 degrees Centigrade) throughout the year. But at the beaches, refreshing breezes moderate the heat. The rainy season is the same as in the Central Valley, but precipitation is heavier. The exceptions are the extreme north and extreme south. The Guanacaste plain suffers periodic droughts, which bother farmers more than visitors. And around Golfito, near Panama, peculiarities in the mountains and winds bring rains throughout the year.

On the Atlantic slope of Costa Rica, storms may blow in at any time, though rainfall is lightest from February through April. Precipitation is over ten feet at Limón in most years, and even higher to the north. Storms appear suddenly and with a frightening fury, but they are usually quickly gone. Temperatures are generally as hot on the Caribbean as on the Pacific, and the humidity is more enervating.

The higher altitudes are cooler. Frosts occur above 2150 meters (7000 feet) during the dry season. And atop volcanoes and in the Talamanca mountains, temperatures may plunge from warm to below freezing in a few hours.

Keep the climate in mind when you pack for your visit. Take a raincoat or umbrella if you'll be outdoors a lot during the rainy season, or if you're heading toward the Caribbean. Taking shelter from the rain for a few hours, however, is no special inconvenience, and during the dry season, around San José and along most of the Pacific, not even the thought of rain occurs.

COST OF LIVING

It will be obvious from prices mentioned in this book that travel expenses in Costa Rica are moderate. Middle-range hotel rooms cost $40 to $50 double in San José, but clean, airy rooms are available for as little as $20 for two. Outside San José, except at deluxe beach hotels, room rates are generally lower.

Four dollars or less will buy a basic, wholesome meal in San José, while a gourmet-quality repast may carry a tab of $15 or more, not including wine, which is expensive. Outside the Central Valley, fine cuisine is usually not available.

While automobile ownership and maintenance are expensive (except for retired foreigners, who may import a car duty-free), public transport is not. The bus fare from San José to any border point is less than $10. Scheduled flights in small planes cost less than $20 to the most distant towns. Hiring a taxi costs about the same as renting a car, or less.

Foreigners who live in Costa Rica find that they save considerable amounts on services and housing, and on the heavy clothing and other items that they can live without because of the mild climate.

Heating and air conditioning are unnecessary in most well-built houses in San José. Many a comfortable home has a fireplace more for esthetic than practical reasons. Lower land taxes and insurance rates further reduce fixed costs. Electric rates are not the bargain they once were, but with fewer appliances, consumption is generally much lower than in North America. Household workers are generally paid $125 per month, or less.

Houses cost roughly half what they do in the United States, sometimes less. But comparisons in this respect are imperfect. The housing market has its ups and downs in Costa Rica as in other countries, and construction methods are different. Most houses come without the appliances and built-in closets and cabinets that one expects in the States, and electrical wiring and plumbing standards are lower. However, better-quality construction is available, and I have seen some condominium units in San José that would make an American apartment dweller cry in envy.

Rental housing is reasonably priced. Two-bedroom apartments with some furnishings start at about $300 per month in middle-class neighborhoods, though in exclusive areas the tab can be much, much higher.

The crunch, when it comes, is in consumer goods. Tape recorders, home computers, cameras, watches, appliances, and almost every other imported, manufactured item costs double to triple what it does in the States. Clothing of local manufacture is priced slightly higher than similar American items, and variety is limited. Cosmetics, whether locally made or imported, are pricey.

At the supermarkets, many packaged and processed items cost more than in the States, while fresh foods cost the same or less. By adjusting eating patterns, one can usually end up with a lower food bill.

Here is a rather unscientific sampling of prices for grocery and non-grocery items at a San José supermarket:

Meat, one-third less than U.S. prices, or lower; fish, one-half to same; cosmetics and diapers, double or higher; local canned foods, same to one-half more; imported canned foods, double or more; eggs, one-half higher; coffee, two-thirds less; dairy products, slightly less; beer, slightly less; fruit and vegetables in season, same to two-thirds less; Gerber baby foods, same to double. Some specific recent prices: cigarettes, 70 to 90 cents per pack; local brands of liquor, $3 per 750 ml bottle; imported wines, $6 and up for a bottle of drinkable French wine, slightly less for Italian or Chilean brands; Scotch whiskey, $10 and up; Spanish brandy, $20; imported American peanut butter, $5 for a 12-ounce jar; sirloin steak, $2 per pound.

In general, persons who are not too attached to mechanical gadgets and pre-packaged, processed foods can maintain a comfortable standard of living for less than in the United States.

ELECTRICITY

Electrical supply is at 110 volts, alternating current, throughout Costa Rica. Sockets are of the American type, usually without provision for a grounding prong. Non-grounded American and Canadian appliances should work without adapters. However, it's always wise to ask about the voltage in your hotel before you plug anything in. In remote locations, such as fishing camps, generators may operate on a non-standard voltage.

FISHING

The marvels of sport fishing in the mountain streams and off both coasts of Costa Rica are still a recent discovery, at least for non-Costa Ricans. Stocks of fish are plentiful, and records are regularly approached, and broken.

On the Caribbean side of Costa Rica, the most notorious species is the pesky and finicky tarpon. Tarpon are caught between January and June in rivers, lagoons and estuaries, and weigh as much as 100 pounds. Other species common to the Caribbean are snook, usually weighing over 25 pounds; the smaller, bass-like machaca and guapote; mojarra, which resembles a bluegill; and shark, mackerel, mullet and jack crevalle. All are found in inland waters, even shark. Deep sea fishing in the Caribbean is limited by the unpredictability of storms.

On the Pacific side, black and blue marlins of up to 1000 pounds are the big attractions, along with sailfish, roosterfish, dolphin, wahoo, rainbow runner, barracuda, a variety of snappers, and jacks, pompano, shark, swordfish, yellowfin tuna, bonito, dorado (mahi-mahi), grouper and corvina, or sea bass. The smaller fish are found in river mouths and estuaries, the larger species out in blue water.

Inland, some of Costa Rica's mountain streams hold trout and smaller fish. The season is May and June for fly fishing, December through March for spoon fishing.

Fishing equipment is in short supply, so serious anglers should bring their own gear. Your fishing camp or resort will recommend specific types of rods, reels and line when you reserve. For tarpon fishing—the big attraction on the Caribbean coast—six- to seven-foot rods with 12- to 20-pound line are used. Reels should hold 200 yards of line. For snook and fly fishing, 10- to 12-pound line is enough. Lighter gear is sufficient for guapote and trout in fresh water. For deep-sea fishing, everything is usually provided by the fishing camp or boat operator.

A permit is required for fishing. If you book a week at a fishing camp, the management will probably take care of this detail. Otherwise, you'll have to buy a permit at the Banco Central (Calle 2, Avenidas Central/1, San José). For offshore fishing, present it for validation with two passport photos to the fishing office (Oficina de Pesca) of the Ministry of Agriculture, Old La Salle Building, La Sabana, San José, office number 33. For river fishing, the permit is validated at the Wildlife Office (Sub Dirección de Vida Silvestre) at Calle 17, Avenidas Central/2, San José, tel. 338112.

For the location of sport fishing operations, see the index of this book under "Fishing."

FLORA AND FAUNA

Costa Rican flora and fauna, and tropical flora and fauna in general, are too varied to be treated justly in a small section of this book, or even in a few books devoted exclusively to the subject. Botanists refer to the natural exuberance of the tropics as "species richness." An area that supports two or three types of trees in the temperate zones might lodge dozens or even hundreds of plant species from ground level to forest canopy in the tropics. Some dimensions of this natural abundance in Costa Rica: More than 2000 species of tree have so far been catalogued, twice as many as in the continental United States. Two-thirds of all known seed plants are found in Costa Rica. And there are over 1000 orchids, ranging from the guaria morada, the purple national flower, down to those with blossoms too tiny to be casually noticed; more than 800 species of fern; and so on, and so on.

One explanation of this variety takes into account the poverty of many tropical soils, which may encourage plants to adapt to compete for nourishment at all levels, up to the tops of the tallest trees. Some draw nutrients from the soil, others feed themselves by sending roots into neighboring plants as parasites, or by capturing dust and decay washed down by rain. All nutrients are continually recycled. Abundant water helps to make this many-tiered world possible. Plants take moisture from the earth, the rain, from pools in large leaves, and from the very humidity of the air around them.

This general tropical description applies to much of the Caribbean lowlands of Costa Rica, and to cloud forest at high elevations. The temperate central valley, with its grassy meadows, pine forests, and rich volcanic soil, will not appear exotic to most visitors. But even here, a number of trees flourish that are so unfamiliar as to be without names in English. The Pacific lowlands, also with rich soil, support their own varieties of forest, which vary according to rainfall.

Here is a rather random sample of wild and cultivated trees and plants found at different altitudes:

Sea level to 2000 feet: Palms (coconut, African oil, American oil, etc.), mangrove, mahogany, cedar, laurel, quinine, banana, rubber, walnut, guanacaste earpod, silk cotton (ceiba), cotton, cacao, sugarcane, rice, bamboo.

2000 to 6000 feet: coffee, corn, beans, pasture grass, wild fig (amate), orchids and bromeliads, citrus, avocado, mango, cactus, pomegranate, papaya.

6000 feet and higher: pine, fir (silvertree,etc.), cypress, alder, madrone, potato, peach, apple.

Many of the plant species of Costa Rica are described in *The National Parks of Costa Rica,* available in San José. Additional species are mentioned in the coverage of national parks in this book.

As a bridge between two continents, Costa Rica is home to animal forms both familiar and exotic. More than 750 species of bird inhabit Costa Rica, as many as in all of the United States. These range from common jays and orioles to large-beaked toucans and macaws, and the exquisite and elusive long-tailed quetzals of the trogon family. The national list includes 50 species of hummingbird, 45 tanagers and 72 flycatchers. A checklist of birds of Costa Rica is available for $2 from Natural History Tours, Box 1089, Lake Helen, FL 32744.

Monkeys abound, among them howler, spider, white-faced and the tiny marmoset. White-tailed deer, raccoons and rattlesnakes, all common in North America, live alongside their South American cousins, the brocket deer, coatimundi and bushmaster. Sea turtles, alligators, peccaries, tepezcuintles (pacas), jaguars, ocelots, pumas and many other "exotic" species are still not uncommon in parts of the country.

Paradoxically, many of these species are difficult to sight. In settled areas, native animals and plants have been wiped out by hunting, land-clearing and poaching. In less-settled areas, the lack of roads and trails keeps out the interested visitor. Fortunately, however, many species may be seen in Costa Rica's national parks.

FOOD

Costa Rica's food holds few surprises. Most restaurants in San José serve what they call "international cuisine," which is a combination of standard North American and European food. *Bistec* (beef), *pollo* (chicken) and *pescado* (fish) are most often encountered on the menu, usually in forms that need little explanation. Genuine native-style food is enjoyed at home, in a very rare city restaurant that advertises its *comida típica* (native food), in simple country eateries, and as snacks.

One of the most common plates in the countryside is *casado*, fish, meat or chicken married ("casado") to rice, beans, and chopped cabbage. *Gallo pinto*, rice and beans, is the staple of poor people's diets, usually served with *tortillas*, flat cakes made of ground, lime-soaked corn. But you don't have to be poor to enjoy the taste of black beans and tortillas, or of *olla de carne* (a stew of beef, yucca and plantain), *chiles rellenos* (stuffed peppers), *maduros,* or *plátanos fritos* (fried plantains), *chilasquiles* (meat-filled tortillas), *pozol* (corn soup), or *tamales* (corn dough with a filling of meat, rice and raisins, steamed in a banana leaf, and served at holiday times). You merely have to search these dishes out, if you're not part of a Costa Rican household. The Cocina de Leña is one San José restaurant that challenges the prejudice against eating Costa Rica's soul food in public.

Traditional snack foods are easier to find. Vendors sell *pan de yuca* (yucca bread), *gallos* (tortillas with fillings), *arreglados* (bread filled with meat and vegetables), *empanadas* (pastry stuffed with meat or some other filling), and various other starchy items at markets, on trains, and at bus terminals. Other favorite snacks are tropical fruits (papayas, bananas, passionfruit, pineapple and many others) sold from carts everywhere in the country, and *pipas*, young juice coconuts, as well as the juice of fruits and sugarcane (*agua dulce*). *Pejivalle*, a pasty palm fruit, and *palmito*, heart of palm, are enjoyed as hor d'oeuvres or in salad. *Cajeta,* a heavy milk fudge, is served sometimes as dessert, as it is in other Latin countries. Hot sauces and peppers—*chiles*—are condiments to be added as desired, and are rarely included in a dish before serving.

Costa Rica's excellent coffee, of course, is enjoyed with all meals, and is often prepared by pouring hot water through grounds held in a sock-like device. Costa Ricans claim all kinds of special properties for their brew—it won't keep you up at night, nor jangle your nerves, but will stimulate you to overall better functioning. This is only understandable chauvinism. Sometimes coffee is served with sugar already added—specify without (*sin azúcar*) if you prefer it that way. *Café con leche* (coffee with milk) is at least half milk. The concept of coffee with cream is understood only in hotels and restaurants that have a foreign clientele.

Gourmet restaurants in San José and nearby cook tender meats to order and serve them in delicate sauces along with crisp vegetables. Chinese, German, French, Italian, Swiss and even the better "international" restaurants produce superb results with foods that are fresh and abundant throughout the year. At the less expensive eateries in San José, and in the countryside, culinary arts and sciences are, unfortunately, not widely diffused. What you'll find can most generously be described as home-style cooking—wholesome, reasonably priced, but not finely prepared—comparable to the fare at Joe's Diner. A *bistec* (steak) will generally be a tough, nondescript slab of meat, served with some of the grease in which it was cooked. The fate of fresh seafood is often similar. Vegetables, other than rice, beans and cabbage, when they are served, will have been in the pot for too long. None of this will do you any harm, especially when you pay only three to four dollars for your meal.

Not that you won't find some pleasant surprises. At one anonymous roadside eatery near Cañas, I had the most exquisite gallo pinto, seasoned with fresh coriander and a hint of garlic, accompanied by a thin *bistec* smothered with onions. There, as elsewhere, the presence of truckers was a good sign. And at a few coastal resorts, standards are as high as in San José. But generally, when you leave the capital, you should lower your expectations.

Fortunately, almost every small town in Costa Rica has a Chinese restaurant, if not two or three, where *chao mein* (chow mein), chop suey and more elaborate plates tease bored palates. These restaurants are not gourmet-class, but they work interesting and edible combinations from Costa Rica's fresh vegetables and meats.

Service in Costa Rican restaurants is relaxed. You'll never be presented with a bill and ushered toward the cash register in order to make way for the next customer. The pleasures of lingering over nothing more than a pastry and a cup of coffee can still be enjoyed. If leisurely dining isn't what you have in mind, you'll have to call the waiter over to place your order, and to ask for the bill (*la cuenta*). A ten-percent tax and a ten-percent service charge will be added on. No additional tip is required.

Costa Rican eating and drinking habits in restaurants may be disorienting. As you have your morning coffee and bacon and eggs, the Tico to the left of you will be starting the day with a whiskey and a chicken sandwich. The Tico to the right of you will be cutting into a steak, accompanied by a beer. The Tico in front of you enjoys a rum and Coke while he ponders the menu. You are too polite (or dumbfounded) to turn to the Tico behind you.

I have no explanations for these customs, except to state that restaurant food is not necessarily derived from what is traditionally eaten at home. *You* were taught that eggs are eaten at breakfast. Maybe they were not. Explaining an affection for liquor is a touchy thing, but there is no doubt that Costa Ricans enjoy their booze in large quantities and at varied hours.

Much of what is consumed is *guaro*, which can be roughly translated as "hootch." Guaro is the cheapest liquor, distilled from sugarcane, and sold in bars for 40 and 80 cents a shot. Sugarcane is also the base for rums of various qualities and agings, some of them quite good. Most guaros and rums are distilled by a government-owned company, but other companies make quite drinkable vodkas and gins. Local whiskeys and liqueurs are also available, but their quality is not as high. The exception is Café Rica, a coffee liqueur, which costs more than other Costa Rican drinks. Imported alcoholic drinks are quite expensive (with the exception of whiskey, which is only moderately expensive at about $10 per fifth), so if you have a favorite brand, bring a bottle or two or three with you. Rum and Coke (Cuba Libre) is Costa Rica's most popular mixed drink.

Local fruit wines are interesting for amusement, but are not taken seriously by anyone who has enjoyed wine elsewhere. Imported wines are quite a luxury. Wine drinkers will have to fork out the money (a few duty-free bottles won't go very far), or else switch to another drink for the duration.

An excellent alternative to wine is beer. Pilsen is a superb brand of beer (in my opinion), and Tropical and Bavaria are almost as good. There are various others to suit different tastes, including a local version of Heineken, that is a ringer for the real thing, but for the health warning—*tomar licor es nocivo para la salud* (drinking liquor endangers health)— which all alcoholic beverages must carry. Beer is inexpensive—as little as 40 cents in some eateries, rarely more than $1. The alcohol content is four percent.

Bars are generally the cheapest places to drink, and they serve a dividend: *bocas*. These are hor d'oeuvres that range from cheese and crackers to little sandwiches that, over enough rounds, will constitute a meal in themselves. In classier joints, you pay for the bocas.

The easiest place to buy liquor, beer or wine is at a supermarket. In small towns with no supermarkets, try the bars themselves or small general stores (*pulperías*), though the selection will be more limited. The deposit on a beer or soda bottle is usually as much as the price of what's inside.

GOVERNMENT

The national government is divided into legislative, judicial and executive branches, each with substantial independence guaranteed by the 1949 constitution.

The president and two vice presidents are elected every four years. To control personal power, the constitution prohibits a president from succeeding himself, and bars certain high officials and close relatives of an incumbent from seeking the office. Incumbents may not take an active part in presidential campaigns, and control of the Civil Guard is turned over at election time to the Supreme Electoral Tribunal, which has broad powers to ensure the fairness of voting.

The Legislative Assembly consists of a single chamber whose deputies are elected for terms of four years by proportional representation. There is one deputy for approximately every 30,000 inhabitants in each province.

The judicial system consists of a Supreme Court and lower courts. Judges are appointed by the legislature. Minor matters in small towns are taken before the mayor or local police agent.

Administratively, Costa Rica is divided into provinces, cantons and districts. The seven provinces are divisions of the central government, with appointed governors. The 80 cantons are local governmental units administered by elected councils. Districts are subdivisions of cantons.

Public order is maintained by civil guards, rural guards, and municipal police. Some units of the civil guard are, in fact, quite military, with helmets, battle fatigues, and anti-infiltration training, while a rural guardsman's daily uniform may consist of Acapulco tourist shirt, sunglasses, and blue jeans with pistol stuffed in the waistband.

HEALTH CONCERNS

The health worries that usually accompany a trip to Latin America—mad dashes to the bathroom, general malaise as unknown microbes attack your insides, long-forgotten diseases like typhoid turning up in the best hotels—hardly apply to Costa Rica, where sanitary standards are generally high and most people are educated enough to have an idea of how disease spreads. Good sense and normal caution should be enough to see you through Costa Rica in good health.

No special inoculations or vaccinations are required or recommended for visitors to Costa Rica. You should, however, get your health affairs in order before you travel. Catch up on immunizations, such as those for tetanus and polio, and consult your doctor if any condition or suspected condition, such as an ear infection, might trouble you during air travel. Take along the medicines that you use regularly, and an extra pair of prescription glasses.

Water in San José and in most of the towns of the Central Valley is chemically treated and safe to drink. Elsewhere, inquire, and if you're still not sure or are simply cautious, stick to bottled sodas or beer. Suspect water is easily treated with laundry bleach (two drops per quart, let stand 30 minutes). Limit exposure to sun if you haven't seen any for a while, and take along some insect repellent for the west coast in the rainy season, and for the Caribbean at any time. Also, take it easy on alcohol until you become accustomed to the higher altitude in San José.

For extensive travel at the budget level or off the beaten track, a dose of immunoglobulin for protection against hepatitis and a typhoid booster are advisable. If you're heading to rural parts of the Caribbean lowlands, take a weekly dosage of a malaria preventative, such as Aralen. Budget travelers should avoid fleabag hotels. Fleas and similar insects are not only unpleasant in themselves but can carry disease. If both top and bottom sheets are not clean and clean-smelling, move on.

HOW TO GET INTO TROUBLE

It's not too likely that you'll get into hot water while visiting Costa Rica. But some customs and practices may differ from what you're used to. Relax and act as if you're on vacation, while keeping in mind some possible sore points.

Drugs, of course, are a touchy item, especially when used by foreigners. Penalties for possession of anything from marijuana on up are severe, so abstention or at least discretion is advised.

Costa Rica is a democracy, but quite security-conscious, more than ever now that neighboring countries are in turmoil. Visitors may be asked for identification at any time, and jailed (yes!) if they do not have proper papers. Always carry your passport or tourist card with you, and arrange prompt replacement if either is lost or stolen.

If there are any black marks against you—traffic tickets, customs duty owed, a debt outstanding—clear them up, no matter how minor. Otherwise, you could be prevented from leaving the country.

Take normal precautions against petty theft. Carry your money in an inside pocket, when possible, and be especially careful on crowded streets and when leaving banks. Be wary of over-friendly strangers.

There are many stories of foreigners having been ripped off, sometimes for considerable amounts of money, in real estate purchases and investment schemes. Be more cautious than at home before parting with your money. You will probably have no legal recourse if your money evaporates in a flurry of documents and contracts that you can't understand.

MONEY AND BANKING

Costa Rica's unit of currency is the *colón*, which is named after Christopher Columbus (Colón in Spanish). Each colón is divided into 100 céntimos. In slang usage, the colón is sometimes called a peso.

In this book, I've quoted most prices in U.S. dollars, based on the current rate of exchange (about 100 colones to the dollar). Costa Rica's currency has an unstable recent history, and devaluations are now a routine matter. You may even find that some prices are *lower*, in U.S. dollars, than those I've indicated. However, rates for hotel rooms, tours, car rentals and other services are fixed in dollars, and then converted to colones at the current rate. You won't get a break on these following a devaluation.

Unfortunately, changing your foreign currency to colones could turn out to be your most unpleasant experience in Costa Rica. The levels of bureaucracy in Costa Rica's banks are unsurpassed. You might have to wait in line for more than an hour while somebody in front of you cashes in sheet upon sheet of winning lottery tickets, or has his loan payments calculated on antiquated adding machines and then transferred to record sheets by a teller with hunt-and-peck typing skills (and how they insist on using typewriters!)

And after waiting, you still might not get your money changed. I once had my travelers checks refused because I had no permanent address in Costa Rica. I was turned down at other banks because my brand of travelers checks was out of favor (they wouldn't say why). Some visitors are refused because they have no passports, although none is required to enter the country.

Unfortunately, there are few alternatives to the banks and their sadistic methods. Severe currency controls are in effect, and visitors may change their money only at banks and at certain hotels. A black market is tolerated, but there is only a small spread between the bank exchange rate and what street moneychangers will give.

With a few precautions, however, you can avoid problems. Some suggestions:

Buy colones before you enter the country. Costa Rican currency is available at exchange dealers in the Los Angeles and Miami airports.

Exchange a substantial amount on arriving at the airport in San José. The airport bank is relatively hassle-free.

Change money at your hotel, if it performs this service. The rate, however, will be slightly less favorable than at the banks.

If you must exchange money at a bank, get there early in the day, and get as much cash as you feel comfortable carrying. Normal banking hours are from 9 a.m. to 3 p.m.

Use credit cards when possible (see below). As a bonus, you'll save the one-percent commission that most banks charge on travelers checks.

Carry a passport for identification.

Take U.S. dollars in cash or travelers checks. Other currencies, such as Canadian dollars and sterling, are difficult if not impossible to exchange.

Only $50 in U.S. funds may be repurchased at the airport bank before leaving Costa Rica. Avoid leaving the country with extra Costa Rican money, which will be exchanged abroad at an unfavorable rate or not at all.

Credit Cards. Visa and Master Card are widely accepted in Costa Rica, American Express to a lesser extent. You may reasonably expect to use your credit card at restaurants where a meal costs $5 or more per person, and at any large hotel that charges $20 or more for a double room. Smaller, family-run hotels and inns generally do not take credit cards, even for $100 rooms. The bank rate of exchange in effect on the date of your purchase will be applied (the card issuer may charge a commission as well).

Money from home may be received by telegraphic or Telex transfer through a bank in San José. Make sure you know through which bank it will be sent—several have similar names. International money orders may also be sent by registered mail, but safety is not assured. Regular money orders and personal checks are nearly impossible to cash.

Business Transactions. Goods should generally be shipped to Costa Rica against advance payment or irrevocable letter of credit (says my publisher, sadly).

NATIONAL PARKS

Costa Rica is one of the leaders in Latin America in preserving its natural treasures. More than eight percent of the country's land area has been set aside in national parks, national monuments, nature reserves, biological reserves, and recreation areas. Park planners have attempted to protect a sample of each climate and ecosystem in the country. While some parks are in remote locations, visitors are encouraged to enjoy all of them. Camping facilities, nature trails, visitors' centers and shelters are provided in most.

The creation of the national parks is part of a double-edged policy regarding the natural environment. Timber operations and land-clearing for farming are proceeding apace, with the encouragement of the government, and destroying native flora and fauna at a frightening rate. A number of parks were last-minute creations that rescued unique areas from farming or touristic development just in the nick of time. But these wild areas of reduced size, even when protected, might not be able to support viable populations of endangered plant and animal species in isolation.

In most of Costa Rica's national parks, visitors will be on their own, with minimal guidance from administrators or interference from other tourists. You'll be freer than in most similar reserves to wander about at your own pace, observe wildlife, and discern the finer features of plants and geological formations. But you'll also have a greater responsibility than elsewhere both to watch out for your own safety and to tread lightly.

Visits to the national parks, except the most frequented and accessible ones (Poás, Irazú, Cahuita, Guayabo and Santa Rosa), should be preceded by inquiries at park headquarters in San José, or the information center in the Bolívar Park Zoo, as to seasonal conditions, the current state of facilities, and access by public transportation. See the San José section of this book for the address. Park headquarters will sell you a good pamphlet guide to the parks and reserves. A more detailed description of the parks and their wildlife, with excellent color photos, is Mario Boza, et.al., *The National Parks of Costa Rica,* available at San José bookstores.

Most of the parks are described in the text of this book. See "national parks" in the index. Parks and reserves not otherwise mentioned are:

Hitoy Cerere Biological Reserve: Rain forest on the Atlantic slope of the Talamanca mountains.

Santa Ana Recreation Area: West of San José, slated to become the home of the National Zoo, when $5 million is found to fund the move.

POST OFFICE

Approximate postal rates are as follows: For light letters, up to 20 grams, via air mail, to the United States or Canada, 25 cents; to Europe, 31 cents. Post cards by air to the United States or Canada, 21 cents; to Europe, 28 cents.

Letters may be received in Costa Rica by having them sent to your name, care of *lista de correos* (general delivery), Correo Central, 1000 San José (or any other city where you may be). There is a small charge for each letter picked up. Tell your correspondents to write neatly. Illegible foreign handwriting is responsible for many a letter going astray.

Enclosure of money, checks, or anything other than correspondence encourages theft of letters. Even registered mail provides limited protection—a $20 maximum indemnity if the letter is sent from the United States. Many businesses in Costa Rica arrange to have their mail from abroad sent to Miami and forwarded by courier.

You may receive parcels at lista de correos, but, except for used books, there isn't much point in having anything sent. The customs duty usually exceeds the value of the merchandise. Tell the folks at home to send a money order instead.

RAFTING

Here's the bottom line: There's plenty of water in Costa Rica's rivers, you can go rafting somewhere in the country at almost any time of year, the sights along the way—exotic macaws, flocks of monkeys, sugarcane fields, dense rain forest trailing vines into the water—are available on comparable trips nowhere else, and, maybe best of all, the water is warm.

There are runs in Costa Rica for every skill level. A trip along the Corobicí River in Puntarenas province—a stereotypical slow-moving tropical river—affords ample opportunity for birding and observing streamside life. It's rated class I-II—unchallenging. On the Atlantic slope, the Reventazón River (Class III), with plenty of rapids separated by sedate stretches, is considered world class, but parts are suitable for beginners. The Pacuare (Class IV), precipitous, with difficult rapids, rushes through gorges billowing with exuberant growth. According to one rafting guide, these three are "technical" rivers—you have to make successive crucial moves in each rapid. But they're not expert runs—if you flip over, you'll be washed onward into deeper, safer water. The General, in the south-central Pacific region (class III-IV), with more volume than any California river, has continuous roller-coaster waves, whirlpools, gorges punctuated by waterfalls, and varying water levels. There are few bugs along the General, which can be rafted for six months of the year.

One-day beginners' trips are offered by two agencies in San José for about $65 (see page 83). Week-long expeditions on several rivers, camping along the way or staying in hotels as appropriate, with some sightseeing, cost about $800. Sea kayaking trips are also available, at similar rates. The organizers provide raft, paddles, helmet, and life jacket. Visitors should wear a bathing suit and tennis shoes, and carry along a change of clothing.

Having encountered a raft of rafters at my hotel on one visit to San José, I had little choice but to enroll in a beginners' trip on the Reventazón River. In true Tico fashion, we were offered beer upon arrival at the put-in point "to calm your nerves." When we started off with a splash fight, I was ready to ask for my money back. I soon changed my mind.

After basic instructions in paddling, and strapping on life jackets and buckling helmets, we were afloat. There was plenty of time to pick out birds, wave to farmers, observe the population of trees and plants that pass by too quickly along a highway, or are hidden in the forest on a hike. We took intermittent rapids paddling, soaking ourselves thoroughly in the first, leaned back in between to watch sugarcane and forest, vines dangling, debris stuck in tree branches in times of high water. A warming, misty drizzle lasted the entire run.

At a midway stopping point, our guides assembled a tropical gourmet picnic of heart of palm, sprouts, paté, cold roast beef, ham, several cheeses, and fruit. It disappeared as quickly as it had materialized. Then we were off for the second act, all rapids, and furious paddling to make it through without capsizing, splashing and gasping, all thoroughly exciting, though in a playful way, for we were assured that a spill would not result in any harm. We arrived upright in any case. And in a couple of hours, after a change of clothes, a sales pitch for t-shirts, and naps in the van, we were quite out of the wild, back in San José.

RETIREMENT

Many retired foreigners make their homes in Costa Rica, and why not? Comfortable houses are available for much less than in many countries. The climate in most areas is agreeable all year. Health care is of good quality, and most people are friendly.

Another attraction is a law that grants special residence status, with all the rights of Costa Ricans except working and voting, to retired foreigners with steady incomes.

Not all retirees find Costa Rica to their liking, of course. Some find it difficult to communicate in Spanish. Trips back home are expensive. Suitable housing is lacking outside of the Central Valley and a few coastal developments. Many goods carry high prices, especially foreign liquor and appliances. Currency fluctuations and inflation make it difficult to predict future living costs. In some cases, the good life can get to be boring.

Obtaining retirement status is an arduous process that can take more than a year. Rules and regulations have changed from time to time, cancelling out some of the tax breaks that lured retireees. And not all Costa Ricans are happy with the presence of a privileged class of foreigners, despite the money that they bring.

Under current law, foreigners may qualify for retirement residence with monthly pension income of $600, an investment income of $1000, or by making a large deposit in a Costa Rican bank. No income tax is due on foreign income. Household appliances and furnishings may be imported duty-free, as well as a car, but duty must be paid when the car is sold.

Do you really want to retire in Costa Rica? It might not be a bad idea. But understand that it's a fair-sized business, too. Many who would sell you on the idea will also take your money for legal services, seminars, property, rentals, or investments that *might* help you qualify for special retirement status. Before you invest your money and effort, make a few extended visits.

Assistance in obtaining retired-residence status is given by the Costa Rican Tourist Board. Information is also available from the Asociación de Pensionados y Rentistas de Costa Rica (Association of Retirees and Annuitants), P. O. Box 700-1011 San José, tel. 338068.

SHOPPING

Costa Rica offers visitors many rewards, but shopping is not near the top of the list.

Only a handful of indigenous crafts—pottery, hand-woven textiles and musical instruments made on a small scale for home use—can be found for sale in stores and museums.

Most of what you see at hotel shops and souvenir stores will be non-traditional handicrafts largely intended for the tourist market—items like miniature painted oxcarts, reproductions of pre-Columbian artifacts, gourd mugs, hammocks, and items made from unusual and attractive hardwoods such as rosewood (cocobolo), teak, lignum vitae (guayacán), and heart of amaranth (nazarena). There's also the usual run of straw hats, t-shirts, macramé, ashtrays and the like. Local production is supplemented by more interesting imports of textiles and basketry from Guatemala, El Salvador, and Panama. You should have no trouble finding these, but just in case, I've given the names and locations of some stores in the shopping section of the San José chapter of this book.

If local crafts aren't overwhelming, don't overlook some of the non-souvenir items that are cheaper in Costa Rica than at home. Utilitarian luggage and other leatherwork can, in some cases, be a good buy. Stop into a supermarket and pick up a pound or two or three of coffee. Most brands are ground too finely for your own coffeemaker, and don't travel well in their cellophane packaging. Volio is one brand available as whole beans to grind at home, Britt is another, at a much higher price.

Tropical delicacies such as *palmito* (heart of palm) are priced reasonably. Hot pepper sauces, chocolates, tropical fruit preserves and much else can fill up those empty spaces in your luggage.

Once you start in at the supermarket, take a look at some general department stores *(almacenes)* and shopping centers *(centros comerciales)*. You might or might not find goods you like at prices to suit your budget, but you'll get an idea of what the Costa Ricans buy and what they have to pay.

STUDY PROGRAMS

Language Schools. The advantage of studying Spanish in a country where the language is spoken are obvious. A number of schools in Costa Rica offer Spanish-language instruction in small groups or on an individual basis. A four-week package of study, room and meals in a private home, and escorted trips around the country, costs about $1100. Instruction in small groups for four hours daily, without accommodations, will run about $700. Write or call the schools for brochures and current prices. A partial listing:

Anglo-Costa Rican Cultural Institute, P. O. Box 8184, San José, tel. 33-8170

Centro Lingüístico Conversa, Apartado 17-1007, San José, tel. 217649.

Forester Instituto Internacional, Los Yoses (P. O. Box 6945, San José), tel. 253155.

ILISA, P.O. Box 1001, 2050 San Pedro. U.S. contact: tel. 213-926-5513.

Instituto Americano de Lenguaje y Cultura, San Pedro (P. O. Box 200-1001 San José), tel. 254313.

Instituto Interamericano de Idiomas Intensa, P. O. Box 8110, Calle 33, Avenidas 5/7 (no. 540), Barrio Escalante, San José, tel. 256009.

Centro Cultural Costarricense-Norteamericano, Calle 37, (just east of San José), tel. 259433. (P.O. Box 1489, San José)

In addition, assorted colleges and universities in the United States offer credit courses in Spanish in Costa Rica. For more information, look at the postings at the Spanish or Romance Languages department at a large university near wherever you happen to be.

Other Programs. The University for Peace, at Ciudad Colón, west of San José, offers masters degrees in human rights, education for peace, and communication for peace, as well as courses on natural resources. Most instruction is in Spanish, though English or French may be used to write exams. For information, write to P. O. Box 199-1250, Escazú, Costa Rica.

The Organization for Tropical Studies, directly and in collaboration with various universities, offers courses in tropical biology, ecology and forestry at its research stations at La Selva and Wilson Gardens. Write to P. O. Box DM, Duke Station, Durham, NC 27706 (tel. 919-684-5774) or P. O. Box 676-2050 San Pedro, Costa Rica (tel. 255064). Biology programs at Monteverde are available through the Council on International Educational Exchange, 205 East 42 St., New York, NY 10017.

Other broad programs in humanities and the natural and social sciences are offered by American universities with campuses or offices in Costa Rica. Generally, you must be enrolled in the university already before you can take its courses.

SURFING

This is not my field of expertise. But according to information supplied by the Costa Rica Tourist Board, steady winds give the northern Pacific coast good waves from early December through April. On the Caribbean, around Limón and to the south, there are good waves from December through February and June through August. Caution and skill are required in this area, as high waves break over coral reefs. In the southern Pacific coastal region, there are said to be high waves throughout the year. Surfing tournaments are held at Playa Hermosa, north of Jacó, and at Manuel Antonio, near Quepos. Pavones, down near the Panamanian border, has become home to some expatriate surfers who have found the perfect wave.

TAXES

Almost all goods and services in Costa Rica are subject to a 10 percent value-added tax ("*i.v.a.*"). Hotel rooms are subject to an additional 3 percent tourism tax. At the airport, the exit tax is approximately five dollars.

TAXIS

In San José, you pay about 70 cents for the first kilometer, 25 cents for each additional kilometer—a bargain! In rural areas, additional kilometers cost slightly more. Waiting time is charged at about $3 per hour. If your trip is over 12 kilometers, you'll have to negotiate the rate with the driver.

TELEGRAMS

International telegrams are handled by Radiográfica Costarricense, Calle 1, Avenida 5, San José. Telegrams may be dictated by dialing 123, or transmitted through your hotel operator. In all cases, the rates are quite high—usually 50 cents per word or more. Domestic telegrams cost only a few cents per word.

TELEPHONES

Costa Rica has a modern, direct-dial telephone system, with more lines per inhabitant than almost any other nation in Latin America. Phones in Costa Rica may be reached from the United States by dialing 011-506, followed by the six digits of the Costa Rican telephone number. From Costa Rica, numbers in other countries can be reached by dialing the international access code (001 for the United States or Canada) followed by the area code and number, or through hotel operators. Direct connections to A.T. & T. operators in the United States are available from Juan Santamaría Airport, and from the Holiday Inn and the telephone company office (Calle 1, Avenida 5) in San José. Calls to the States cost $2 to $3 per minute at the daytime rate; to Canada, $3 to $4 per minute; to Europe, $4 per minute. If calling from a hotel, ascertain first any additional charges, or else call collect.

Within Costa Rica, there are no area codes. Any number can be reached simply by dialing its six digits. Dial local numbers carefully to avoid erroneous long-distance charges! In a few remote locations, your call will reach a local operator, who will connect you with your party. Rates are modest. From San José to Jacó, for example, a three-minute call from a public phone will cost about 25 cents. From a private phone, the charge is about 65 cents. You'll pay more if you call through your hotel operator.

The service numbers for telephone number information, etc., given in the San José section, are valid throughout the country.

TICO TALK

Recurrent words that might not be in your Spanish vocabulary:

Batidos   A beverage of liquified fresh fruit and milk.

Bomba   Gas (petrol) station

268

Cabinas	Usually basic, cold-water beach accommodations. But cabinas can also be middle-range motel-style units. The common denominator is an outside or courtyard entrance to the room.
Campo	Space (as on a bus)
Cien metros	One block
Cruda	Draft beer
Faja	Belt. In other countries, a faja is a sash. Not that you need a belt, or a sash, for that matter; this is just by way of illustrating that the Costa Rican language is in some ways stuck in the past.
Fila	Line; Haga fila: line up
Frescos	Fruit drinks
Gallo	Gallo pinto (rice and beans)
Hueco	Pothole
Macho	American, or big shot; literally, "male." But the term doesn't connote men exclusively. The American ex-wife of an ex-president is known as "La Macha."
Mi Amor	My love. Don't take it to heart if that smashing lady at the ticket counter or that incredible hunk calls you "mi amor." It's a common form of address, like the cockney "luv."
No se aceptan excursiones	Busloads of holiday-makers not welcome (a good sign at any beach hotel)
Palenque	Thatched shelter (equivalent to the Mexican palapa)
Pulpería	Corner Store
Salón	Saloon
Soda	A basic luncheonette.
Sudada	Stewed, as *carne sudada*, stewed beef.
Tico	Costa Rican
Típico	Native-style, Costa Rican-style, as *comida típica*, a native-style meal.

TIME

Costa Rica is on Central Standard Time, equivalent to Greenwich Mean Time less six hours.

TIPPING

A ten-percent service charge is added, by law, to all restaurant bills, so there's no need to leave any additional amount unless service is especially good.

At hotels, give the porter 25 to 50 cents per bag for carrying your luggage. Chambermaids will appreciate your leaving the equivalent of a dollar or two if you've stayed for a few days.

Taxi drivers are never tipped, nor are tour guides, except for special kindnesses. Some guides will tell you otherwise, but you pay quite enough for most tours in Costa Rica.

When in doubt about whether or how much to tip, remember that a tip is a reward for good service. Poor service means no tip.

WEIGHTS AND MEASURES

Costa Rica is firmly on the metric system. Gasoline, juice and milk are sold by the liter, fabrics by the meter, tomatoes by the kilo. Gone are the days when visitors were confused by a hodgepodge of yards, varas, manzanas, fanegas, caballerías, gallons, and assorted other English and old Spanish measures.

Old usages survive mainly in giving directions. People will usually say 100 *metros* (meters) to indicate a city block, but you'll sometimes hear 100 *varas*. In fact, a block is closer to 100 varas, a vara being an old Spanish yard, equivalent to 33 inches or .835 meters.

WHAT TO TAKE AND WEAR

When packing for your visit to Costa Rica, keep in mind that the climate is moderate. For San José and the Central Valley, take what you would wear during the spring at home. A light sweater or jacket may be required for the evening, especially during the dry season. For early-morning excursions to the frosty heights of volcanoes, you'll do best to dress in layers, perhaps a sweater over a shirt and t-shirt, with layers coming off as the temperature climbs.

For visits to either coast, you'll want lightweight clothing, preferably all-cotton, or else cotton blends. Essential items will be a bathing suit, a few shirts or blouses, shorts, and a pair of sandals. Take one long-sleeved top and slacks in case you overexpose yourself to sun. The sultry coasts also require sunglasses, and a hat to keep the sun off your head. Cheap straw and cotton hats are widely available in Costa Rica, but the fit is often tight on gringos.

In the rainy months, from April to December, and for trips to the Caribbean, you might want to take a folding umbrella or a light raincoat, though neither is essential if you won't be straying far from your hotel or tour bus.

If you'll be traveling by bus and train, a travel alarm will come in handy for early departures. Hotel wake-up calls are unreliable.

In general, informal clothing is suitable. Even in San José, you may dine at your hotel in slacks and sport shirt or blouse. At the best restaurants, however, and at formal events, such as concerts at the National Theater, a dress or jacket and tie are appropriate. Costa Ricans value a neat appearance (just look at how they dress!) and regard visitors who wear patched clothing with puzzlement. Shorts are generally not worn in San José, except for sports or around the house, though customs are slowly changing.

Campers, and those staying at budget hotels in the lowlands, will want to take insect repellent. Good, comfortable shoes are necessary if you plan to do any walking. Tennis or jogging shoes will do.

Bring a moderate amount of reading material if your visit will center on San José, where English-language books and magazines are available (though expensive), or a pile of books for a beach holiday. Take more film than you think you'll need. Bring your own cigars or pipe tobacco. Pick up a few duty-fee bottles of liquor on the way down if you have a favorite brand. Take sufficient deodorant, shave cream, etc. Sportsmen will want to take all the equipment they anticipate needing for fishing or camping.

In general, remember that anything imported or mechanical is likely to be much more expensive in Costa Rica than at home. So if your Walkman or some other gadget is indispensable to your being, take it along.

MORE INFORMATION

Costa Rica's Tourist Board (Instituto Costarricense de Turismo) is one of the more cooperative and helpful organizations of its type. Conveniently for U.S. residents, it has a toll-free number, 800-327-7033 (in Florida, 305-358-2150). For information by mail, write to 1101 Brickell Avenue, ground floor, Miami, Florida 33131; or to the branch office at 3540 Wilshire Blvd., no.404, Los Angeles, CA 90010 (tel.800-762-5909, or 800-762-5900 in California); or to the main office at Apartado Postal 777, San José, Costa Rica (tel. 231733).

Items available from the tourist board are a basic map of Costa Rica, brochures for hotels in various price ranges, and general information folders. For detailed maps, include a check for $2.

For fishing, horseback riding and other special-interest travel, contact one of the travel agencies listed earlier (see page 232). Travel agents who are familiar with Costa Rica are a good source of general information as well.

Useful books about Costa Rica include:

John and Mavis Biesanz, *Costa Rican Life*. New York: Columbia University Press, 1944; reprinted by Editorial Lehmann, San José, 1976.

Richard Biesanz,et. al., *The Costa Ricans*. Englewood Cliifs: Prentice Hall, 1982; reprinted by Editorial Universidad Estatal a Distancia, San José, 1983.

(Both of the above books cover many aspects of Costa Rican society. The first is regarded by many as a classic; many of its observations are still valid today.)

Beatrice Blake and Anne Becher, *The New Key to Costa Rica*. San José: Publications in English (Box 7-1230), 1988. An affectionate guide, frequently updated, especially useful for its coverage of San José and information relative to long-term stays. Includes such topics as hiring a maid, the excruciating details of extending your stay, how to find a lawyer for obtaining residency, details of study programs, etc.

Ellen Searby, *The Costa Rica Traveller.* Juneau: Windham Bay Press, 1988. Numerous photos, and comparative tabular summaries of hotel amenities.

Mario Boza, et. al., *The National Parks of Costa Rica.* Madrid: Incafo, 1981. Imperfectly rendered English version, but the color photos and information on flora and fauna are solid.

Hilary Bradt, *Backpacking in Mexico and Central America.* Boston: Bradt Enterprises, 1983. Includes descriptions of hikes in Costa Rica's national parks.

J. P. Panet, *Latin America on Bicycle.* Champlain, N.Y.: Passport Press, 1987. Includes a chapter about a bicycle trip through Costa Rica.

Most of the above titles are available in San José bookstores.

The *Tico Times,* published on Fridays in San José, is one of the best English-language newspapers in Latin America. Articles cover events in Costa Rica and Central America, as well as local traditions, business, fishing, and items of human interest. The On the Town column reports on restaurants and entertainment. The letters column is a free-for-all. Ads for lodging and services will interest many visitors and potential visitors. Investment promotions—sometimes with wildly exaggerated claims—are also prominent. An annual subscription in the United States or Canada costs about $50. Write to P.O. Box 145450, Coral Gables, FL 33114-5450. A tourist edition is published annually in October. (One oddity of Costa Rica: with an excellent English-language newspaper, and a number of businesses that advertise in it heavily, you might get the impression that there are more and better facilities out there than actually exist.)

Costa Rica Report is a personal, independent newsletter published monthly in San José. There is no advertising whatsoever to influence the reportage. Coverage includes people, events, economic developments, investment opportunities, and scams. If you are even thinking about living or investing in Costa Rica, you owe it to yourself to read a few copies. I glean lots of useful information from every issue. An annual subscription costs about $42. Write to P. O. Box 6283, San José.

If you want to *see* the product before you go, several tourist videos of Costa Rica are available. One that you can order by mail is *Costa Rica Today*. Send a check for $30 to Cota International, P. O. Box 5042, New York, NY 10185.

INDEX

278

Playa Ocotal, 183-84
Playa Panamá, 169, 183
Playa Potrero, 185-86, 187
Playa Tamarindo, 187-89
Playas del Coco, 169, 180-81
Poás volcano, 82, 91, 111-14, 221
Poasito, 112, 114
Portete, 103, 128, 135-36
Postal service, 76, 261-62
Potrero Cerrado, 98
Protestants, 24
Publications, 71, 273
Puerto Barrios, 129
Puerto Jiménez, 216
Puerto Vargas, 147
Puerto Viejo de Sarapiquí (Heredia province), 141, 225-26
Puerto Viejo (Limón province), 144, 148
Puntarenas, 4, 122, 117, 151, 152-57
Punto guanacasteco, 167

Quakers, 158
Quepos, 155, 202-210
Quetzal, 162, 212
Quitirrisi, indigenous group, 88

Races, 22, 26-28, 123, 126-27, 128-29
Rafael Lucas Rodríguez Caballero Wildlife Refuge, 166
Rafting, 212, 233, 262-63
Railroads, 80, 241; to Limón, 80, 121-27, 128; to Puntarenas, 80, 155
Retirement, 263-64
Reventazón river, 101, 102, 104, 125, 262
Rincón de la Vieja, volcano and national park, 170
Río Frío, 227-28
Río Grande de Orosi (river), 101
Río Macho (river), 102

Río Cuarto, 224
Rip currents, 195
Rodríguez, José Joaquín, 15

Sámara, 190-91
San Antonio de Escazú, 82, 88
San Carlos region, 221-26; town, 117, 164, 166, 221, 222-23, 224
San Gerardo de Dota, 211
San Isidro de Coronado, 86-87
San Isidro de El General, 212-13
San José, 12, 14, 31-85
San José de la Montaña, 107, 108
San Juan river, 141, 225
San Lucas island, 156-57
San Miguel, 224
San Pedro de Barva, 107
San Pedro de Poás, 114
San Rafael, 87
San Ramón, 117
Santa Cruz, 169, 175-76
Santa Elena, 155, 158, 159-60
Santamaría, Juan, 110
Santa Rosa national park, 169, 171-73
Santa Teresita, 106
Santiago Puriscal, 82, 88
San Vito de Java, 219
Sarapiquí river, 141, 225
Sarchí, 115-17, 222
Savegre River, 211
Settlement of Costa Rica, 4, 7-13
Shopping, 76-78, 264-65
Sierpe River, 216
Siquirres, 126
Sixaola, 147, 148
Soto, Bernardo, 15
Spain, colonizes Costa Rica, 9-13
Spanish language in Costa Rica, 23, 268-69
Study programs, 265-67
Sugar cultivation, 6
Surfing, 267
Swampmouth, 127

Tabacón, 223
Talamanca, indigenous group, 27, 106; mountain range, 4, 151, 210
Tamarindo, 187-89
Tambor, 156, 193, 194
Tárcoles, 197
Taxes, 267
Taxis, 78, 267, 241
Telegrams, 78, 267
Telephones, 79, 267
Tempisque river, 164, 166, 177
Theaters, 59-60, 74
"Tico," explained, 23
Tierra Blanca, 98
Tilarán, mountain range, 3, 151; town, 164-66, 223
Time of day, 270
Tinoco Granados, Federico, 16
Tipping, 270
Tortuguero canal, 136-37, 139-40; national park, 122, 137-41, 225
Tourism, 18, 27, 29-30
Tourist Office, 29, 61, 80, 272
Tours, 81-85, 232-34, 242
Train travel, 80, 122-27, 155, 241
Travel agencies in Costa Rica, 83-85; abroad, 232-34
Travel, general advice, 29-30, 36, 119-20, 229-73
Tronadora, 164

Tropical Agronomic Research and Education Center, 104
Tropical Science Center, 158, 163
Turrialba, town, 103-105, 126; volcano, 91, 105, 106
Turtles, nesting, 137-38, 139, 173, 189

Ulate, Otilio, 16, 17
Ujarrás, 103
United Fruit Company, 123
Uvita island, 10, 128

Valle Central: see Central Valley
Vanderbilt, Cornelius, 141
Vara Blanca, 224
Vásquez de Coronado, 11, 95
Venecia de San Carlos, 224
Veragua, 10
Villa Nueva, 33
Visas, 234-35
Volcanoes: see National Parks, individual volcano names

Walker, William, 14, 110, 142, 171
Weather: see Climate
Weights, 270
Wilson Botanical Garden, 219

Zarcero, 222
Zoos, 64, 115

Travel Guides from Passport Press

Guatemala Guide, by Paul Glassman

"Filled with useful information, both general and specific, on Guatemala's culture, geography, history, customs and hotels. Glassman thoroughly explores the territory and subject."

Booklist

"My highest recommendation."

Carl Franz, *The People's Guide to Mexico*

Latin America on Bicycle, by J.P. Panet

"Delightful, informative and unusual... essential to anyone planning a bike trip in the region – and even to many contemplating less rigorous tours."

Americas

Belize Guide, by Paul Glassman

"Invaluable... don't leave home without it."

International Travel News

Costa Rica, by Paul Glassman

"If a visitor had to limit himself to just one book on Costa Rica, this would certainly be my recommendation... accurate, detailed, and practically oriented... the combination of writing style, common sense and wry good humor make this book a pleasure to read."

Tom Sloan, San Jose, Costa Rica *Tico Times*

For a list of current titles, write to Passport Press, Box 1346, Champlain, New York 12919. Passport Press guides are available at most travel bookstores.